398.2 SEGA
Segaloff, Nat. MAR 1 6 2002
The everything tall tales,
legends, & outrageous lies
0245
12.95

THE
EVERYTHING®
TALL TALES,
LEGENDS,
& OUTRAGEOUS LIES
BOOK

CALEDONIA PUBLIC LIBRARY
CALEDONIA, OHIO

THE

EVERYTHING®
TALL TALES,
LEGENDS,
& OUTRAGEOUS LIES
BOOK

Nat Segaloff

Adams Media Corporation
Holbrook, Massachusetts

Copyright ©2001, Adams Media Corporation.
All rights reserved. This book, or parts thereof, may not be reproduced
in any form without permission from the publisher; exceptions
are made for brief excerpts used in published reviews.

An Everything® Series Book.
Everything® is a registered trademark of Adams Media Corporation.

Published by Adams Media Corporation
260 Center Street, Holbrook, MA 02343
www.adamsmedia.com

ISBN: 1-58062-514-2
Printed in the United States of America.

J   I   H   G   F   E   D   C   B   A

Library of Congress Cataloging-in-Publication Data
Segaloff, Nat.
    The everything tall tales, legends, and outrageous lies book / by Nat Segaloff.
       p. cm. — (The everything series)
    Includes bibliographical references and index.
    ISBN 1-58062-514-2
    1. Urban folklore. 2. Tall tales. 3. Truth and falsehood. 4. Imposters and imposture.
I. Title. II. Series.
GR79 .S44 2001
398.2'091732—dc21   2001022404

Many of the designations used by manufacturers and sellers to distinguish their products are claimed as trademarks. Where those designations appear in this book and Adams Media was aware of a trademark claim, the designations have been printed in initial capital letters.

This publication is designed to provide accurate and authoritative information with regard to the subject matter covered. It is sold with the understanding that the publisher is not engaged in rendering legal, accounting, or other professional advice. If legal advice or other expert assistance is required, the services of a competent professional person should be sought.

    —From a *Declaration of Principles* jointly adopted by a Committee of the
    American Bar Association and a Committee of Publishers and Associations

Disclaimers: (1) The anecdotal nature of this book is that the probity of some of the people and/or institutions may once have been in doubt. Where credible historical record has clarified such questions, it has been noted. Notwithstanding the above, the inclusion of any person, product, idea, location, enterprise, or other entity in this book does not imply a challenge to its honesty, and none should be inferred. (2) All Web sites, pages, and information are included as of the date of this writing, and neither the publisher nor the author can assume responsibility for any changes that may have occurred since then.

Caution: The schemes, beliefs, and other details presented in this book are offered strictly for the entertainment of the reader. Laws, social mores, and just plain good taste may prohibit certain practices recounted herein, and nothing in these pages should be construed as permission, authorization, or inspiration to attempt them. In other words, don't try this at home.

Illustrations by Barry Littmann and Kurt Dolber.

*This book is available at quantity discounts for bulk purchases.
For information, call 1-800-872-5627.*

Visit the entire Everything® series at everything.com

Dedication

To Norman R. Poretsky, Harvey Appell, Paul A. Levi,
Karl E. Fasick, John Markle, Nico Jacobellis, and Carl Ferrazza,
all of whom taught me ethics in a business
that wasn't supposed to have any.

CANCELLED-NO LONGER PROPERTY
OF MARION PUBLIC LIBRARY
(OHIO)

Acknowledgments

Bob Adams, Publisher; Pamela A. Liflander, Editor; Agnes Birnbaum, Bleecker Street Associates, Inc., Agent.

Grateful thanks for contributions and counsel in addition to that which is credited herein: Robert W. Abramoff; Robert E. Baskin, Bob Bulmash; The Coca-Cola Company; David Chapman; Robin Cohn, Robin Cohn and Company; Sally Cragin; Colin Criminger; Ami Lachmani; John de Lancie; Ron Evry; Gary H. Grossman; Arnold Herr; Internet Fraud Watch; Mark Kermode; Don Kopaloff; Emily Lockman; Paula Lyons; Rebecca Madeira, National Consumers League, The Pepsi-Cola Company; Barbara and David Mikkelson; Leonard Nimoy; Stephen F. Rohde; Rob Rosenberger; Helen Sanders, Carson Productions; Leigh M. Simons; Clark F. Smidt; Mason Locke Weems; Kietryn Zychal.

Particular thanks are extended to Christopher Darling, Stan Levin, and Loren Rose for their expert counsel on specific sections.

. . . plus those who shared information on condition that their stories could be used, but not their names.

Contents

Chapter 1
Mythtory / 1

Chapter 2
Old Wives' Tales, or Bad Advice from Well Meaning Relatives / 19

Chapter 3
There's One Born Every Minute (America's Best Cons and Con Artists) / 43

CONTENTS

Chapter 4
Mass Hysteria: Historic Hoaxes and Classic Urban Legends / 89

Chapter 5
Internet Hoaxes / 120

Chapter 6
Hollywood and Bust / 147

Chapter 7
Modern Urban Legends / 186

Chapter 8
Damage Control / 214

Appendices

Introduction

The great masses of the people ... will more
easily fall victim to a big lie than to a small one.
　　　　　　　　　—Adolf Hitler, <u>Mein Kampf</u>

✓ **REALITY CHECK**

What Are These?

Throughout this book you'll see items called "reality checks." They will point out lapses of logic, corrections of fact, additional comments on nearby topics, or just stories that seemed like a good idea at the time.

This is a book about lies, not truth. When someone lies, he or she corrupts the Truth. That's not necessarily a bad thing if it's done for the right reasons, such as sparing someone's feelings or achieving a higher moral purpose, although it's sometimes tricky making the call. For instance, in John Ford's 1962 Western, *The Man Who Shot Liberty Valence,* a reporter is asked to bury a story because printing it would damage the reputation of a hero, and America needs its heroes. "When the legend becomes fact, print the legend." This line, written by Willis Goldbeck and James Warner Bellah, has been frequently quoted to justify political "spin."

But what if a lie is told for the wrong reason? As political activist Noam Chomsky has pointed out, "The right to lie in the service of power is guarded with considerable vigor and passion." The question then becomes, Whose power? Is it for "good" or "evil"? Who decides? Now define your terms.

Philosophers (and sometimes juries) make a distinction between *conscious* and *unconscious* lying. Conscious lying is sometimes obvious, frequently immoral, and—when it is used to defraud—usually illegal. Unconscious lying can be determined only in hindsight—that is, after the Truth becomes known—and it is seldom punishable, although it may be embarrassing ("Golly, I didn't know that was a toupee!"). It is also what makes this book possible, because it is *unconscious lying* that gives rise to rumor, myth, urban legend, and folklore—in other words, that uniquely human recreation known as *gossip.*

✓ REALITY CHECK

Word History: Gossip

The word *gossip* is derived from the Anglo-Saxon words *God* and *sib*, referring to a close friend or protector, such as a godfather or godmother. Gradually it was familiarized to *gossip*. By Elizabethan times, gossip had lost its religious significance, thereafter referring to someone who was known to enjoy a good time.

Gossip is the lie that contains its own disclaimer; nobody really accepts it, but everybody wants it to be true. People couch their skepticism by saying, "I don't believe this, but . . . " or "Someone just told me that . . . " It's like saying, "This joke is offensive, but it's so funny I'm gonna tell it anyway."

When journalists print gossip, they tag it with the word *reportedly*, as in "The XYZ company *reportedly* admitted that one of its products is faulty." Check it out. The dictionary defines *reportedly* as "according to a report." In other words, *reportedly* is the journalistic equivalent of "Trust me."

"Trust" is conditional. We *trust* facts but *believe* rumors. Maybe it's because facts are provable, but rumors come to us through someone we . . . er . . . trust. Before the invention of writing, human culture was transmitted by oral tradition. The veracity of the information depended entirely upon the credibility of the person imparting it. If Ugg the Caveman was known to exaggerate how many wildebeests he slew during the hunt, why should the tribe believe his account of a strange, flickering red-orange substance that lit up the cave and hurt when you put your hand in it? But if Gronk, who was never off on his wildebeest count, said he saw something called "fire," everybody believed him. Thereby did Gronk become the king, while Ugg went on to start the *National Enquirer*. A modern corollary is, If space aliens are so smart, how come they always show themselves to the people who are least likely to be believed?

The answer is that human beings are, by nature, curious. We are drawn to (1) money, (2) sex, (3) shiny objects, and (4) juicy stories, and if number 4 contains some combination of the other three, so much the better. What separates us from the beasts is that we are supposed to be able to tell what's true from what's false, or at least what's right from what's wrong, and, what's more, to care which is which.

In the end, it comes down to morality, and morality is usually a function of Faith. Not necessarily religious faith, but Faith as in *assurance*. How many times have you heard the wisecrack, "My mind is already made up. Don't confuse me with the facts"? Although, in some cases, Faith can include fact, it doesn't have to.

As many a creative writer has said, "Never let the facts get in the way of the Truth." What is important—and what this book is about, underneath all the stories—is why we so often embrace lies as if they were the Truth. How can normally intelligent human beings be seduced into being abnormally unintelligent? Is there something deep inside that allows our innate curiosity to be deflected into the comfort of fantasy? Is it like yin and yang? Like Satan and God? Matter and Antimatter? Holmes and Moriarty? Captain Kirk and his Evil Twin?

Lies can be seductive. As a test, read this paragraph straight through:

> During the 1990s, the national crime rate fell, yet that same period saw an exponential increase in the construction of prisons and the birth of a movement to fill them using the "three strikes" and "truth-in-sentencing" laws. Does society actually need criminals so much that politicians pass laws making more things illegal, and police justify themselves by going out to catch the offenders? Is there a connection between tougher laws, more prisons, and campaign contributions by the prison guards' union? Most Americans believe that the government's war on drugs is warranted by the prevalence of controlled substances in our society. Yet a growing number of people believe that the government purposely controls certain substances in order to get people to approve laws that will incarcerate nonviolent drug users, oppress minorities, seize people's assets, undermine the Fourth Amendment (search and seizure), engage in domestic spying, and—oh, yes—help the tobacco companies who, as everybody knows, long ago trademarked all the popular names for marijuana so that, when pot is eventually legalized, they can control the market.
>
> *Danger, Will Robinson! Danger, Will Robinson!!*

Whoa! Take a breath. Did anything in that paragraph sound like a lie? If, *for even one moment*, you believed *any* part of it to be true, then you are beginning to understand the power of myth on

---

✓ REALITY CHECK

Bonding

What makes human beings trust one another? Perhaps it's the simple need to bond with someone, as when tourists who would never pay attention to each other in the States become fast friends when they meet in a foreign land. Baby ducks follow the first thing they see once they come out of their shells; scientists have even trained newborn Rhesus monkeys to think of a warm washcloth as their mother. People who speak with their palms upturned inspire trust, as do those who, in conversation, constantly repeat the name of the person they're talking to. On the other hand, people distrust those who have three names (such as Lee Harvey Oswald, Mark David Chapman) or two first names (most AM radio disc jockeys). Oh, and never trust anybody who says, "Trust me."

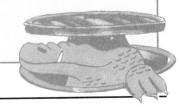

the human psyche. (By the way, depending on whom you ask, part of it actually *is* true.)

On a less paranoid level, remember when you were a kid and you heard that if you swallow aspirin with a bottle of Coca-Cola, you become intoxicated? Or if you smoked baked banana skins, you'd get high? Or that Joan Crawford once made a porno movie called *Ballin' the Jack*?

None of the above is true. At least, not per se. All you get if you chug aspirin and Coca-Cola is stomach gas. Smoking baked banana skins, if anything, gives you a headache. And if Mommie Dearest ever made a "groin grind" film (as *Variety* used to call them), you'd think a copy woulda turned up over the last 70 years—unless they're being hoarded by the guys in the black helicopters, of course. And yet how many times have we heard those stories, or repeated them because the person who told them to us swore they were true? Or because they sounded as if they *could* be? Or because we felt important knowing something that our friends didn't?

So this book doesn't presume to explore Truth. Leave that to the philosophers. The examples that follow captured the popular imagination of their time. Not everybody in here is a crook, and not every story is a crime, but they are fascinating examples of society's frailty, and the need that people have to believe.

Nat Segaloff
Los Angeles, California

✓ REALITY CHECK

Quotable

The ever quotable Oscar Wilde said, "The aim of the liar is simply to charm, to delight, to give pleasure. He is the very basis of civilized society." In Walt Disney's *Pinocchio*, the Blue Fairy warned, "A lie grows until it's as plain as the nose on your face." Finally, Mark Twain put the cork in the bottle when he wrote, "Always do right. This will gratify some people and astonish the rest."

Chapter 1

Mythtory

What is a lie but a kind of a myth?
What is a myth but a kind of a truth?
—Don Quixote de la Mancha

Unlike other animals, humans transmit culture through language. Lion and wolf parents teach their offspring how to hunt by example; papa pigeons coax their chicks to fly by prodding them from the nest; mama seals protect their pups and show them how to fend for themselves. Every animal that nurtures its young relies on eons of instinct provided through on-the-job training to ensure the survival of its species.

What gave *Homo sapiens* a unique rung up on the evolutionary ladder was the ability to communicate complex ideas. First, the humans communicated by making identifiable sounds, but so do prairie dogs. Cave drawing may have played a part in this process; maybe there was no name for "wild boar," but there certainly was a blood painting of one. With the passage of time—who knows how long and what physiological changes took place in the human larynx?—sounds became codified into speech, and were later (much later) unified with drawing to become representational language.

Each advance in communication enabled ideas and facts to be set down in a form that could be conveyed to people who were not in the immediate vicinity of the storyteller, whether at that moment or in that generation. As society advanced, so did the complexity of its language. Animals may have depended on a combination of instinct, experience, and pheromones, but human civilization developed grammar, slang, abstract thinking, and even humor ("Why did the platypus cross the road?").

For centuries, humans transmitted life knowledge orally, embellishing tales from simple reports of the hunt into seminal epics such as *The Iliad, The Odyssey, Beowulf,* and *The Song of Roland.* Holy teachings, too, were refined through repeated telling until they were affixed in writing. The stories might change subtly as they were transported and translated from one tribe's language into another's, or as the lucidity of the storyteller waned with age and infirmity.

When the first pen (or feather or charcoal or chisel) touched the first paper (or papyrus or stone or clay), human knowledge at once became both finite and infinite: finite because it could be expressed and preserved with precision, and infinite because it no longer had to be memorized before it could be repeated. Movable type (circa A.D. 1454) further expanded knowledge by greatly reducing the cost of books, thereby enabling the masses to afford literacy.

Writing did not stop the oral tradition entirely, however; it merely changed its nature. Printing was expensive and was controlled by a powerful minority, usually royalty or the clergy). Even more intimidating, printing carried the responsibility of permanence. Once something appeared in black and white, it assumed a power of its own—and a liability, as anyone who dared print something without the royal imprimatur quickly learned to his detriment. Thus began the separation of news and gossip: News was what the Establishment deemed to be in its interest, gossip was what people really thought. That may be a simplification, but it suits the purpose of this chapter, which is about where rumors, myths, urban legends, and other stories come from.

Why do humans tell tales? Filmmaker Joseph L. Mankiewicz (*All about Eve*) claimed in *More About "All About Eve"* that storytelling arose out of *homo sapiens*' need to fill " . . . the few hours that stretch endlessly between Mankind's Evening Meal and Mankind's Bedtime." According to Mankiewicz's fanciful theory, one of our earliest ancestors suddenly got it into his head to jump up, smear his face with mud, and strut back and forth "making like a chicken." He got a laugh, and did it again: "The first Encore!" Mankiewicz continues, "[He] must have pranced and danced and cackled himself into total exhaustion that first First Night when—we mustn't forget—the Audience, too, was born."

Whether it was tribal warriors regaling the stay-at-homes with grandiose memories of the hunt, or medicine men inventing reasons not to venture too far into the woods, stories have at once

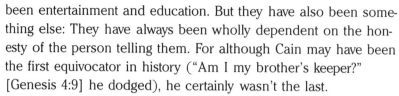
✓ REALITY CHECK

Playground Myth #1

According to Art Linkletter, "Kids say the darndest things." For 50 years, the jovial broadcaster quoted youngsters saying that "alimony is a disease you get from marriage" and "a skeleton is a person wearing his bones on the outside."

There are, however, things that kids still tell each other that they would never reveal, even to Art Linkletter. The Reality Checks in this chapter report—sometimes for attribution, sometimes not—Life Lessons overheard on playgrounds, in summer camp, and on the streets. Here are some medical "facts":

- If you swallow chewing gum, it sticks to your heart.
- If you swallow a watermelon seed, it grows inside your stomach, which is how girls have babies.
- If you sneeze with your eyes open, your eyeballs fly out.

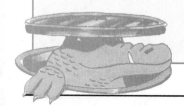

been entertainment and education. But they have also been something else: They have always been wholly dependent on the honesty of the person telling them. For although Cain may have been the first equivocator in history ("Am I my brother's keeper?" [Genesis 4:9] he dodged), he certainly wasn't the last.

Myths exist to explain things that cannot be resolved through observation or reason. Why does the sun rise and set? Before Copernicus and Galileo observed that the Earth rotated on its axis, it was easier to believe that the Sun God drove it across the sky in a golden chariot. Where did fire come from? Well, originally Prometheus stole it from the gods on Mount Olympus. Where does the world itself come from? Why, it rests on immense elephants that stand on a huge tortoise. Why is the Earth the center of the universe? Because if it isn't, then humankind shrinks to insignificance in the cosmos.

If "seeing is believing," why do people believe what they cannot see? Certainly no man in colonial America in 1692 would have bought a horse he could not inspect himself, yet he (and others) were more than willing to accept the word of some teenage girls in Salem, Massachusetts, that their town was rife with witches. And what if seeing is *not* believing—as in the 1969 furor that Paul McCartney of the Beatles had died in 1965, and his "appearances" since then have been a series of impersonations? If Lois Lane and Jimmy Olsen were too thick to realize that Clark Kent was Superman, who's to say the Walrus *wasn't* Paul?

We believe in some things because we *want* them to be true (like Santa Claus). When maturity, enlightenment, or experience finally leave no doubt that we were wrong, it can take us awhile to get over it. Multiply that by tens, hundreds, and thousands of people who fall prey to the same illusion ("Say it ain't so, Joe!"), and you've got a pretty fair idea of why we cling to our beliefs with a passion reserved for life itself.

Where do we hear myths today? Certainly there are television dramas, talk radio, tabloid newspapers, and fiction books. But there are still the back fence (and its electronic reincarnation, Internet chat rooms), social clubs, locker rooms, beauty parlors, sales meetings, barrooms, and—perhaps most seminally—school playgrounds. As long as people in authority talk to people who will listen, human imagination will never be lonely.

"An invasion of armies can be resisted," wrote Victor Hugo in 1852, "but not an idea whose time has come." He might have added, "Nothing dies so hard as an idea whose time has passed, but it won't lay down and die."

The Telephone Game as Urban Legend Paradigm

Groucho Marx believed that "if you want a reporter to print a joke right, you have to tell it to him wrong." To gain such wisdom, the Grouch must have played "telephone," a party game that demonstrates with the speed of an insult how rumors start.

Here's how it works. One person whispers a message into another person's ear, then the second person whispers the message as he heard it into a third person's ear, and so forth. With each transfer, the message can be whispered only once. The longer the chain or the louder the party, the more the message is bound to go awry. By the time the last person announces to the others what he's heard, the original words have usually become hopelessly mangled.

If language is so precise, what has happened? Plenty, and it all illustrates how gossip works. A player might misunderstand the message and pass it along dutifully but erroneously; or she might hear it accurately but slur it while repeating it. A player might deliberately change the message as he hands it off, compromising both the truth and the game itself. Conversely, if it's a common saying, a subsequent player might recognize it and change it back. Usually, though, "telephone" screws up even the most innocent message, and gets big laughs by the time the circuit finishes.

As with many games, "telephone" has a real-life counterpart. The original message is exactly that: an observation, a comment, a fact begun or discovered by someone, and then conveyed in

✓ **REALITY CHECK**

Playground Myth #2

"A guy slapped a girl so hard on the back that her falsies came out. The second time I heard this (maybe 5th grade), the doofus who told me the story said that her 'false teeth' came out. I had to correct him. And then explain to him what falsies were, precocious brat that I was."

—submitted by Stan Levin, Maryland

5

conversation. The person who hears it may or may not remember it fully, so she passes along as much as she remembers—whether it's accurate or not.

Someone with an agenda may intentionally alter a story; another may simply forget a part and fabricate something to fill in the blanks. The only defense against either occurrence is a corrective intervention, the modern counterpart of which is a letter to the editor or a press conference.

Unless you happen to be one of those people who has no interest in gossip—in which case the only thing to do is hang up the phone—you would probably rather heed the famous advice of Alice Roosevelt Longworth: "If you can't say something good about someone, sit right here by me."

✓ REALITY CHECK

Playground Myth #3

"There is a famous (or infamous) story of the man who picks up a girl at a bar (or dance club). Later, at home, he awakens, with no sign of the lady still present. He goes into his bathroom to brush his teeth, and on the mirror, scrawled in blood-red lipstick, is the note: 'Welcome to the world of AIDS' or alternately 'Thanks for the sex, you now have AIDS.'"

—submitted by David Chapman, New Jersey

Aesop

The world knows very little about Aesop other than his fables, which describe human nature as freshly now as when he first told them in the sixth century, B.C. Aesop is believed to have been a slave who lived in ancient Greece from 560 B.C. to 520 B.C. Regardless of his intellect or political acumen, his slave status doomed him to a lifetime of servitude. It is also thought that he was of African origin.

Popular myth holds that Aesop's storytelling skills made him so beloved by the Greeks that he was permitted to travel as a free man. When he arrived in the realm of King Croesus, he was invited to stay as a citizen. There Aesop ingratiated himself, using his illustrative fables to reconcile people. His ambassadorial skills inspired Croesus to send him on a mission to Delphi to dispense a quantity of gold to the populace. But the greed displayed there so offended Aesop that he threatened to return the gold to Croesus. This action enraged the Delphis and they executed Aesop.

The Curse of "The Scottish Play"

Myths are sometimes invented out of whole cloth, but on occasion there may actually be enough fabric to warrant them. Ask any actor to say the name of Shakespeare's *Macbeth* and, if he or she has any experience at all on the boards, you'll likely hear in response, "The Scottish Play." M-a-c-b-e-t-h, it seems, is the title they dare not mention by name.

Actors are, by dint of their tenuous profession, superstitious. But the curse of *Macbeth*—hereinafter referred to as "The Scottish Play"—is one myth that has every indication of being true. Fittingly enough, it started on opening night in 1606 when the actor (yes, actor) playing Lady "The-Scottish-Play" fell ill, and Shakespeare himself had to go on in his place (shades of the movie *Shakespeare in Love*). Fortunately, there were no theater critics in those days; unfortunately, there was the unhappy patron who had hired the Bard to write the play. When he hated it, the work was pulled from the repertoire.

Theater historians confide that there has rarely been a production of "The Scottish Play" since then that has not added to the legendary curse. In 1849, in New York, 23 people were killed when a riot broke out at the Astor Place Opera House. According to Carl Sifakis's *The Encyclopedia of American Crime,* Orson Welles's 1936 Harlem stage interpretation of a *Voodoo Macbeth* (transposed from Scotland to Haiti) was a smash, but the lead actor fell ill and Welles had to go on—in blackface. The Old Vic's 1937 Laurence Olivier version sidelined its director (traffic accident), its producer (his dog died), and its star (Olivier's voice). Just to make it binding, the head of the Old Vic died on opening night. In 1981 the New York Lincoln Center revival was likewise cursed when its star, Philip Anglim, lost his voice for two weeks.

Not even the movies have been spared. Roman Polanski's bloody 1971 incarnation was the first motion picture from Playboy Productions—and the last.

So the next time somebody announces he or she has been cast in "The Scottish Play," don't say the customary "break a leg." In this case, it just might come true.

✓ **REALITY CHECK**

Playground Myth #4

"Shortly after the Cyclone roller coaster opened at Six Flags Magic Mountain (known at the time only as Magic Mountain), it is said that 'a really fat woman' got into the car, but could not bring down the safety bar over her rather excessive front lap. Supposedly, as the coaster takes its first big leap, so does she. She went flying out and landed with a crash, necessitating the temporary closing of the ride (and a rather large coffin)."

—submitted by Robert W. Abramoff, California

Poor Richard's Almanack

Written and published by Benjamin Franklin between 1733 and 1758, *Poor Richard's Almanack*—ascribed to "Friend and Servant Richard Saunders"—contained wisdom, discourse, maxims, meteorological predictions, how-to hints, and a little hokum. Considering that the multitalented Franklin, who would live to be 86, was only 27 when he wrote his first edition, his folksy insights were remarkable:

> *Eat to live, not live to eat.*
> *He that lies down with dogs shall rise up with fleas.*
> *Men and melons are hard to know.*
> *He's a fool that makes his doctor an heir.*
> *Beware of meat twice boiled, and an old foe reconciled.*

So, as it turns out, was his sense of fun. For as honorable as Franklin was in his politics and as publisher of *The Philadelphia Gazette*, he was not above allowing "R. Saunders" to pull a prank. Case in point: Titan Leeds.

In a back-and-forth that went on in the pages of the Almanack for eight years, Richard and an old schoolmate named Titan Leeds sniped at each other over something that should have been settled early on: the date and time of Leeds's death.

According to the 1733 edition, Leeds passed away on October 17, 1733, at 3:29 P.M. Because the Almanack was published well ahead of that date, Leeds responded to Richard in time for the next year's edition: "I have by the Mercy of God lived to write a Diary for the year 1734 . . . " Richard duly published it, adding with a straight face, " . . . whether he be really yet dead, I cannot at this Writing positively assure my Readers."

The fact that Leeds published a competing almanac didn't escape Richard's notice. Yet, until he stopped the hoax in 1740 (in *Poor Richard's Eighth Almanack*), he insisted that "W.B." and "A.B." have "continued to publish Almanacks in his Name ever since; asserting for some Years that he was still living; At length when the Truth could no longer be concealed from the World, they confess his death in their Almanack for 1739, but pretend that he died not till last Year, and that before his Departure he had furnished them with Calculations for 7 Years to come."

As "proof" of Leeds's 1733 demise, Franklin reports that, while napping in his office one day, Leeds paid him a visit from the Other World and slipped him a note containing three predictions for the following year:

1. About the middle of June next, J. J——n, Philomat (resident of Philadelphia), shall be openly reconciled to the Church of Rome, and give all his Goods and Chattles to the Chappel, being perverted be a certain Country Schoolmaster.
2. On the 7th of September following my old friend W. B——t shall be sober 9 Hours, to the Astonishment of all his Neighbours;
3. And about the same time W.B. and A.B. will publish another Almanack in my Name, in spite of Truth and Common-Sense.*

With that, Richard/Franklin left it to his "Courteous Readers" to decide when Titan Leeds really died, never raising the question of whether he had ever lived.

An Authentic American Legend: Johnny Appleseed

His given name was Jonathan Chapman, but he is better known as Johnny Appleseed; and for once in American folklore, everything they say about him is true. Unusual for a national hero, he didn't win his reputation by fighting wars or forging the new nation. Instead, he planted trees.

Chapman seems to have been born in Boston in 1775. However, his legend begins 26 years later in the Territory of Ohio,

---

*Spelling is of the period.

✓ **REALITY CHECK**

Playground Myth #5

"When I was in second grade or so, a prim little school friend noticed I was chewing on my nails while waiting for the ball to come my way (the vicissitudes of playing deep defense for a strong team in soccer). Laura calmly noted that *she* knew of a girl who *loved* to chew her nails, and since nails were made of a different material you couldn't digest them and they just stay in your stomach. What happened is that after *years* of nail-biting, the rogue nails had collected in her stomach and formed an *evil ball*. One time she tripped, and the ball was so sharp "like razor blades" that it tore through the wall of her stomach and emerged. Of course, the girl died."

—submitted by Sally Cragin, Missouri

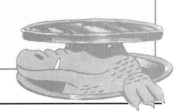

where he appeared with a horseload of apple seeds and began planting them on the farm of Isaac Stadden. Chapman's saga became hazy for another five years until he was seen passing through Jefferson County, on the Ohio River, rowing two canoes that were lashed together and loaded with apple seeds. By this time Jon Chapman had become "Johnny Appleseed." He continued westward to the state of Indiana, then to western Pennsylvania, and on to Michigan, stopping at every fertile spot along the way to plant trees. Observers recalled that he planted the trees by hand, walking barefoot along the grass and scrub brush, his buckskin seed bag hanging from his shoulder. He always told the settlers where he was sowing so they could prepare clearings in which to transplant the saplings once they sprouted.

Johnny's life was as ascetic as his crop. He was, by all accounts, a strict vegetarian and deplored any waste of food. His scholarship was altruistic. He would cut apart a book into chapters and distribute them among homes as he walked through a territory, always returning in the same order to deliver the next chapter to the waiting readers on his circuit.

By 1838, civilization encroached upon Johnny's sensibilities so heavily that he went even farther west. His last recorded story dates from 1847 when he entered the household of a now-nameless settler in Allen County, Indiana. Although he arrived at suppertime, he accepted only some bread and milk, sitting in the sun-drenched doorway to eat it. By morning, he had fallen ill, and a doctor was summoned. The doctor reported that he had never seen anyone so ready to accept death, that there was almost a beatific glow on the man's face. Jonathan Chapman died shortly thereafter, at the age of 72. He had spent 46 years traveling across hundreds of thousands of square miles of the newborn nation, leaving a legacy of food that sustained the pioneers who followed him. He died knowing no one, yet everyone knew him.

And if this story isn't true, it ought to be.

American Semi-heroes

For the generation growing up in the atomic age, television replaced the dime novel in forming the image of America's frontier past. Sure, the movies did their job to etch the archetypes of the Old West (*Stagecoach*, *Gunfight at the O.K. Corral*, *Red River*), but as big a star as John Wayne was, did he ever have his own theme song?

They don't make TV shows about bad guys, or at least they didn't used to. That's why, when early TV producers told stories to the baby boomers, they sometimes had to disguise a dark past with a white hat. Here's the truth about our childhood "heroes":

1. **Wyatt Earp (1848–1929).** The lyrics of his TV theme song said he was "brave, courageous and bold," and he was, sort of. But the legendary marshall of Tombstone, Arizona, and Dodge City, Kansas, was also—with his brothers James, Morgan, Virgil, and Warren—a vicious shakedown thug who demanded a share of any illicit business that went on in his town.

2. **"Bat" Masterson (1853–1921).** William Bartholemew Masterson was a natty dresser who "wore a cane and derby hat," which was very daring in the 1880s when western streets had as many road apples as gunfighters. Apropos the latter, "Bat" Masterson (he changed his name because he hated "Bartholomew") was, by all accounts, so fast on the draw that adversaries knew never to challenge him. A buffalo hunter, hero in the "Indian wars," and an itinerant lawman who occasionally helped out his friend Wyatt Earp, Masterson's reputation exceeds him. Of the dozens of men he supposedly shot in his long career, he killed only one, and the other guy drew first.

3. **"Texas" John Slaughter (1841–1922).** The "Disneyland" TV miniseries starring Tom Tryon was a colorful twist on the life of this cattleman-turned-lawman

✓ **REALITY CHECK**

Playground Myth #6

"There was an elderly couple who lived in our neighborhood when I was a kid who were never home on Halloween eve, but left a shopping bag full of candy on their doorstep. Rumors had it that they had once been frightened and tormented almost to death by kids one Halloween years ago so they refused to be home, and they left the candy to keep from having their house burned down as a 'trick.' When we grew up we finally learned that Halloween eve was a family anniversary so they always spent it out, but they were kindly enough to leave candy out anyway. Naturally, those of us 'in the know' got there early and emptied it before any of the other kids came by."

—submitted by Emily Lockman, Massachusetts

("Texas John Slaughter made 'em do what they ought-er"). The real Slaughter was a well-heeled rancher who chased rustlers off his land by any means possible, including shooting them. When he was made sheriff of Cochise County, Arizona (where Tombstone was located) in the late 1880s, he picked up the pieces after the messy Earp–Clanton showdown at the O.K. Corral. Although Slaughter himself was honest, he was a bad judge of employees. His deputy, Burt Alvord, turned out to be one of the most corrupt lawmen in the territory. Slaughter retired in the 1890s.

4. **"Judge" Roy Bean (1825?–1902).** He called himself "The law west of the Pecos," and he was. He covered all the bases from policeman to judge to jury, as well as saloon keeper and whorehouse owner. Bean's sole qual-ification to administer the law in the town of Vinegaroon was that he owned a copy of *The Revised Statutes of the State of Texas*. Like many territorial "judges" of the era, Roy Bean was really a gangster who happily accepted fines from the varmints he and his henchmen hauled in. His reign came to an end in 1896 when he ran for re-election and the ballot box wound up with more ballots than there were voters.

5. **Daniel Boone (1734?–1820).** Whether you believe that "Daniel Boone was a man, yes a biiiiiig man" (Lionel Newman and Vera Montson's TV theme) or that he laughed "Elbow room!" (as poet Arthur Guiteman rhymed in "Daniel Boone"), he was still very much a pioneer. Following the French and Indian War of 1856, North Carolina–born Boone went through the Cumberland Gap and saw a lake containing a large salt lick (the signifi-cance of this salt lick is that it attracted a huge amount of game). The region had been declared off limits to colonists by a 1763 decree from King George III, but when news of Boone's discovery "leaked" to whites, the

✓ **REALITY CHECK**

Playground Myth #7

"My friend Charlie, of St. Paul's School and Princeton pedigree, said that a kid in his class picked on a booger, which turned out to be a worm that had grown in the sinus cavity on his face and it was three feet long by the time he finished pulling it out, and he had to be careful not to let it break, because then they would have to operate. Quite possibly he was pulling my leg, but he was a junior at Princeton; isn't that a little old for fibs?"
—submitted by Kietryn Zychal, California

scramble incited feuds among resident Native American tribes. By 1773, Boone was leading settlement parties into the Cumberland Gap, claiming the region as "Kentucke" and further displacing the original residents.

6. **Davy Crockett (1786–1836).** Davy Crockett was a renowned storyteller, but what is remarkable about his legend is that the broad strokes of it are true. According to B. A. Botkin's *Treasury of American Folklore*, he did, indeed, come from Tennessee, which he described as "born in a cane break, cradled in a sap trough, and clouted [clothed] with coon skins." He ingratiated himself to one and all as a good ol' boy by telling folksy tales, many of which he saw fit to write down in almanacs, which means that he was literate. According to Crockett, he once tied a wolf's tail through a knothole in a tree, skinned a b'ar and forced her to run around nekked, and talked a raccoon into surrendering rather than take a bullet. With such skills of persuasion, it was natural that Crockett would run for Congress. He won election in 1829 and, once in Washington, became known more as a humorist than a politician. After two terms he "lit out" to Texas where he heard of a fight raging between a Mexican general and some American squatters who refused to surrender a building they were occupying in San Antonio. Thus did Davy Crockett, a Tennessean, die giving birth to Texas—and his own legend—at the Alamo.

7. **John Henry (1836?–1875?).** Everybody knows about "steel-drivin' man" John Henry, and perhaps can even sing a stanza or two of the famous folk song about how he beat the steam drill. But there appears to be little hard information about exactly what happened in that contest in the early 1870s that gave Americans—and especially African-Americans—a true hero. What is reported is that Henry, 34, weighed between 200 and 225 pounds and was the best driver on the Chesapeake & Ohio Railroad. A "driver" was responsible for drilling holes into the rock to hold dynamite charges. To blast through the

Big Bend Tunnel in Talcott, West Virginia, the C&O obtained a steam-powered drill that was advertised as capable of doing the job of any laborer. When John Henry swore he could beat the steam drill, the contest was on: Whoever made the most headway in 35 minutes would win the $100 prize. Using two 20-pound sledge hammers, Henry sank two 7-foot holes, compared to the machine's single 9-foot hole, making him the clear winner. Unfortunately, the strain was too much for him, and he died that night. His statue now stands atop the tunnel.

8. **Paul Bunyan (1914–).** Fabled woodsman Paul Bunyan, who traveled the forests of the northern United States with Babe, his blue ox (blue because Bunyan discovered him nearly frozen in the snow), is a staple of the American landscape. He stands guard over diners, lumber yards, and miniature golf courses; his legend was further visualized as a 1958 Disney cartoon. Far from having a frontier past, however, Bunyan was actually born in 1914. His "father" was W. B. Laughhead, an advertising writer, who created the legendary lumberjack for a sales brochure for the Red River Lumber Company of Minneapolis, Minnesota.

9. **Francis Marion (1732?–1795).** The American Revolutionary War general better known as "The Swamp Fox" (played by Leslie Nielsen, for those who remember him from before his comedies), gained fame for leading colonists in guerrilla tactics against the British army. Part double agent and part visionary, Marion made it a point to pester and outwit the Redcoats. The movie's portrayal of the legend raises two questions. First, did the American colonists really hide behind rocks and fire at the Redcoats who remained standing in neat rows out in the open waiting to be shot? Second, did the colonists still have British accents?

10. **Butch Cassidy (1886-1911? or 1937?).** Butch Cassidy, whose real name was Robert Leroy Parker, was the

outlaw scallawag who invented train robbery. He formed The Wild Bunch in the late 1890s and founded their hideout at Hole-in-the-Wall, also known as Robber's Roost. By all accounts, Cassidy was a great shot, a clever leader, and a brilliant strategist. He also never actually killed anybody. After he robbed a Union Pacific train, Pinkerton detectives tracked him down, not to arrest him, but to offer him, on behalf of the railroad, a job as a security guard. In other words, a payoff to stay away from their trains. Unfortunately, while he was in negotiations, his gang robbed another Union Pacific train, and the chase was on. In 1901, Cassidy, the Sundance Kid (Harry Longbaugh) and Etta Place (who was not a school-teacher as in the movie, but a "working girl") began a trek that ended in either Bolivia in 1911 (if you saw the movie) or in Washington State in 1937 (if you believe Cassidy's sister, Lula Parker Betenson) when he died of old age.

Parson Weems and George Washington

Perhaps George Washington couldn't tell a lie, but Mason Locke Weems could, and it has lasted 200 years. Thanks to "Parson" Weems, every schoolchild thinks that the young father of our country chopped down a cherry tree and then nobly 'fessed up to it.

Weems, a clergyman-turned-book peddler, published *The Life and Memorable Actions of George Washington* in 1800, the year after Washington died, intending to affirm and celebrate the legend of the general, plantation owner, and first U. S. president. Although the famous cherry tree story did not appear until the fifth of more than seventy editions of his work, it has stood the test of time, not to mention attempts at verification.

✓ **REALITY CHECK**

Playground Myth #8

"All my life I've heard that this works, but I've never heard of anybody who actually succeeded at it: If you stick somebody's hand in warm water while they're sleeping, they'll wet the bed. Supposedly this happens a lot at summer camp and boarding school, and the next morning the poor kid gets the nickname 'Midnight Sailor.' Maybe it's a guy thing."

—submitted by Liane Brandon, Massachusetts

In point of fact, Weems credits the story not to Washington or to himself (though it almost certainly could be), but to "an aged lady" whom he had met 20 years earlier. She was "a distant relative, and, when a girl, spent much of her time in the family." It is therefore possible that the woman in question was a slave (like other early presidents, George was a slave owner). The story is set in 1738 when Washington was six. He had been testing his hatchet on "the body of a beautiful young cherry tree" and accidentally felled it.

"George," said his father, "do you know who killed that beautiful little cherry tree yonder in the garden?"

This was a tough question, and George staggered under it for a moment: but quickly recovered himself and looking at his father, with the sweet face of youth brightened by the inexpressible charm of all-conquering truth, he bravely cried out, "I can't tell a lie, Pa; you know I can't tell a lie. I did cut it with my hatchet."

"Run to my arms, you dearest boy," cried his father in transports, "run to my arms; glad am I, George, that you killed me tree; for you have paid me a thousand fold. Such an act of heroism in my son is more worth than a thousand trees, though blossomed with silver, and their fruits of purest gold."

Weems was not a man otherwise known to spin yarns, so his efforts on behalf of Washington have been seen as his contribution to the folklore of the young country. Ironically, Weems was "out of town" when America itself was formed. Born in Anne Arundel County, Maryland, in 1759, he studied medicine, and, according to his family genealogy, may have spent the Revolutionary War as a surgeon in service to the British Navy. Notably, on his father's death in 1779, Weems freed the family's slaves, then proceeded to England to study for the ministry. With the help of John Adams and Benjamin Franklin, Weems obtained ordination, then returned to Maryland to preach. After his retirement, he started writing, and spent his later years overseeing revisions of what had become his bestseller. He died in 1825. *(Thanks to Mason Locke Weems for his permission to use selections from his research and family history.)*

Ned Buntline, the Legend Builder

For starters, Ned Buntline's name wasn't Ned Buntline, it was Edward Zane Carroll Judson. But that doesn't matter, because he also lied about William Frederick "Buffalo" Bill Cody and James Butler "Wild Bill" Hickok. What the heck, it sold dime novels.

Judson and Buntline lived separate lives, even though they were the same person. Born in 1823 in the Catskills town of Stamford, New York, Judson was an adventurer. When his father, a failed writer, insisted on moving the family to Philadelphia, young Ed spent his time learning the streets of the new city, then took to the sea at age 14. He returned in 1842, when he felt he could settle down. By then he already had a reputation as a hellion, having gotten in trouble for talking back to a ship's officer, starting brawls, fighting duels, stealing from the mess—and then writing about it. When magazines rejected his stories as too crass, he printed them himself, taking the pseudonym "Buntline" after the name for the rope at the foot of a square sail.

Over the next few years, Judson married several times and dallied several more, always squeaking through encounters with the law. Judson's closest call came in 1844. He killed a man who had discovered him *in flagrante* with his wife. Testifying in his own defense at his murder trial, Judson narrowly missed assassination in the courtroom by his victim's brother. As Buntline, he then embellished the story to make it sound as though he had barely escaped lynching (a lynch crowd had indeed formed, but that was just for show; Judson remained in protective custody until he quietly left town).

Meanwhile, Buntline started and folded several periodicals that naturally featured his own writing. He finally began the magazine that people remember, *Ned Buntline's Own*, in the mid-1840s,

---

✓ **REALITY CHECK**

Playground Myth #9

"In the third grade there was an older guy named Max whose older brother shared all the secrets of sex with him, which made him the worldliest of third graders, bar none (there was never anything forthcoming from Max, but he seemed to thrive on the publicity). One day Max brought a rubber to school. He spent the day with the thing rolled down over his index finger, chasing the girls around with it and giggling maniacally. When we asked Max about it, he said his brother had given it to him, and it was used for sex. None of us could figure that out. Well, soon after that the movie *Goldfinger* came out, which made quite a stir for being dirty and full of sex. Now it was clear to us: if *Goldfinger* was a movie full of sex, and if Max chased girls around with one of those things on his finger, then obviously sex was something that a guy did to a girl by touching her somewhere with one of those things on his finger."

—submitted by Ron Harris, New York

gleefully printing one exaggerated story after another, cashing in on easterners' fascination with the "romantic" West and westerners' nostalgia for the decadent East. During this time, Buntline's most important (and lurid) book, *The Mysteries and Miseries of New York*, was published and became an enormous success. While researching New York nightlife, Ned found himself attracted to the city and started making connections at every level within it. One of the connections turned out to be a political upstart named Captain Isaiah Rynders, who detested the British as much as Buntline did. On May 7, 1849, Buntline, Rynders, and others fomented a riot during a performance of *Macbeth* at the Astor Opera House in New York, and 23 people were killed. Just before he was taken away to serve a year in jail for his part in the debacle, Buntline's fourth wife, Annie, divorced him.

On his release, Judson found his life in a shambles. Politics was out, business was impossible, and decent society shunned him. Ah, but there was always Ned Buntline. Writing for his own magazine as well as *The New York Mercury*, Buntline drew from Judson's life and cranked out a series of dime novels, each brimming with purple prose and rough-hewn ideas, and venerating not only himself but the men he had met while on his life's odyssey. At the same time, paralyzed with fear at the number of people he had hurt during the first 30 years of his life, Judson fled the city in the mid-1850s for the Adirondack Mountains. There he married again, was widowed again, and kept writing. During this time, he celebrated the adventures of "Wild Bill" Hickok, "Buffalo Bill" Cody, Sitting Bull, Annie Oakley (nee Phoebee Mozee), Yellow Hand, and other actual figures he turned into flamboyant heroes with his pen. He died in 1886, still in print.

Edward Z. C. Judson lived a life of extraordinary daring. But only as Ned Buntline did he burn his way into history, bringing the Old West along with him by virtue of having practically invented it.

Old Wives' Tales, or Bad Advice from Well Meaning Relatives

✓ REALITY CHECK

Knock on Wood

When people "knock on wood" or "touch wood" for luck, they are continuing a medieval superstition. At that time, people believed that evil or mischievous spirits hid in hollow trees. If these spirits overheard a human's plans, they would interfere. If the person knocked on the tree trunk, however, he or she could frighten the spirits and then continue the conversation without fear of eavesdroppers.

Nothing ever becomes real until it is experienced—Even a proverb is no Proverb to you till your Life has illustrated it.

—John Keats

Old wives' tales were the first urban legends. They took hold because they represent some kind of truth, or at least seemed to make sense at the time. But who are these "old wives" everybody talks about? Why should they know more than the experts?

Pop quiz: Who would you believe more, a scientist or a bunch of Peruvian Indians? Okay, now add this: In the 1640s, the Peruvian Indians ground up cinchona tree bark and fed it to the sick to lower a fever. A team of Jesuit missionaries noticed this practice, told others about it, and, as a result, the Peruvian Indians' primitive remedy taught the rest of the world about quinine. Too bad that British Lord Protector Oliver Cromwell—a fierce Protestant at a time when Protestants were at war with Roman Catholics—refused the Indians' life-saving medicine because it was defended by Catholic missionaries. Cromwell died of malaria in 1658. As the old wives' tale says, "Civilization advances funeral by funeral."

Scientists have often been astonished that those old wives really had their act together. Nevertheless, the difference between folk knowledge and "acceptable" scholarship is a conflict that can be traced throughout history. It's still creating tension, even in today's presumably more enlightened times. In fact,

- How many medicines are we losing to the commercial destruction of the rain forest?
- Maybe food additives aren't good for us after all.
- Why did our mothers tell us not to sit too close to the TV set when we were kids, yet as adults we all face a computer monitor a foot away?

So where were the old wives while the experts were in college? They were watching, and doing, and sharing with other old wives through the normal activity of conversation. How else, you may ask, would the average person living in medieval times know that the foxglove plant contains digitalis, a drug that (we know today) treats heart disease? Probably by trial and error, and by observation conducted throughout centuries of unrecorded history—the same way that primitive man learned that some mushrooms kill you and others don't, that the tides flow in predictable patterns, that salmon swim past the cave at the same time each year, and that when Bernie ate that plant over there, he stopped having chest pains. But when Caleb ate that other plant, he died. So let's hear it for Bernie.

Before the scientific method became accepted as an orderly means to codify the wonders of the world into a useful guide to life, human knowledge wasn't recorded in books. It was handed down by shaman, medicine men, practitioners, midwives, servants, priests, rabbis, gurus, and Mom and Dad.

That having been said, although some folk knowledge is right, some of it is just plain wrong:

- Disease is not caused by "evil humours" that envelop the body, but by germs, which Louis Pasteur posited in 1861.
- "An apple a day keeps the doctor away" works only if the illness happens to be constipation, since apple juice is a mild laxative.
- "The doctor brings babies in his black bag" is a sweet way to distract children from learning about birth control. Still, you'd be surprised that many unwed mothers today tell obstetric nurses, "Gee, I didn't know *that's* what caused babies."
- "If you lose something, you will always find it in the last place you look for it." Well, duh.

There is always a germ of truth in the aphorisms that inform our culture, even if sometimes you have to blast for it. This chapter explores some of the most pervasive of these maxims and tries to establish or debunk their veracity. Don't be surprised if Grandma was smarter than Einstein, even if the only theory of relativity she ever proposed was to your grandfather.

Is It True What They Say About Men with Big Feet?

It's true: Men with big feet wear big shoes.

Milk Soothes Ulcers

Stomach ulcers are disruptions of the mucous membrane of the stomach lining caused, in part, by the overproduction of the stomach acid used to digest food. Milk, a substance containing complex proteins, is harder to digest than most compounds. Thus, drinking it to soothe a stomach ulcer may actually trigger the production of more acid.

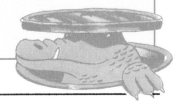

Chicken Soup Cures Colds

Chicken soup is good for everybody but the chicken. Although there is no scientific proof of the medicinal value of *potage poulet*, it is universally accepted as being "good for what ails you." Scientific data is conspicuously sparse, but several theories abound:

- Chicken soup is a more palatable way of getting fluid into the body.
- The steam rising from the bowl enters the nose and clears the sinuses.
- The salt in the soup promotes fluid retention.
- Your mother serves it to you, and it's her attention that helps cure the cold, not the soup.
- It's just mind over matter—or mind over mucus.

There are just as many people who insist that hot and sour soup is a palliative for the common cold. Certainly the spices used in this soup open the nasal passages. Ask anyone whose healthy nose has started running during a spicy Asian, Indian, or Mexican meal. For those whose stomachs can't tolerate the heavier pork or beef stock base of some hot and sour soup recipes, the comparatively milder chicken stock base can have a more soothing effect. So we're back to chicken.

But is it an actual curative? You know what "they" say: If you take something for your cold, it will last seven days. If you do nothing, it will last a week.

Don't Sit So Close to the TV Set

How ironic that the first generation raised with television—and which was constantly warned by their parents not to sit too close to the TV set because it would hurt their eyesight—now spends 10 hours a day sitting in front of a computer screen, and nobody seems to care.

In point of fact, there is increasing anecdotal evidence—though it's not yet codified into a formal study—that computer screens may, indeed, affect vision. Some consumer watchdog groups have also indicated that it is a good idea to avoid standing behind a computer screen because of the possibility of low-level radiation leakage.

There certainly seems to be an increase in carpal tunnel syndrome and tennis elbow. This is the result (some say) of resting the hands on the keyboard all the time instead of having to stop at the end of every line to slap the typewriter carriage back to the left-hand margin.

Your Face Is Going to Freeze That Way

Unless one is afflicted with a form of paralysis such as Bell's palsy or myasthenia gravis, there is little chance that one's face will ever "freeze" in a specific position. This advice falls into the same category as "Don't cross your eyes. I knew a kid who did that and his eyes stayed that way forever." For either change to occur, one's muscles would have to become detached and replaced, or lock in spasm. And either contingency can be surgically corrected.

(*Hint*: The next time Mom says that, say, "Oh, yeah? Name him." If your face isn't already unstuck, her surprised look should finish the job.)

Truck Drivers Know the Best Places to Eat

What is it about the dining public that they will buy cookbooks, watch TV cooking shows hosted by Cordon Bleu chefs, pay outrageous prices to be mistreated at hoity-toity restaurants, and then say, "Truck drivers always know the best places to eat"?

Professional interstate truck drivers have demanding and lonely jobs. Often they must pay expenses out of their own pockets, so the profit margin is tight. Add in the dangers of the road and the

Copper Bracelets Have Curative Powers

The only thing a copper bracelet does is turn your wrist green. No jewelry or other external application has the least effect against arthritis, rheumatism, epilepsy, pleurisy, or any other medical condition, even though various gizmos have been sold throughout the ages with the promise that they have curative properties.

Chemicals in human perspiration combine with the copper to produce that greenish tinge that looks rather unbecoming (unless you're a Vulcan). To eliminate it, paint the underside of copper jewelry with clear nail polish.

✓ REALITY CHECK

Dead Man's Hand

"Aces and eights" in poker are called a "dead man's hand" because James Butler "Wild Bill" Hickok was holding a pair of each when he was shot to death by Jack McCall on August 2, 1876. Known to taunt challengers into gunfights so that he could kill them fair and square, Hickok had settled into Deadwood Gulch in the Dakota Territory, gotten married, and planned to search for gold. He was enjoying a card game in the Number 10 Saloon when McCall, who held Hickok responsible for his brother's death, put a bullet in the back of his head.

size of the average rig, and drivers are forced to select roadside dining that is:

- Cheap
- Safe (to park and catnap)
- Convenient (and easy to exit and re-enter the highway)

And there's something else you hear around truck stops: Drivers park, not necessarily where the food is hot, but where the waitresses are. It gets lonely on the road.

The Death Penalty Is a Deterrent to Murder

Does the death penalty act as a deterrent to murder? According to the Death Penalty Information Center, as of this writing, 609 people have been put to death since individual states resumed executions in 1976. Yet people go right on killing each other.

"The facile notion that there's a link between the death penalty and deterring people doesn't hold water," argues attorney Stephen F. Rohde, president of the American Civil Liberties Union of Southern California and a Board member of Death Penalty Focus. "Countries with the death penalty have higher crime rates than countries without the death penalty; states with the death penalty in the United States have higher crime rates than states without the death penalty; there's even evidence that . . . crime rates go up after an execution."

If death penalty advocates are so convinced that the punishment is a deterrent, why aren't executions televised?

"I think they realize," adds Rohde, "that it would put the death penalty in people's homes. It's reminiscent of news footage of Vietnam; when we finally saw the horror of Vietnam, that actually led to greater opposition to the war."

Moreover, social and religious groups can't agree on the fine points of the morality involved. Some insist that it's wrong to take *any* human life (unborn children and convicted murderers alike).

Others believe that it's wrong to take an *innocent* human life (*e.g.*, a fetus), but it's okay to take a *guilty* human life (*e.g.*, a murderer). Still others support abortion as a matter of choice, yet oppose the death penalty because of flaws in the legal system.

The fact is that most homicides in America are not premeditated. They are crimes of passion committed "in the heat of the moment" between people who know each other. In such circumstances, deterrence doesn't enter into the equation.

As quoted in David Rintel's *Clarence Darrow for the Defense*, "attorney for the damned" Clarence Darrow once explained his absolute opposition to the death penalty: "I never hesitated to defend a man accused of murder, if only to prevent a second murder, by the state." Darrow's admittedly liberal logic is helpful in explaining the fallacy of the death penalty as a *deterrent*:

> If people are really kept from punishment through fear, then the more terrible the punishment provided, the greater the fear. The old forms of torture should be brought back. (. . .) Our . . . lawmakers even seek to make death by the State as painless as possible, and thus take away most of the fear that is supposed to prevent the weak from committing crime.

Instead, the opposite is true, as states spend millions of tax dollars annually housing death row inmates and prosecuting their appeals through the court system. Ask the grieving, angry families of murder victims. At the heart of the capital punishment controversy is not deterrence, but revenge.

In explaining why the U.S. government had not executed any federal prisoners since 1963 while various states had been proceeding with their executions since 1976, U.S. Attorney General Janet Reno announced at a January 21, 2000, Justice Department news briefing (reported by *Reuters*): "I have inquired for most of my adult life about studies that might show that the death penalty is a deterrent. And I have not seen any research that would substantiate that point. Before I authorize anything such as that, I make sure that the facts and the law justify it."

"If You Puts a Knife under the Bed, It Cuts the Pain in Two"

This may have been the medical advice given to Prissy in *Gone with the Wind*, but it has absolutely nothing to do with easing the pain of childbirth. It does, however, suggest why the first thing out of someone's mouth in a movie childbirth scene is, "Boil some water." Presumably the water is to sterilize the instruments (it certainly isn't to cook the baby!), but those scenes seem to take place only in homes or stables where there are never any medical instruments around. Prevailing wisdom (there's that term again) seems to be that husbands are ordered to "boil some water" to give them something to do so they'll stay out of the way of the "wimmenfolk."

You Can Catch a Bird by Putting Salt on Its Tail

If you're close enough to dump salt on a bird's tail, you're close enough to use your hands! And what exactly is the salt supposed to do?

Salt is a good way to get rid of snails and slugs, though. It kills them by rapid dehydration. In fact, you can watch them sputter and dissolve right before your very eyes. Alas, the salt changes the salinity of your garden, so it is not suggested for pest control on soil. But if the critters slime their way up onto the sidewalk, sprinkle away.

Which brings up the old joke about a guy who comes home from work one night and finds a snail crawling on his newspaper. He picks up the snail and lobs it across the street, then takes his paper and goes inside. Three months later there's a knock at his door. The guy opens the door, and the snail says, "What was that all about?"

You Can Lead a Horse to Water, but You Can't Make Him Drink

It is a common presumption that the ready availability of knowledge in and of itself is not sufficient to inspire learning. In his play *Man and Superman* (1903), author George Bernard Shaw posited, "Those who go to the racecourses can stay away from them and go to the classical concerts instead if they like: there is no law against it. . . . A mere physical gulf they could bridge; but the gulf of dislike is impassable and eternal." Similarly, the purveyors of popular culture seem to think that "the masses" will reject entertainment that stimulates the mind as well as the adrenaline. As proof, look what's on TV.

There is, however, just as much indication that someone who enjoys reading one book will immediately read another, and that literacy is the greatest incentive to learn that one person can ever bestow upon another. Parents glow when they hear their child utter his first word; teachers report the elation of seeing a student sparkle at the moment of discovery; and what kid hasn't beamed from ear to ear when the teacher calls on her and she has the right answer?

Alexander Pope, in *An Essay on Criticism* (1711), offered the following caution against shortchanging the educational process:

> A little learning is a dangerous thing;
> Drink deep, or taste not the Pierian spring;
> There shallow draughts intoxicate the brain,
> And drinking largely sobers us again.

Thus, the saying "You can lead a horse to water, but you can't make him drink" denies the existence of human curiosity. The only reason people won't think is that they have been discouraged from doing so by those people who want to keep them uneducated. Yet the history of the disenfranchised in America (African-Americans, Irish, Italians) who have thrived, and even set up their own educational systems after being cut out of society's

✓ REALITY CHECK

Senior Citizens and Dog Food

As baby boomers dominated American commerce in the 1960s, rumors began circulating that senior citizens on fixed incomes were being driven to eat dog food. The image of Grandma and Grandpa being saved from starvation by a $1.15 can of Fido Food was disturbing. Ironically, it may have been fed by an old episode of *The Honeymooners* in which Ralph Kramden and Ed Norton feasted on what they thought was Alice's paté, but which turned out to be—well, you get the idea. Although dog food is manufactured to health standards that would make it fit for human consumption, no studies support this as a standard practice.

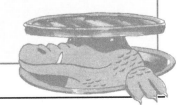

schools, proves the contrary. Maybe you can keep a good horse down, but not a good person.

You Can Catch VD from a Toilet Seat

Sexually Transmitted Diseases (STDs) received this name precisely because they are transmitted through sexual contact. The list of STDs includes syphilis, gonorrhea, genital herpes, chlamydia, and HIV. Although the bodily fluids of an infected person can theoretically carry STD bacteria or viruses, most of these germs have an exceedingly short survival rate when exposed to light, heat, or air. Therefore the chance of catching anything from a toilet seat is nonexistent—unless, of course, that's where you had sex. And you can't "get infected" by swimming in the same pool as someone who is infected, as long as the chlorine concentration is at least 1.5 parts-per-million; in the open sea, the sun and salt essentially counteract the risk. Likewise, you know that girl everybody heard about in school who sued the pool owner because she got pregnant by swimming near a boy who ejaculated in the water? It didn't happen—at least, not in the pool.

The Shortest Distance Between Two Points Is a Straight Line

The shortest distance between two points is a straight line only in the abstract world of plane (Euclidean) geometry. As any airline pilot knows, a curved line is always the shortest distance between two points on the curved globe, such as London and New York, where the "Great Circle Route" adds the third dimension to Euclid's postulate. In the 1960s, a third mathematical theorem was offered by the highly respected scholarly journal, *MAD* magazine: "The shortest distance between two points is a taxi."

Truth Shall Be a Defense in a Libel Suit

First, let's make one distinction. *Slander* is when you *speak* a defamatory statement; *libel* is when you *print* it. Libel is therefore taken much more seriously because of the relative permanence and power of the written word.

That having been said, truth is, indeed, a *defense* to a lawsuit brought by someone who feels that he or she has been libeled. "Defense," however, is not the same as "exoneration." In addition, just because an allegedly libelous statement may be proven true in a court of law, it must still meet the U.S. Supreme Court's test under *Sullivan* v. *New York Times*, 1964:

1. Injury to the person or his reputation
2. Reckless disregard for the facts
3. Actual malice

He Drinks like a Fish

Although it looks as though they are constantly swallowing water, fish don't drink. They absorb any water they need from the food they eat. The mouth action is to force water over their gills, where oxygen is extracted so they can breathe. In any event, fish certainly don't "drink" in the sense of consuming alcohol.

The Two Airplanes Had a Near Miss

Let's hope not. By definition, *near miss* means that they *nearly missed hitting*; in other words, they collided.

By the same logic, when something or someone is accidentally ignored, it is said to have "fallen between the cracks." Using the imagery of flooring, if something "fell *between* the cracks," it landed on a floorboard. The expression should be, "fell *through* the cracks."

✓ REALITY CHECK

Bumblebees Shouldn't Fly

Bumblebees are aerodynamically unsound. Fortunately, they don't know anything about aerodynamics, so they can fly. There are two presumptions at work in this old saying. The first is whether bumblebees are capable of flight; obviously they are, even if they don't look like a 767. The second is somewhat more existential; namely, whether knowing their aerodynamic shortcomings would make them drop out of the sky. This is one case where ignorance is not only bliss, it buzzes.

✓ REALITY CHECK

Rape and Prostitution

The sexist remark that "you can't rape a prostitute" is not only offensive, it's uninformed. Prostitution is a consensual act involving sex (disregarding, for the sake of this example, the social and economic forces that may lead to prostitution). Rape is nonconsensual sex by means of force or coercion. Not only is it possible to rape a prostitute, but the ignorance shown by this locker room saying may encourage it.

Finally, how often have you heard the expression *desert island*, which conjures up the cartoon image of a bedraggled shipwreck survivor languishing beneath a lone palm tree on a circle of land the size of a Buick, surrounded by limitless ocean? Close, but no coconut. The geographic definition of *island* is "a body of land surrounded by water." A desert is "an arid region capable of supporting only a few life forms." This doesn't mean just sand. A desert can include such barren terrain as the polar ice caps. Although, theoretically, it would be possible to have an island in the desert, more accurate expressions might be *deserted island* or *tropical island*.

If You Feed Birds, They'll Forget How to Find Food for Themselves

Scattering seeds on the ground or placing a bird feeder in the backyard is a thoughtful gesture, but it doesn't replace birds' normal foraging. Think of it as cheese and crackers at a supper party. The birds just consider the feeder as another source of food, but that doesn't keep them from pursuing their normal activity. Further, a bird feeder in the snow does not prevent migrating birds from their seasonal schlep. Nature provides in many more ways than humans—even bird watchers—can imagine.

Every Cloud Has a Silver Lining

This refers, of course, to being optimistic, not to a meteorological phenomenon. Taken with sayings such as "It's always darkest just before the dawn" and "Put on a happy face," it means that one should always try to find something good in a bad situation. Before this starts to sound like a sermon, remember that "everyone loves a winner" and, human nature being what it is, nobody wants to hang around a loser. A positive attitude may hide the sad truth, but being upbeat is contagious and helps to provide emotional relief during painful times. Not surprisingly, good news follows good attitudes.

Just try not to sound like a moron. There's the story about the little boy whose parents were too poor to afford a Christmas gift, so they filled his stocking with horse manure. The boy was so optimistic that, when he saw what he got, he said, "Wow! Santa Claus brought me a pony, but it got away!"

To Get Rid of a Wart, Rub a Potato on It

Rubbing a potato on a wart and burying the spud in the ground does one thing: It sows a potato plant. The only way to get rid of a wart is with medicine. Warts are caused by viruses. Some viruses may be herpes, many may be contagious, and a few may be precancerous. This is why "a change in a wart or mole" is one of the warning signs of cancer and should be immediately referred to a physician.

The potato may be referred to a chef.

Also, frogs and toads have nothing to do with warts, but they may have something to do with Budweiser.

A Bad Penny Always Turns Up Again

The only "bad" penny is a slug, or a bent coin, or one that falls through a coin-operated vending machine without counting toward the purchase of the merchandise. Other than in gum ball dispensers, some of which still cost 1¢, the odds of receiving the same penny as change twice in one's lifetime is minuscule.

The expression refers to the unpleasant ability that troublesome people have of bothering those who have tried to get them out of their lives. The mooching relative, the money-grubbing friend, or the boring office worker never grasps that he or she is not wanted, and always seems to show up at the most inopportune time.

The Apple Doesn't Fall Far from the Tree

Children learn from their parents, not only through intended lessons but by example. The parent who says, "Do what I say, not what I do" hopes the child will ignore hypocrisy. But kids miss nothing, especially things that are forbidden; that's why parenting is such an important responsibility.

Unfortunately, the saying also includes bad apples. There is no question that biases are passed from parent to child. Corrective classroom lessons or television commercials alone cannot break the chain. To change these beliefs, the child must repudiate the parent, and that takes personal intervention.

The human race has survived because each generation learns from the preceding one and passes the knowledge on to the generation that follows. Sayings such as "like father, like son," "like mother, like daughter," and our apple adage reflect this legacy.

Mark Twain wrote, "When I was a boy of fourteen, my father was so ignorant I could hardly stand to have the old man around. But when I got to be twenty-one, I was astonished at how much the old man had learned in seven years."

So maybe there's hope after all.

Never Eat at Any Restaurant Called "Mom's"

Novelist Nelson Algren first gave this advice, which has been expanded over the years. Here's a recent version: "Never eat at any restaurant called 'Mom's,' never accept third-party checks, never sit down to play poker with any guy named after a city, never buy a ticket to any movie with a Roman numeral in the title, and never, ever—even if you ignore the other advice—never go to bed with anyone whose troubles are worse than your own."

Folksy as these cautions sound, they all involve trust. No restaurant cooking can possibly be as good as Mom's, and any that says it is, is full of scrapple. (For that matter, what the heck is "home-style cooking"?) Third-party checks are now so suspect

✓ REALITY CHECK

Flushing Down Under

For some reason, many people believe that water swirls down the drain in one direction in the Northern Hemisphere and in the other direction in the Southern Hemisphere. They are probably confusing the swirling action of a tub full of water with a phenomenon first noted by a civil engineer named Guastave-Gaspard Coriolis in 1835. The "Coriolis Effect" or "Coriolis Force," as it has come to be known, addresses why a moving object appears to change direction depending upon where one is standing while viewing it. For example, a ball tossed from a moving car will appear to veer backwards to someone inside the car, yet the ball will appear to fly in a straight line to someone standing on the curb as the car goes by.

(continued on next page)

that even banks refuse to accept them. Guys named after cities are, by tradition, superb gamblers (even if they sometimes can't go back to their namesakes without inspiring the melting of tar and the plucking of feathers). Movie sequels are well-known travesties of the originals (with the notable exception of *The Godfather Part II*, *Aliens*, *Terminator 2: Judgment Day*, even-numbered *Star Trek*s, and odd-numbered *Nightmare*s *on Elm Street*.

You Can Take the Lad Out of the Country but You Can't Take the Country Out of the Lad

Each of us is the sum of his or her experiences. Unless we purposely change our behavior (and sometimes even if we do), we will always reflect our heritage.

Sociologists, behaviorists, and other scholars have endlessly debated which carries more weight: Nature or Nurture. Erik Erikson and other psychologists suggest that human beings travel through developmental stages, any one of which can offer a variety of stimuli, and the aggregate of which forms a unique individual.

American speech is a perfect example of the way people cling to their roots. Various studies report that the average child spends between two and eight hours a day in front of the TV set, which is populated with people who speak standard, unaccented, and generally correct English. Well, if television is such a powerful tool, why do we still have regional accents? Why can't kids write term papers or talk about politics, and still know everything about the latest fads and rock groups?

It's because no single cultural event can change a person's basic personality. That includes giving Clem Kaddiddlehopper a bus ticket to New York City.

One famous movie star—okay, it was Cary Grant—even acknowledged that he was his own invention (he was born Archie Leech). He answered a female fan who gasped, "You're not Cary Grant!" with the rejoinder, "Truly, madam, nobody is."

✓ **REALITY CHECK**

Flushing Down Under

(continued from previous page)

The Coriolis Force does, however, affect great air masses as the earth rotates beneath them once every 24 hours. For this reason, hurricanes rotate counter-clockwise in the Northern Hemisphere and clockwise in the Southern Hemisphere. But the force is too weak to alter the way water spirals down the drain; that motion is the result of the way the basin was filled, imperfections in the porcelain, and subtle currents in the standing fluid. It also dispels the myth that you couldn't flush at all if you lived exactly on the equator.

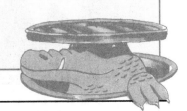

Ignorance Is Bliss

When Thomas Gray wrote "Where ignorance is bliss, 'tis folly to be wise" in 1742, he was commenting on how much more human beings accomplish because no one knows the date of his or her own death. Nowhere did Gray say that uneducated people are happier. In fact, as America becomes more drastically divided between the haves (as in, "I'll have a café latté") and the have-nots ("Do you want fries with that?"), the question of whether ignorance is bliss becomes a greater concern than ever before.

The premise here is that people can be kept happy by not telling them how bad things really are. Certainly governments seem to follow this lead, frequently under the rubric of "national security." But, for example, as airline personnel discover when they fail to make timely announcements and passengers are stranded on the runway, there are limits to both ignorance and bliss.

Existentialists posit that the more we know about our situation, the more powerless we are to affect it. That is reflected in a 1961 statement by John F. Kennedy: "When I became President, what surprised me the most was that things were just as bad as I'd been saying they were." Had JFK not become the most powerful person in the world the moment he took the Oath of Office, he might have been frustrated by his sudden loss of ignorance.

For everybody else, a University of Kentucky study (reported by Alfie Kohn in *You Know What They Say*) might apply: People with less education were somewhat more likely to sound hopeless about life. Indeed, social unrest (*i.e.*, blisslessness) may stem from the perceived gap between what one group sees others receiving and what it receives. In other words, "I know how the system works, but I don't know how to make it work for me." Under such a yardstick, ignorance does not produce bliss; it produces revolution.

✓ REALITY CHECK

Skin Breathing

Although Shirley Eaton—the poor "golden girl" who succumbed to solid body gilding in the James Bond movie *Goldfinger*—might think otherwise, humans do not "breathe" through the pores in their skin. If that were the case, swimming would be just as suffocating as being body-painted. Unless there is a poisonous substance in the paint, the chief effect would be overheating, since pores are involved in cooling the body by perspiration, and covering them for any length of time (as in the weight-loss fad of being swathed in plastic wrap) might be unhealthful.

Don't Swim for an Hour after Eating

For about an hour after eating, the body focuses its energy on digesting the meal: the blood goes to the stomach, the energy supply dips, and the metabolism thinks food. But this has nothing to do with the dreaded "stomach cramps" that every mother warns her child about. There is no such thing as a stomach cramp. And there is no connection to a muscle cramp that may, indeed, endanger a swimmer. Most likely, Mom just doesn't want you to blow lunch.

More People Commit Suicide During the Holidays

Contrary to widely held belief, the suicide rate does not increase before, during, or after the Christmas, New Year's, or Fourth of July holidays. If anything, it decreases, probably because more intervention is available.

This misconception may have grown out of the movie *It's a Wonderful Life*, in which George Bailey (James Stewart) contemplates jumping off a bridge on Christmas Eve. Or, it may be reinforced by the media, which often dwells on holiday irony. According to the National Center for Health Statistics, however, the peak suicide month is actually April, a season that has to do with spring, rebirth, and, coincidentally or not, love.

Breakfast like a King, Lunch like a Knave, Dinner like a Pauper

The days of eating "a healthy breakfast with one item from each of the four basic food groups" are over. On the other side of the plate, Pop Tarts don't cut it either. Still, eating *something* in the morning cuts hunger and provides enough energy to make it through the first part of the day. Most agree that schoolchildren

who are denied breakfast have trouble concentrating, lack energy, and fall behind in their studies.

On the other hand, if you eat a big meal late at night, you feel sluggish and gain weight because there's not enough time to work off the calories before bed. What's a body to do?

That's how the expression, "Breakfast like a king (large), lunch like a knave (medium), and dinner like a pauper (small)" came about. The theory is to eat when you need the energy and practically fast when you do not. Informal diet advice adds that you should never eat after 8:00 P.M. That gives your metabolism four hours to work before you hit the sack.

If You Have Water Bugs, You Won't Have Cockroaches

Before we begin our delightful discourse on invasion versus infestation, let's meet our cast:

1. German cockroaches (*Blattella germanica*) are ¾ inch long and pale brown or tan. They are most prevalent in American homes and businesses. They usually live near food and are difficult to exterminate. They also reproduce exponentially. In several generations one fertile female can produce 30,000 descendants a year. Like Nazis, they are invaders.
2. Brownbanded cockroaches (*Supella longipala*) are ½ inch long and dark brown. These fecund insects prefer warmer environments and can thrive on the protein found in casein glue. One brown supermarket bag can feed several families. They also invade and stay unseen.
3. American cockroaches (*Periplaneta americana*) are 2 or more inches long and pale brown or yellowish. They crave a warmer, humid home and prefer sewers to houses, although if there is construction in a residential area, they have been known to invade nearby homes and businesses.

4. Oriental cockroaches (*Blatta orientalis*) are 1 to 1½ inches long (or longer), and are a dark reddish brown. They are often called "water bugs." Like their American cousins, they do not generally live indoors, although they can crawl inside a house through an opening the thickness of a penny. Their presence is more properly called an "invasion" rather than an "infestation." Small comfort.

Sadly, cockroaches do not feed on each other so it is entirely possible that two or more species can coexist in a single environment. Although they are unsightly and offensive, they are not poisonous. But they do tend to dwell in filth, which makes them, their egg pods, and their droppings dangerous to humans and pets. Pest experts advise that, while spray insecticides can provide initial control of roach populations, the more effective control is through spraying boric acid and similar powders.

Marijuana Leads to Heroin

There are many variables which come into play when an individual takes drugs: pain, peer pressure, depression, financial ability, medical necessity, and, of course, opportunity. Smoking one marijuana cigarette today won't lead to shooting heroin tomorrow, although the people with whom one associates—and the conviviality in doing so—may make further experimentation attractive. Once you're already in a restaurant, as the saying goes, why not try the whole menu? On the other hand, nobody can force you to eat Brussels sprouts.

Society has long held that a drug is a drug is a drug, even if the legal inconsistency borders on hypocritical. The two most addictive drugs in the arsenal—alcohol and nicotine—are widely available and culturally accepted, even encouraged through advertising. Indeed, a frequent argument is that more people (politicians, the police, lawyers, and the prison industry, not to mention the drug dealers) benefit from the drug problem than from preventive drug education.

✓ **REALITY CHECK**

Congressional Medal of Honor

There is no such award as the Congressional Medal of Honor. There is, however, the Medal of Honor, which is presented by an act of Congress. It represents the highest gratitude that the nation can pay to an individual who has served his or her country in action against an enemy in time of war. The Medal of Honor has been awarded 3,429 times since it was created in 1863. As of this writing, the medal was last awarded for action in Somalia in 1993. No Medals of Honor were given in the Gulf War.

There is no medical proof that the body automatically craves progressively "harder" drugs. Each drug produces its own high or low. Many long-term drug users (primarily cannabis, or "pot," smokers) report being perfectly satisfied with what they've got. A 1988 study by the National Institutes on Drug Abuse* revealed that only 10 percent of drug users will become addicted to the drug they sample. There was only one exception: tobacco was found to be 90 percent addictive.

Lawmakers and parents, however, fear that, as an individual builds up a tolerance for one drug, he or she will move on to another. Depending on the drug, the problem may be more psychological than physiological. Certainly the cost of drugs drives some people to commit crimes to obtain them, and that is another cause for concern. But one drug in and of itself is not a catalyst to another. The political and social environment that surrounds drug use, however, may lead to escalating usage.

Dogs Don't Sweat

Of course, dogs sweat. You would, too, if you had to wear a fur coat in hot weather. Dogs excrete moisture through the pads on their paws. Any excess moisture (not "sweat," although it sure smells as bad) leaves Fido's body through his mouth in the form of vapor and a slobbering, wet tongue. That's why dogs pant so much in hot weather.

Gout Is Caused by Eating Too Much Rich Food

Gout is an inflammation of the joints (frequently the big toe). It is not caused by rich food, although its actual cause is not definitively

*Michael S. Gazzaniga, professor of Neuroscience, Dartmouth Medical School, interview by William F. Buckley, *National Review* (February 5, 1990), quoted in McWilliams (op. cit.).

known. What is known is that gout is a crystalline deposit of purines ($C_5H_4N_4$) stemming from an excess of uric acid in the blood. Caffeine may also be involved. If eating rich foods or consuming alcohol causes an individual's metabolism to produce uric acid, that acid might exacerbate an existing condition, but it's after the fact.

The image of an old man, his gouty foot wrapped in bandages, banging into walls and screaming in pain may have been a mainstay of silent comedies. But it certainly is not funny to those who suffer from the affliction.

Ice Cubes Made from Hot Water Freeze Faster Than Ice Cubes Made from Cold Water

Thermal conductivity is one of the constants of the universe. The amount of energy required to lower the temperature of water to 32°F (0°C) will increase with the temperature of the water put into the tray. Hot water has "farther to go" than cold water.

In any event, the process of freezing is not that of an external source (*i.e.*, the freezer) "lowering" the temperature of the water, but of the freezer permitting energy within the water to escape into the colder environment. If the water has been boiled first, the boiling may purge some of the air normally suspended in the water, making it slightly more dense (which is why boiled water tastes flat) and therefore more conducive to energy loss.

Beer on Whiskey Rather Risky; Whiskey on Beer, Never Fear

Different people react to alcohol in different ways. The only hard-and-fast rule is that drinking gets you drunk.

The "beer on whiskey" ditty would put the hearty Boilermaker out of business, just as the adage "never mix, never worry" would

✓ **REALITY CHECK**

Saltpeter as a Sexual Suppressant

"Don't eat the eggs," one soldier whispers to another over breakfast in the mess hall. "They spike them with saltpeter."

Saltpeter (potassium nitrate, KNO_3) is legendary as a sexual suppressant. It is a tasteless substance that is secretly mixed with food served to soldiers, submarine crews, Boy Scouts, college athletes, and any group of males who "they" want to keep from getting too randy before a big event (war, jamboree, homecoming, etc.). As with Spanish fly, there is no such thing. Saltpeter has some medical use as a diuretic to increase the flow of fluid from the body. Unfortunately, the fluid happens to be urine.

P.S. "They" also don't put Ex-Lax in chocolate pudding.

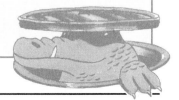

doom Long Island iced tea. There are also myths about the drinking order of wine and liquor ("grain and grape" versus "grape and grain"), scotch not affecting some people, carbonation in beer and champagne forcing alcohol into your bloodstream faster, and brandy giving the sloppiest hangover.

Several years ago, liquor manufacturers caught flack for introducing a line of milkshake-like cocktail products that seemed geared toward introducing young people to alcohol. Indeed, cocktails such as the Sombrero, Grasshopper, and White Russian seem to have been designed for people who hate to drink but want to get drunk.

Sugar, preservatives, additives, or impurities may cause differences between one kind of inebriation and another, and contribute to the lore of drinking. As with the effects of any alteration of body chemistry, the determining factor is the person, not the poison.

Lightning Never Strikes the Same Place Twice

Let's start by defining lightning. It is a sudden electrical discharge moving from a positive charge to a negative charge. This usually means that lighting strikes, not from the sky downward, but from the positively charged Earth upward to a negatively charged cloud. The speed of travel is so fast—often 1,000 miles per *second*—that it breaks the sound barrier and creates a sonic boom, which we call thunder. The temperature surrounding the lightning strike (often called a "bolt") can reach 50,000°F.

Like any flowing force, lightning seeks the path of least resistance—a hill, a tree, a metal broadcast tower, a skyscraper, a home lightning rod, a goal post, a golfer standing on a putting green raising his nine iron—and the closer to the clouds, the better. Therefore, lighting will theoretically keep striking in the same place until that place is either moved, lowered, destroyed, or heads to the clubhouse.

A Criminal Always Returns to the Scene of the Crime

This old wives' tale has as much to do with semantics as it does with criminality. In the sense that many crimes of violence (spousal abuse, child abuse) are committed by people who know each other, the accuracy of the saying is obvious. Young people involved in misconduct such as shoplifting, school vandalism, joyriding, or breaking and entering "return" to the scene of the crime because it's in the community where they live.

But if the saying is taken to mean a cosmic compulsion that mysteriously draws criminals—particularly murderers—back to the scene of the crime, the only time that is likely to happen is if he or she is brought there by the police for questioning. In many cases, a murderer does not even leave the scene of the crime, but comes to his or her senses and summons the police to let justice (and the American Bar Association) take its course.

It's probably also time to dispose of the myths that "the dead man's eyes hold the image of the killer in them" or that "the ghost lingers in the murder room until the killer is caught." If lie detector evidence isn't admissible in court, why allow the other booga-booga?

People Go Nuts During a Full Moon

According to journalist Paul Katzeff in *Full Moons*, there is some truth to this assertion, though scientists differ in their explanations. The murder rate does spike during lunar fullness, but so does romance. The birthrate rises slightly during a full Moon, but so does female ovulation.

The word *lunacy*, meaning insanity, derives from the Latin words *luna/lunaris*, for the Moon. Anecdotes abound of people doing strange things every 29 days, 12 hours, 44 minutes, and 3 seconds when it glows full in the sky. Emergency room personnel and paramedics report that their business picks up during the full Moon, and supervisors in psychiatric institutions also insist that their patients grow restive at those times.

There may be some chicken-and-eggism going on here. Do people act differently during the full Moon, or does the full Moon serve as a convenient timing device to peg behavior that goes on all the time? If the brightness of a full Moon keeps light-sensitive people from sleeping, their behavior may well be affected. Some people insist that the gravitational pull of the Moon and Sun on Earth's tides also affects the human body, which is "98 percent water." On this point, the jury of scientific research is still out, but its collective mind is finally looking into quantifying what the average nonscientist has "known" all along.

Middle Children Are Ignored, so They Grow Up More Independent

In a family of three children, the firstborn is egocentric, the third-born is the perennial baby, and the secondborn learns to be independent because nobody pays any attention to her. Right?

The firstborn is insecure at having been pushed aside by the secondborn, who then gets all the attention. Then the thirdborn becomes the independent one, because everybody is still paying attention to the first two.

Or maybe the firstborn is the independent one. She helps raise the secondborn and teaches him how to raise the thirdborn when the time comes.

No, wait! Maybe all three get together and form a singing group. Studies of the psychological effects of birth order are as varied as the personalities of the subjects they try to analyze, and just as irregular. Many other factors contribute to a child's personality—for example, the age of the parents, the stability of the marriage, the socioeconomic circumstances, and the years separating the siblings' arrivals. The only thing that can be proved beyond a doubt is that, in a family with three children, the firstborn will be the oldest.

Chapter 3

There's One Born Every Minute
(America's Best Cons and Con Artists)

✓ REALITY CHECK

James Reavis, Fake Land Baron

The genius of swindler-forger James Addison Reavis was that he collected rent on land he didn't own, and he had the paperwork to back it up. Operating in the 1880s, during the time of the westward expansion, Reavis forged deeds to show that he owned Spanish lands in the American Southwest. He charged settlers, businesses, and even the government for their use. His scheme, which may have netted him as much as $10 million, was eventually discovered when a suspicious investigator examined Reavis's documents and proved that the watermark on the paper hadn't been in use until well after the documents were supposedly signed.

Believe It or Not!

—*Robert LeRoy Ripley*

When Robert L. Ripley started publishing "Believe It or Not!" in the *New York Globe* in 1918 he was a 24-year-old sports cartoonist with an obsession for odd information. Who can run the fastest backward? Who can jump the farthest on ice? Can a chicken really choose lottery winners? Today it would be called trivia, but in a world still in shock from the reality of the Great War, it became a phenomenon. Within five years Ripley moved his immensely popular feature to the *New York Post*, and before long it was syndicated in 326 newspapers in 38 countries. It had also expanded its ken to include curiosities such as eggplants shaped like Queen Victoria, five-leaf clovers, and sheep with a map of Australia on their wool. Today the Ripley legacy includes newsreels, TV shows, museums, and books, all based on the challenge, "Believe It or Not!"

Think about that phrase. Nowhere does it say these things are true. It just says that you can believe them if you want to. This makes Ripley, for want of a better term, an honest charlatan. Legions of others have not been, and this chapter will introduce some of the most notorious—and successful. They are often people you would love to have dinner with, even if they'd stick you with the check.

According to *Bartlett's Familiar Quotations*, newspaperman and curmudgeon H. L. Mencken wrote in 1926 that "No one in this world, so far as I know . . . has ever lost money by underestimating the intelligence of the great masses of the plain people." Indeed, though it may still be true that if you invent a better mousetrap the world will beat a path to your door, the way to make the really big bucks is to sell the mousetrap for $5 and make sure that it wears out in a year. For that matter, why not make home computers that cost $1,500 and are obsolete in a few months?

But the most delicious tales—at least, as long as you're reading a book on urban legends and scams—are those that excite the imagination, capture the spirit, and, in general, lead the public into a forbidden world. In pioneer days, this was called "seeing the elephant," an expression used by settlers of the American West who were driven by a hearty blend of bravery and curiosity to wonder what was over the next ridge. Sometimes this wanderlust was rewarded by Mother Nature with natural marvels like the Grand Canyon. At other times, the reward was paid by average people who were snookered into below-average land deals, gold mines, and get-rich-quick schemes. Not just in America, but the world over, there have always been elephants worth seeing, and people who contrive ways to make money showing fake ones.

Shamefully, the media often go along with these fantasies; they sell papers and build ratings. A century ago, most major cities managed to support between two and eight daily newspapers, and competition for readership was fierce and sometimes bloody. As a result, news commerce frequently ignored the truth in an effort to increase circulation. The Age of Science that capped the 19th century brought with it a fascination with anything new, preferably technological, and the press's traditional skepticism went by the boards.

The summit of that arrogance would become the tragedy of the *Titanic*, which proved to be a floating Tower of Babel. But before that horrible chastisement, many a breathless newspaper article would champion the water engine, the Cardiff Giant, and the Piltdown Man, only later issuing sheepish retractions once these "magnificent scientific discoveries" turned out to be frauds. The attitude of "sales over sanity" was so pervasive that, in 1895, reporter Louis Stone of Winsted, Connecticut, began testing it. Stone wondered whether people automatically believed everything they read in newspapers. As an experiment, he invented stories about freaks of nature and sold them to newspaper editors as though they were true. The experiment was so effective that it became his profession. Over the next two decades Stone made a tidy income planting such unchallenged reports as a tree that produced baked apples, a squirrel that shined its master's shoes with its tail, and a cow, owned by two women, that was too embarrassed to allow men to milk her. As obviously false as those stories seem today, they went unchallenged a century ago, for if

✓ REALITY CHECK

Lyndon's Friend

Lyndon Baines Johnson was no stranger to the fringes of the law, but it was his friend Billy Sol Estes who got caught, and LBJ couldn't do squat to help him. Johnson's association with Estes nearly cost him his place on the 1960 Democratic Party's ticket with John F. Kennedy, and it dogged him throughout his administration. A fellow Texan, Estes gained notoriety in the 1960s for convincing farmers to invest in fertilizer tanks that didn't exist. He served time, and then stepped in even more fertilizer by borrowing money using collateral—oil fields—that didn't exist, either. When he was duly convicted again for fraud in 1979, he told the judge that not only would he serve his time, he would also pay $10 million in back taxes by asking his friends for help.

✓ REALITY CHECK

Speaking of Ethics

"Though he slay me, yet I will trust him."
—Book of Job, 13:14

"Men trust their ears less than their eyes."
—Heroditus, *Histories*, Book I, Ch. 8

"It's better to be quotable than to be honest."
—Tom Stoppard

"Honesty is a strategy like any other. In a pinch, I have been known to use it myself."
—Jean Anouilh

"Honesty is the most important part of acting. If you can fake that, you've got it made."
—George Burns

Edison could make sounds come out of a box, who's to say a cat couldn't do calculus?

Yet such pranks could also do real damage. Around 1886 to 1888, *Appleton's Cyclopedia of American Biography* unwittingly published at least 84 erroneous biographies of fictitious persons, all of which had been sent in by mail. Apparently *Appleton's* had a policy of blindly trusting anything that anybody had the gumption to send them. As a result, the anonymous hoax went unnoticed until 1919, when 14 fake bios were discovered. An investigation turned up 70 others by 1936, but even today no one knows the extent of *Appleton's* gullibility or the fate of others who depended on its research.

Meanwhile, the sobering reality of World War I drove the public to seek credibility instead of sensationalism, and journalism resumed its historic duty to, in the words of humorist Finley Peter Dunne, "comfort the afflicted and afflict the comfortable." (One wonders when a similar shift in public taste will begin afflicting today's television scream-fests, right-wing talk radio shows, and supermarket tabloids.) Despite such diligence, a few remarkable cases have managed to slip through the cracks and capture public attention. The people profiled in this chapter are not all crooks, phonies, or fakers. Some of them merely saw what the public wanted and gave it to them—for a price.

John E. W. Keely and His Water Engine

According to legend, "Years ago a brilliant scientist invented an engine that runs on water, but the greedy automobile industry found out about it, had him killed, and destroyed both his prototype and his patent."

That sounds like the stuff of high drama. Indeed, playwright David Mamet even wrote his own version of the story. Along with such myths as "the tobacco companies copyrighted the names of marijuana" and "Elvis lives," the persistent legend of a water engine has fueled many an urban legend. It remained for a Philadelphia con man named John E. W. Keely to convert the water engine into gold—for himself, at least.

In 1874 Keely, then 47, began claiming that he had invented an engine that could power a 30-car train 75 miles in 75 minutes on a quart of water. He even had a demonstration model of the engine in his workshop, and invited investors to witness its amazing performance. Almost immediately four well-heeled financiers—Henry Sergeant (Ingersoll Rock Drill Co.), Charles B. Franklyn (Cunard Steamship Line), lawyer Charles Collier, and banker John J. Cisco—came aboard. The four men even formed the Keely Motor Company and began trading stock in what they were certain would be a lucrative future. According to at least one source, John Jacob Astor even begged to invest $2 million.

Over the next quarter century, and despite attacks in the prestigious *Scientific American* magazine, Keely talked hundreds of people into putting money into his device, which ran on water—but was never *quite* perfected. Only after Keely died in 1898 and his laboratory was razed was it discovered that his engine ran, not on water, but on a compressed air system in his basement that fed power to his machine through pipes buried in the floor. It was then revealed that Keely, who had worked as a journeyman carnival barker, had mastered the use of valves, bells, and whistles while building and running the sideshows and fun houses of his younger days.

Three-Card Monte/Monty

It litters the streets of New York City like dog-do, and its purveyors are appreciated just as much. It's three-card monte, a variation on the ol' shell game with a similar track record.

> The angle: Find the winning card (usually a queen) among three facedown cards that are being shifted back and forth on a flat surface.
> The buildup: It looks easy because other people are winning.
> The catch: It gets hard as soon as you put your money down.
> The secret: The other "winners," or "cappers," are shills.

What's most amazing about three-card monte is that the dealer has to be reasonably skilled, not only in playing the traditional game but also in varying it as the need arises. If there doesn't seem to be a sucker in the crowd, he or she may "accidentally" place an obvious mark on the winning card (a piece of dirt, a fleck of paper, a bent corner) to complete the seduction. Naturally, as soon as the victim has chosen the marked card, it is deftly switched for a losing card, which is similarly marked.

If the victim happens to choose the winning card, the shills' job becomes especially important. They must be equally adept at improvising innocence, joy, victimization, or outrage—and sometimes all four—to claim that they had their bet down first, that one of them is going to call the cops, or, in a real pinch, to start a fight that breaks up the game.

A distinction for quibbling aficionados: When three-card monte is played outdoors it is called open monte. When it is played indoors, such as in a big store, it is called closed monte.

Chicago May

The woman believed to have perfected the "badger game" was Chicago May. May Churchill Sharpe was born in Dublin, Ireland in 1876. She spent six years in a convent school before running off to America at the age of 12 with £60 stolen from her father. By 1889 she was in New York and living as the underage mistress of a man named Dal Churchill.

Dal was as much a crook as May. He taught her well, posing as her outraged husband (to shake down her johns) right up until he was hanged in Phoenix, Arizona, for train robbery in 1891. At the time, May was 15. That's when she lammed it to Chicago and quickly took her place as "Queen of the Badger Game." As such, she would extort payoffs from her male customers, steal securities (which she would ransom back to the owner), and earn the odd prestige of never double-crossing anyone she had already double-crossed. As fame impinged on her operation, she varied her routine by employing a "mother" and "husband" to shake down her tricks.

Soon even that game became so well known that imitators moved in on it.

In the early 1890s, Chicago got too hot for May and she moved to New York. There she plied her trade until her death in 1935.

Panel House

If it sounds like the beginning of a haunted house nightmare, you're right on all three counts: it haunts people, it happens in a house, and it is unquestionably a nightmare. The "panel house" is an embellishment of the badger game involving a specially built hotel room or, more commonly, a "house of ill repute." Surreptitious access is through a sliding wall panel from an adjacent room, generally near the chair or dressing cabinet where the man hangs his clothing while enjoying the charms of his lady friend. While the man and woman are otherwise engaged, her operative slips in through the secret panel and picks the man's trousers clean. If he turns out to have a wallet the size of a softball, though, the rip-off may escalate into a badger game.

If it sounds like a lot of trouble to build a house just to rip off a few traveling salesmen, the example of Shang Draper should settle all doubts. Draper was a saloonkeeper in New York in the 1870s, but he also ran a panel house near Prince and Wooster Streets in Greenwich Village. Crook that he was, he was also a showman. His variations on the badger game included hiring young girls (ages 9 to 14) who would have their "parents" break in on their trysts. To frighten the pedophile even more, the girl would slip a cackle badder (see the sidebar on this page) into her mouth so she'd bleed when her "mother" slapped her. That usually did the trick to the trick, and he paid up rather than risk exposure.

Ben Marks

They say that success has a thousand fathers while failure is a bastard child. Somehow Ben Marks worked it the other way around, which stands to reason since Ben Marks was a confidence

Cackle Bladder

Originally a small bag filled with chicken blood, the miracle of invention has now allowed this timeless prop to be filled with anything from food coloring to theatrical special effects blood. Latex condoms have also been known to work. It is placed in the mouth of a make-believe "victim" who, at the proper time, bites down on it and allows the blood to seep (or spurt) through his or her lips. (Watch how Robert Redford slips one into his mouth in his hotel room as he readies himself for the final act of the movie *The Sting*.)

Motion pictures and reality-based television shows have pretty much educated the public at large about the clinical result of injury to the human anatomy, making cackle bladders a relic of a more naive—and arguably, less violent—past. (*Note:* It still works like a charm in car insurance scams.)

The Short Con Versus the Long Con

"Short" and "long," in relation to the confidence game, has as much to do with the length of time it takes to commit the swindle as with how much can be scored by pulling it off. Short cons are designed to bilk the victim of the money he is carrying at the time. Long cons are far more complex and may involve having the victim go home or to her bank to fetch more money (called a "send") to trigger the next stage of the con. Prior to the "send" comes the "breakdown," which is when the con artists determine how much money the mark can raise before they make the "sting" (spring the trap).

man. The success he's generally credited with is the invention of the "big store."

Think of the big store as a shopping mall of crime. It is an actual location that looks like a legitimate retail business; in reality, it is a "cleaning" establishment devoted entirely to removing *filthy lucre* from the pockets of its customers. It can be a fight club, a gambling parlor, a saloon, or a farmer's market. But in Marks's design, it was a general store where the bargains were literally too good to be true.

Little is known about Marks himself. Supposedly born in Council Bluffs, Iowa, before the Civil War, he supported himself from an early age by gambling as he conned his way across the American West. He was an engaging fellow, redheaded and hefty, with a twinkle in his eye that made him look like a youthful Santa Claus. It was the era of the Iron Horse (the railroad) tooting its way to California, giving birth to boom towns populated by the thousands of unsettled laborers hired to build them—men with lots of money and no way to spend it, and more brawn than judgment.

That's when Ben Marks arrived. Starting with a portable game of three-card monte played on a platform dangled from his neck and braced against his broad chest (like cigarette girls in 1930s nightclubs), he was always frustrated by seeing the *real* money wander off into saloons where the poker games were going on. By the time he got to Cheyenne, Wyoming, he had devised a way to beat the odds at the professional gambling houses by making the house itself the game.

In 1867, Marks opened his first Dollar Store, a commercial establishment whose windows were festooned with displays of bargains, none costing more than a buck. Of course, a dollar went a lot further in those days, but still . . . ! Once a customer went inside to examine the merchandise, he was fair game. Milling throughout the store were independent grifters, short-con specialists, and other gamesmen who would strike up a casual conversation with the newcomer, distracting him from the reason he had ventured indoors with the promise of quick riches. In a twisted way, it was the forerunner of "environmental theater," because most of the customers were shills working with their partners-in-crime to create the appearance of an ongoing business solely to bilk the one or two suckers who came in of their own volition. Unlike today's legitimate casinos where the customer plays against the house and knows that the odds are against him or her, Marks's big store pitted the customer against each of the confidence operatives (from whom he secured financial tribute).

Marks experimented with a variety of games besides monte, stacked decks, faro bank games, loaded dice, and similar short cons. He installed a boxing ring and a dirt footrace track so that he could entice even bigger wagers through fixed athletic competition.

Before long, Marks's enterprise was doing so well that he opened another in his hometown of Council Bluffs. The idea even spread as far north as Chicago where, it is said, a big store owner did so well selling the prop merchandise that he gave up gambling altogether to concentrate on retail. The result is now one of the Windy City's most respected department stores!

Marks's Dollar Store was little more than a den of thieves, but it spawned some important variations that became mainstays of the confidence art. One was the "mitt store," an illegitimate room found in the back of a legitimate business, where customers were lured by a "roper" or "steerer" who, like Orpheus, acted as an envoy between both worlds. When farmers came to town to sell their goods, for example, the mitt store was there to snare them while they were waiting in the (legitimate) main room to meet buyers.

Yet another variation, the "wire store" (also called the golden wire), took the form of a big store betting parlor, staffed entirely with confidence operatives. The mark was lured in by a "friend" (actually the "roper") who slipped him tips from an inside contact at Western Union. The scam worked because Western Union provided a "golden wire" that carried bona-fide track results to bookmaking parlors across America.

Wire stores were based on the swindle that an "insider" at Western Union could stall the reports so that the mark could slip in a last-minute bet on a horse that had just won but hadn't been announced yet. The scam worked because the

people who ran it tapped into telegraph lines that reported legitimate results from several racetracks. The only difference was that they were also part of the same team as the inside tipster. So the mark, who was allowed to win some small bets early on, was convinced that the place was on the level.

When it was time to spring the trap, the confidence operatives would purposely mess up the signals in a way that made the victim think it was his fault. For example, as he hurried to the betting window to place his wager, three "customers" would suddenly cut in front of him until it was too late to bet. Or the phone message would be garbled and he would put his money on the wrong horse. Or the slip of paper containing the winner's name would fall into a puddle and be rendered illegible. Astonishingly, each slip-up would hook the mark even more deeply. And if he dared protest or become surly, it was time to reach for the cackle bladder.

Another variation on the big store was the flat-out fake business where the furnishings, the signage, and all of the patrons were part of the swindle—except for the lone victim for whom the whole thing was thrown together. The big store was the setting for the long con, an elaborate ruse that could net upward of $100,000 if the con artist was able to "send" the mark to a bank to fetch a lump sum. By design, everything in the big store was portable. When the mark wasn't there, neither was the store, lest the authorities stumble on it by chance. Of course, immediately following the "sting"—that is, once the mark handed over the money and walked out—the entire big store and the people in it instantly became a memory.

Ben Marks not only brought larceny in off the streets, he trained a generation of young confidence men who fanned out across the country and brought the art of the swindle to the four corners of the ever-expanding United States.

The Ducats

Show business has adopted the term *ducats* to mean "tickets" for a show. In the parlane of confidence men, however, *ducats* refers to a short con play with five cards (business cards will do if playing cards are not available).

Truth to tell, it's a pretty nifty scam involving nothing more than picking one of five equal-looking cards out of a dealer's hand. The person who sets up the con (called the "roper") conspires with the victim to place a mark on one of the cards. Bets are placed. When it comes time to choose the "marked" card, however, the cards have been turned around so that the wrong marked card is now facing out of the dealer's hand. The victim dares not complain and never learns that the roper and the dealer are working as a team.

Joseph "Yellow Kid" Weil

The most successful American con artist—not only in his own immodest opinion but also according to many police department bunko authorities—has to be Joseph R. "Yellow Kid" Weil.

Born in the mid-1870s, Weil drew his nickname from the popular Yellow Kid character in Richard Outcault's newspaper comic strip of the day. The cartoon character was a plucky survivor, and so was his human namesake. After being introduced to the grift (con games) as a shill for a snake-oil salesman named Doc Meriwether, Weil saw how easy it was to bilk the unsophisticated rural population. By the time he had worked his way to Chicago at the turn of the century, he had learned a more important lesson: City folks were just as easy to cheat, plus they had more money.

More important, they also had savvy—they knew that confidence games existed—and as such fell through a specific crack in Chicago law that defined a "confidence game" as one that takes advantage of an unwary stranger. Since the denizens of Chicago's racetracks, betting parlors, and banking firms—in other words, Weil's prime sucker list—were anything *but* unwary, Weil had free reign on the Windy City's rich and famous.

And he used it. At Garfield Park racetrack, he bought a nag called Black Fonso, which was a perfect look-alike for a real-life winner. He accepted bets for the winner, switched it for the laggard Fonso, and kept the "losses."

✓ **REALITY CHECK**

Yellow Kid's Last Scam

One of Weil's last scams was to write a magazine article about his early days as a confidence man. The publisher paid him his $100 fee by check, but when he saw his bank statement he was surprised to see that Weil had shamelessly altered the document to read $1,000. The publisher declined to prosecute, figuring (correctly, as it turned out) it would probably be the guy's last con, and it would make a great dinner table story.

His real-estate scam, "Oceanic County," involved giving away hundreds of free deeds to vacation land, then collecting $30 apiece (instead of the municipally mandated $2) to register the lots with the city (which, of course, he never did). Weil's partner in that gambit was the redoubtable Colonel Jim Porter who made a fortune during the 1920s in Florida's real-estate boom.

Weil's investment scheme in a worthless mining operation, in which he posed as the famous mining engineer Pope Yateman (see page 63) wasn't the only time that the Yellow Kid used a printer to his benefit. He always kept a supply of fake letterheads, billing heads, stock certificates, business cards, and other stationery. He determined early on that people are trusting to a fault, always their own.

"I have often thought about banks and the confidence which people have in the very word," Weil told his biographer, W. T. Brannon. "The big sign BANK and the cages inside quieted any fears they might have had as to the authenticity of the institution."

Accordingly, Weil once dutifully set up a big store sting in a building that had just been vacated by the Merchants National Bank of Muncie, Indiana. But first, to make his big store look legit, he had his operatives visit the *new* Merchants National Bank building to liberate a supply of their deposit slips. He then stenciled "Merchants Bank" on canvas bags, filled them with metal washers, and left them stacked in the old vault to make the place look rich. Weil peopled the bank with workers and customers (all gang members) whenever the mark was present.

Despite the damage he caused countless people throughout his life, most of whom wanted a piece of his hide, Weil never suffered for his dastardly deeds. By 1975, he was 100 years old and had outlived the era that had created and sustained him. When reporters and historians tracked him down in his Chicago retirement, they not only brought away stories of his exploits (some of which, they realized with a smile, might have been a tad exaggerated), but his lament that modern-day con men just didn't have the imagination, knowledge, and background that he possessed.

And probably not his success, either.

The Pedigreed Pooch

All good cons presume a high level of venality on the part of their victim, but the pedigreed pooch swindle is one that has a special place in the hearts of animal lovers. This one was perfected by two of the most skillful con artists of all time: Joseph "Yellow Kid" Weil and Fred Buckminster.

Here's how it went. Weil struts into a barroom leading a well-groomed dog (this was in the days when dogs and cigars were allowed into eating and drinking establishments). He chats up the bartender and announces that he is killing time before "the most important business meeting of my life." Unfortunately, he can't bring his beloved pet. Weil whips out pedigree papers attesting to the value of the dog, and offers the bartender a fast $10 if he watches the animal for an hour. Of course, the bartender agrees, and Weil leaves for his crucial meeting.

Not 10 minutes later, Fred Buckminster enters the bar. His eye is immediately caught by the dog, and he excitedly asks the bartender, "Do you know how valuable that animal is? Why, I'll pay you a hundred dollars for it right this instant!"

The bartender, of course, refuses.

"I'll make it two hundred," Buckminster enthuses.

Hanging on to whatever vestige of honesty he has, the bartender says, "But it isn't mine to sell."

"Nonsense," counters Buckminster. "I'll make it three hundred if you can persuade the owner to sell it." He hands the bartender a $50 bill, adding, "Here's a down payment. I'm in room three-fifteen at the Plaza Hotel. Call me when you've made the deal." Then he leaves.

After the bartender stews for 45 minutes, Weil returns looking utterly crushed. "I'm ruined," he confesses. "My business meeting was a complete washout. I have no money."

At this point the bartender's wheels start turning and he says, "Let me help out." I'll pay you a hundred bucks for your dog."

"Oh, I could never let go of my beloved pup," Weil says, near tears.

"I'll make it two hundred," the bartender offers, secretly computing that he already has $60 ($10 from Weil and $50 from Buckminster, who had promised to pay him an additional $250 upon delivery). So, after paying the $200, he will still clear an easy $90.

"Well," says Weil, "okay."

The bartender hands Weil $200 for the dog and heads over to the Plaza to complete the transaction. Naturally, there is no Buckminster staying there, and the bartender finds himself the owner of a stray mutt that has cost him $140.

Weil and Buckminster, meanwhile, cleared $140 on an outlay of $60. Since they were effortlessly pulling the pedigreed pooch scam on 10 bartenders per afternoon, they had no trouble raising a fair-size bankroll before the word got around.

✓ REALITY CHECK

Charley Gondorf

Charley Gondorf was a swindler who, around 1900, specialized in a long con called a "rag" scam. A rag scam is a confidence game that is similar to a wire store (which consists of a fake gambling parlor that intercepts race track results), except that a rag scam intercepts stock market reports.

What made Gondorf's rag scam ingenious was that he used real brokerage offices. He gained access to them by bribing guards or using skeleton keys, and ensured his privacy by always meeting his marks after business hours. Rather than make his victims suspicious, such precautions made them feel as though they were being granted an inside track. The only track they wound up traveling was the one to the poorhouse—courtesy of Charley Gondorf.

Fred Buckminster

It takes a true con artist to con another con artist, but that was Fred Buckminster's claim to fame. He devoted his life to his motto: "When I see a crook, I see nothing but dollar signs."

Buckminster also worked for 20 years with the legendary Joseph "Yellow Kid" Weil, perfecting such long and short stings as the fixed prize fight, wire stores, and the "pedigreed pooch" scam. Later, working with a gimmick man named "Kid Dimes," Buckminster devised a ploy that allegedly netted them $750,000 from a number of illicit gambling dens. But we're getting ahead of ourselves.

Fred Buckminster began his life of grift when he was still a teenager, around 1880. He discovered that the easiest people to cheat were those who were already cheating others, primarily corrupt bankers, whom he would lure into stock swindles. One of his biggest scores was against George "Palmer House" Ryan who ran the Stockade, a wire store in Springfield, Illinois. Buckminster knew that a wire store operated by delaying the telegraphic reports of actual racetrack results. So Buckminster bribed a locomotive engineer to toot the train's whistle in a code containing the race results as the train passed Ryan's gambling hall. Then Buckminster slid in a last-minute bet!

But his most ingenious swindle, as recounted by Carl Sifakis in *The Encyclopedia of American Crime*, was the one he worked in 1918 with Kid Dimes against Chicago's corrupt King George Club. The Kid was hired by the King George Club to rig their roulette wheel to allow the croupier to press a button that would drop its ball on three specific magnetized numbers. Buckminster had the Kid rig a second button underneath the customer's end of the table. This second, even-more-secret button would cancel the croupier's button and direct the silver ball to a fourth number chosen by Buckminster, who was posing as a customer. Buckminster steadily raised the stakes. The club was more than happy to accommodate him, expecting him to lose. But then he pressed his button, stinging the horrified house for thousands of dollars that they dared not challenge. Predictably, the King George Club's owners angrily summoned Kid Dimes to justify the loss. Ostensibly examining the table (but actually removing all traces of the second button), the Kid tossed a dead battery at the owners and admonished them for being too cheap to keep their equipment in shape. Afterwards, Kid Dimes and Fred Buckminster split their score.

Despite his success at cheating others, Buckminster spent his money as easily as he won it and wasted many of his working years in prison. He finished his last sentence in 1939, after which he retired from the rackets at the age of 76. He died four years later, probably of boredom.

Panhandling

Begging for money on a street corner is not usually considered a crime, although it can be raised to the level of a con, if not an art. Its mere existence belies the presence of what financial experts call a "healthy economy."

By and large, the public has become inured to the vagrant who bums change on the street corner, or holds up a "help me" sign at a freeway exit ramp. In reality, an alarming number of these men and women are Vietnam war veterans, homeless, or mentally ill people whom society has come to ignore. They are not criminals, even if local lawmakers sometimes try to pass laws that criminalize what they do.

But there are also folks who make a tidy living exploiting others' guilt. As a Los Angeles civic improvement poster stated in the mid-1990s, "Some of the best actors in Hollywood aren't in the movies."

Panhandling supposedly gets its name from the fact that, when you reach for a handout, your arm looks like the handle of a pan. It may also be a crude reference to the extension handles used on church collection plates that allow them to be passed along the pew from the aisle.

At the turn of the century, an expert panhandler names George Gray would stalk well-dressed people and throw fits in front of them, embarrassing them until they gave him money. Similar forms of "aggressive panhandling" are being addressed legislatively in many cities even today.

The best current scam is the guy in a business suit who needs $5 for a cab because he just had his wallet stolen, or who hangs around a parked car and stops passersby for change for the parking meter. You'd think that someone who is able to show up at the same spot ever day, or who is ingenious enough to invent such a creative story, would be able to hold a regular job. But the true con artist (as opposed to the genuine victim of society) can make more money with his or her wits than with a W-2, and that's why the game stays afoot.

Harry Hoxsey

People with terminal disease often fall prey to hoaxers, making them victims a second time. This is understandable; in a country where pharmaceutical companies are accused of jacking up medical costs and the Food and Drug Administration (FDA) is under constant assault, who can blame sick people for seeking alternative treatment?

The quest for cures is nothing new; history recounts scores of ersatz "professors" touring the country in medicine shows, selling "snake oil" guaranteed to cure everything from baldness to black plague. Now regarded as colorful mountebanks, these charlatans dispensed restorative "elixirs," which, if you were lucky, only contained pepper, molasses, alcohol, and maybe a little laxative (so you'd think they were doing something useful). All too often, however, the term *snake oil* was pathetically accurate; the potion didn't cure snake bite, but it made you as sick as if you'd been bitten. That brings us to Harry Hoxsey.

Could Harry Hoxsey really cure cancer with the herbal remedy that was handed down to him? Or was he "the worst cancer quack of the century" as the American Medical Association (AMA), the FDA, and American Cancer Society charged?

Hoxsey's treatment was an empirical formula that his own great-grandfather John, an Illinois horse breeder, had developed in the mid-1800s after observing a diseased stallion apparently cure himself by eating certain plants. According to Hoxsey's memoir, *You Don't Have to Die,* John successfully treated other similarly afflicted horses with a melange consisting of buckthorn, red clover, alfalfa, prickly ash, and folk medications. The formula was bequeathed to Harry, who regarded it as a family secret and for years refused to divulge its contents.

In 1924, Harry opened his first clinic and began ministering to an ever-growing circle of patients who had given up medical hope of being cured. He reportedly had some success with external tumors by applying a powder containing cascara, potassium iodide, barberry root, burdock root, buckthorn bark, and other plants. For internal cancers, he concocted a brownish liquid whose effectiveness remains debated.

In the days of snake oil salesmen, the sight of a tub-thumping medico being tarred, feathered, and run out of town on a rail was the way the sheriff kept order and protected the interests of the people. By the 20th century, the tar and feathers were applied by the courts. In Hoxsey's case, it wasn't only his "cure" that drew fire, it was his enthusiastic personality and secretiveness. Although he won a libel suit against the Hearst papers in 1947 after they referred to his income as "blood money," the federal government, urged by the medical establishment, took up the cudgel. In 1950 a reinterpretation of the Food, Drug and Cosmetic Act of 1938 enabled the FDA to prosecute him; only then did Hoxsey reveal his chemistry.

Supporters have noted that many of Hoxsey's herbal components have since become part of accepted cancer therapy, yet maintain that the AMA, FDA, and other organizations have steadfastly refused to test them. For their part, the medical authorities (including the American Cancer Society, which added Hoxsey's remedy to its Unproven Methods list in 1971) refer to his imprecise methodology and staunch secrecy as reasons to doubt his motives.

Hoxsey had closed his U.S. clinics by the mid-1960s and relocated to Tijuana, Mexico, where his nurse-aide Mildred Nelson took over as his health began to fail. He died in 1976. Rumors persisted for years that a Chicago-based cartel of medical investors (some of whom were members of the AMA) approached Hoxsey early in his career to buy his interests in the formula. It was his refusal to sell, Hoxsey claimed, that led to his lifelong prosecution. Can Nature succeed where Science has failed? That is the question at the heart of every alternative medical regimen, whether it's chiropractic, acupuncture, faith healing, or "the Hoxsey cure."

Car Insurance Scams

Although it's illegal to operate a motor vehicle without insurance, as insurance rates skyrocket, drivers try to find alternate routes. Some car owners simply don't buy insurance. The insurance industry responds by offering "uninsured motorist coverage" to those who do, while state motor vehicle departments continue to issue licenses to uninsured motorists. It's a vicious circle.

The auto insurance scam involves ne'er-do-wells who disconnect the brake lights of their cars and then position themselves in front of high-priced vehicles. At an opportune moment they slam on the brakes. Since there are no taillights showing, the mark rear-ends them. The scam artists will then generously offer to accept an on-the-spot cash settlement from the luxury car owner "instead of notifying our insurance companies, because all they'll do is raise our rates."

Princess Caraboo

Princess Caraboo's tale sounds like something right out of a movie, but it took 177 years to reach the screen (in 1994, starring Phoebe Cates). Even then, people didn't believe it could have really happened.

On April 3, 1817 (the last verifiable fact in the case, as it turned out), a strange young woman knocked on the door of a small house in Bristol, England, and, in a language no one had heard before, weakly asked for food. When questioned by British authorities, including Crown magistrate Samuel Worrall, the girl responded in her unknown tongue and wrote answers in a hand that no one could read. Fortunately, Manuel Eyenesso, a traveler from the East Indies, was present, and he correctly interpreted the stranger's replies. Her name was Caraboo, and she had been born in Java.

She was a princess who had been kidnapped by pirates, forced to sail as their slave, and managed to escape to England.

All society—encouraged by a pamphlet published that year by J. M. Clutch of Bristol—became intrigued by the woman they called Princess Caraboo, although no one quite knew what to do about her. Other than Mr. Eyenesso's translations, Caraboo had not explained herself in any way. Oxford scholars were contacted, but failed to identify her writing and even raised doubts about her Javanese dialect.

Gradually the truth emerged. Princess Caraboo, it seemed, was not the fake. The faker was Eyenesso, who didn't speak a word of her language, but simply made up whatever he pleased in lieu of a translation. Indeed, it developed that Caraboo was one Mary Willcocks who was born in Devonshire in 1791. She had run away to London at the age of 16, married once if not twice, and learned snatches of her foreign language from one of her male friends. Her mother identified her from newspaper reports, and came to Bristol to collect her. Meanwhile, the mysterious Eyenesso disappeared.

So, eventually, did Princess Caraboo. A collection was taken up on her behalf and she was shipped to America.

Or so the story goes.

Banco/Bunko

"Banco" is an elaborate confidence ruse involving a card game in which everybody is in on the trick except the victim. It rose to prominence during the gold rush era of the 1850s until California vigilantes drove it east, where it settled in New York City under the expert application of men such as George P. Miller ("King of the Banco Men") and Hungry Joe Lewis. It was also known as a "faro bank game" after the mechanical device that held the cards so they could be dealt easily.

The swindle involves betting on the order in which playing cards will appear from a stacked deck. Everybody in the game knows the order except, obviously, the victim. At first, the mark is allowed to win a little, inspiring him to place larger and larger bets

✓ **REALITY CHECK**

Judge Crater

Two disappearances in the 1930s stunned and puzzled the world: Amelia Earhart vanished while attempting to fly around the world in 1937; and Joseph Force Crater, a New York Supreme Court judge, left for work on August 6, 1930, and was never seen again. Throughout the 1930s a continual effort was made to find Judge Crater, with police chasing a succession of false or useless leads. No motive for his disappearance was ever discovered, although there were rumors of corruption among his political associates. In 1937, Judge Crater was ruled legally dead; but for many people who followed his story during the Depression, it remains very much open.

against the other players. When he begins to think that he has a feel for the game (sometimes encouraged by other "players" who disclose that the dealer told them what the last card will be), he places a very large final wager—and loses.

The term *banco*, incidentally, appears in several forms including *bunkum* and *bunko*. Some etymologists trace its origins to the 1820 congressional debate about the Missouri Compromise. A particularly long-winded and meaningless speech was given by the representative from Buncombe County, North Carolina, inspiring reporters to transform the name *Buncombe* into the word *bunkum*, which then mutated into *bunk, debunk,* and the rest. The term became formalized when it was self-applied by police department "bunko squads" who investigate illegal confidence activities.

(*Note*: Except in name, this swindle is unrelated to a popular board game which is also called Bunko.)

Michael Milken

When the crime is so big that no punishment is sufficient, or when the crime is committed with public acquiescence, society has no alternative but to declare the criminal a hero. Such was the case with Michael Milken, the brilliant Drexel Burnham Lambert Inc. stock manipulator of the 1980s, who discovered the legal loophole that made junk bonds possible. Although Milken pled guilty to securities fraud and related charges in 1990, he made so many people rich that, on his release from jail, he remade himself as a philanthropist.

Milken's original "crime"—junk bonds—was not illegal. Junk bonds were simply high-risk securities issued on undervalued or questionable companies that made it possible to finance leveraged transactions. For example, Milken would buy 100 percent of a stock with 10 percent of the money, then take over the company and sell off its assets to pay the bill. His loophole enabled investors to sidestep the requirement, put in place following the Wall Street crash of 1929, that anyone buying stock on credit had to have money to back it up. Milken made possible the immense corporate mergers that have consolidated world finance over the past 20 years and sent the Dow Jones Industrial Average into the stratosphere.

In 1998, Milken agreed to a settlement with the Securities and Exchange Commission for allegedly advising MCI on its 1995 investment in News Corp. and Ted Turner on his merger with Time Warner. Banned from trading in securities under the terms of his 1990 plea bargain, Milken paid $47 million in fines for his purported role in the $8.9 billion transactions. Despite the fine, sources still placed his net worth at $700 million.

Stock Swindles

Today's stock market is fraught with frenetic commodities brokers, instant billionaires, merger-mania, the uncertainty of day trading, and persistent whispers about insider tips. But it's still nothing like the virtually unregulated securities industry just before the stock market crash of 1929. In fact, it was that atmosphere of unfettered trading—much like what's going on in dot.com Internet companies as this book is being written—that seduced countless people into investing in the financial security of such legendary con artists as Joseph "Yellow Kid" Weil.

Weil himself boasted about it in his 1948 memoir *"Yellow Kid" Weil* (with W. T. Brannon): "Until the market crash of October, 1929, nearly everybody believed there were big fortunes to be made in stock. Consequently, many folks who ordinarily would not have dabbled in stocks were easy victims of my schemes."

Weil's complicated, but effective, stock swindle took place in the days when people could still believe the items they saw in print. It began when Weil saw an article in *McClure's* magazine about a mining engineer named Pope Yateman who had wrung money out of a supposedly worthless mine in Chile. Weil bought as many copies of that issue as he could find and had a friendly counterfeiter/printer reprint the article, substituting Weil's photograph for Yateman's. Weil then rebound the fake pages into the real magazine, which he thoughtfully sent to all the public libraries in the towns in which he would work his con.

✓ REALITY CHECK

What's In a Name?

Nicknames for grifters didn't start with Damon Runyon or end with the Mob. "Monikers" have been part of the vocabulary of grifters ever since Monte went into the three-card business. Guys like "Brickyard Jimmy" once laid brick in the slammer; the "Brass Kid" sold cheap jewelry; "Bow-Legged Lip" had bow legs and a harelip; the "Narrow Gage Kid" could lie across railroad tracks and just touch both rails; and "Kissing Sam" could pick a pocket while talking to his victim face-to-face. Even a woman could earn a professional name; Chicago's "Duck Walk" Kelly won her less-than-flattering sobriquet because that's the way she waddled when she had her twin pistols stuffed in her garter belts.

His next step was to snare victims who would gladly invest in a stock offering that the knowledgeable Yateman (Weil) proposed. If anyone questioned his veracity, he simply referred them to their local public library to check him out in *McClure's*.

Selling the mark the fake stock was a cinch after that. And before he skipped town, Weil would go to the local library to switch the fake *McClure's* for a real one, further confounding the victim's efforts to sic the authorities on him.

"In general, though," Weil said in his autobiography, "my 'customers' seldom complained. They preferred to take their losses rather than let the world know that they had been so gullible."

The Drop Swindle

Pop quiz: you and a stranger happen across a wallet lying in the street. You both see it at the same time. The wallet is loaded with cash.

The stranger says, "Wow, I'll bet the guy who dropped this wallet would pay a big reward to get it back." When you agree, the stranger says, "If I wasn't in such a hurry, I'd go with you to return it and share the reward. Tell you what: you return the wallet, just give me fifty dollars now and you can keep whatever the reward is." What do you do?

Guys like Nathan "Kid Dropper" Kaplan (1891–1923) correctly realized that most people would simply give him $50 to get rid of him, then turn around and keep the wallet without bothering to find the owner. That made it a good deal for Kaplan, because it was his prop wallet and it was filled with counterfeit bills.

The "drop swindle" is still used today by scam artists who hang around ATMs. Police admit that they never know how many people are actually ripped off this way because victims are too embarrassed to report it.

As for "Kid Dropper" Kaplan, he gave up dropping wallets in the 1920s and started dropping people. Kaplan was credited with the murders of at least 20 men during the labor union wars in New York's garment district. He was assassinated in 1923 by a hood named Louis Kushner, leading to a power struggle that eventually allowed Louis "Lepke" Buchalter to take over the union rackets in 1927.

✓ REALITY CHECK

Peter Christian Barrie

Peter Christian Barrie worked the horse tracks from 1926 to 1934. Taking a cue from "Yellow Kid" Weil, Barrie would buy two horses: one a champion racer, the other a nag. He would paint the nag to look like the champ and enter it in races which, of course, it would lose. When the odds were sufficiently heavy against the nag, he would enter the champion and collect the outlandish winnings that would always follow. Since the authorities were only on the lookout for doped horses and fixed races, they never suspected Barrie's switcheroo. By the time the Pinkertons finally caught up with Barrie at Saratoga, prosecutors were stymied because the laws against race fixing were hard to enforce, so Barrie was shipped off to Scotland where he died in 1935. The next year, the racing industry went on to institute more reliable credentialing.

Laying the Note

A lightning-fast short con called "laying the note" (and sometimes "the switch") involves swapping paper money before the mark realizes what has happened. A perfect example was expertly enacted by actors Ryan O'Neal and Dorothy Price in director Peter Bogdanovich's 1973 film, *Paper Moon*, adapted by screenwriter Alvin Sargent from the book *Addie Pray* by Joe David Brown.

In the scene, O'Neal buys two hair ribbons for his daughter in a general store. They cost 15¢, and he pays with a $5 bill. Now pay attention.

1. Engaging the clerk (Price) in conversation, O'Neal accepts the $4.85 change. He pockets the 85¢ but keeps the four $1 bills visible.
2. He then adds another $1 from his pocket to the four $1 bills to make a total of five $1 bills. He asks the clerk to exchange his five $1 bills for a $5 bill from her register.
3. The clerk hands him the $5. She keeps the five $1s, all while O'Neal continues his distracting banter.
4. Next, O'Neal hands the $5 back to the clerk, gripes about having too much paper money, and asks her to add his $5 to the five $1s and give him a $10 bill. She does.
5. The O'Neals are out the door, in their car, and down the street before the clerk even begins to suspect that something strange just happened. What has happened is that he has just made $4.85 and two hair ribbons.

Clifford Irving

When *The Autobiography of Howard Hughes* was announced for publication by McGraw-Hill Book Company in 1971, nobody was more surprised than Howard Hughes. The bashful billionaire, who had fled America rather than pay a judgement levied against him by a California court over a stockholder dispute, didn't seem like the sort of person who would give his life story to anyone. And yet, supposedly, he had told all to Clifford Irving, a 42-year-old novelist living the expatriate life on the Mediterranean island of Ibiza.

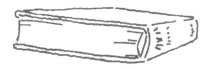

But, then, Hughes had always been considered a nutcase, hadn't he? Didn't he buy a Hollywood movie studio (RKO Radio Pictures), walk in the front gate, say "paint it," and leave forever? Didn't he rent Cary Grant's house and live in it without furniture? Didn't he grow 8-inch-long fingernails and pad around his hotel room in Kleenex boxes because he was afraid of germs? Or was that just stuff in the autobiography that Irving sold to McGraw-Hill for $765,000 with excerpt rights going to *Life* magazine?

Although Hughes wasn't talking, others were. *Time* reporter Frank McCulloch vouched for the manuscript's believability, as did CBS-TV's Mike Wallace. *Publishers Weekly* said the same thing, and Albert Leventhal, editor-in-chief of McGraw-Hill, dismissed attacks on the book's veracity by opining, ". . . it would take a Shakespeare to invent such a work." Clifford Irving backed up his credibility by explaining that he and Hughes had arranged repeated meetings in the Bahamas and Mexico to talk about the book. As proof of Hughes's collaboration, Irving produced a manuscript laden with corrections in the billionaire's own handwriting.

It was, as they say on Publishers' Row, sexy stuff. Hughes finally told all about his relationships with starlets, his friendship with Ernest Hemingway, his exploits as an adventurer, and other sure-fire page turners. The controversy was fanned by assertions in the book that Hughes had loaned President Richard Nixon $405,000, and hints that the Watergate break-in may have been the result of the White House's paranoia that Hughes may have revealed this to the Democratic Party. Later, when graphologists certified the authenticity of Hughes's handwriting, McGraw-Hill scheduled a 400,000-copy run.

Then Howard Hughes called.

"This must go down in history," he said through a speakerphone in a press conference arranged by his Summa Corporation. "I only wish I were still in the movie business, because I don't remember any script as wild or as stretching the imagination as this yarn has turned out to be." He then denied both the autobiography and Clifford Irving. In reaction, Irving denied Howard Hughes, implying that the secretive mogul had made the public announcement to indemnify his corporation from the book's revelations.

By the end of January 1972, however, Irving admitted that he had perpetrated a hoax. "I never met Howard Hughes," the writer said. "It was a caper, nothing more." Irving explained that he and his Swiss wife, Edith, had cashed the publisher's checks (written to Hughes) in Switzerland. He also said that he had written it (with Richard Suskind) based upon careful research, vivid invention, and a calculated risk that Hughes would never emerge from exile to denounce it. Further intrigue arose when Nina van Pallandt, a Danish beauty who was identified as Irving's mistress, stepped forward and testified against him at his fraud trial. On March 13, 1972, Irving pleaded guilty to federal conspiracy charges. He was sentenced to two and a half years, served 17 months, and returned whatever of the publisher's money was unspent.

There were also those who insisted (and still do) that it was not Hughes who made the phone call.

Astonishingly, for a book that gathered so much publicity, it was never published. The rights reverted to Irving, who reportedly kept the manuscript in a box that he carried around from residence to residence. In 1999 an Internet company called Terrificbooks.com announced plans to offer what the *International Herald Tribune* called "the most famous unpublished book of the 20th century."

As for Howard Hughes, he died in 1976 on a private plane flying between Acapulco and Houston, leaving behind the "Mormon Will," but that's another story (see Melvin Dummar, page 69).

Janet Cooke and Her Brethren

The scoop was too good to be true: Jimmy, an eight-year old heroin addict, survived on the streets of the nation's capital through his wits, his luck, his habit, and the attentions of a *Washington Post* reporter. There was only one thing wrong: Jimmy didn't exist. He was the invention of Janet Cooke, a talented reporter for Washington, D.C.'s leading daily newspaper, the home of Woodward and Bernstein. Real or not, "Jimmy's World" sold papers and drew attention to the District of Columbia's horrendous drug problem. On

✓ **REALITY CHECK**

The Autograph Con

The autograph con is used on celebrities and public officials. Someone asks you for your autograph and then converts the piece of paper into a negotiable check. Don't laugh. Although banks prefer their own checks with the funny computer symbols, by law in most states a check can be written on *anything* that can be processed. As many an actor has been told by his or her agent, "Never sign an autograph the way you sign your checks or contracts."

April 13, 1981, Cooke's passionate profile won her and the paper a Pulitzer prize.

Two days later, Cooke confessed her chicanery, explaining that, while "Jimmy" was a fabrication, he was nevertheless an amalgam of a number of child drug addicts she had met while researching her story. The *Post* was scandalized. Not only was it embarrassing for them ethically, but Cooke was black, and had gained her position on the prestigious paper not only because she was a good writer, but (as her detractors claimed) because she helped correct the *Post*'s minority hiring statistics. After an internal investigation and a great deal of criticism from self-righteous colleagues, Cooke was fired and had to forfeit her Pulitzer. In 1995 she was working in a Michigan department store. The next year, a former boyfriend wrote a *GQ* magazine article about her ordeal and sold the film rights to her story, for which she reportedly received a share.

Fate worked a little differently for three other journalists who invented the news instead of covering it. In 1998, *New Republic* writer Stephen Glass was dismissed for some 27 alleged violations of the magazine's ethics code, primarily for fabricating information. Around the same time, two *Boston Globe* columnists, Mike Barnicle and Patricia Smith, were drawn into a firestorm when it was asserted that Smith had fabricated quotes, and that Barnicle had engaged in plagiarism (of a George Carlin book) and had written about two cancer patients whose existence he was unable to later prove. When Smith (a black female) was fired but Barnicle (a white male) was not, there were cries of racism. Finally the *Globe* demanded Barnicle's resignation, pleasing numerous people who had challenged his veracity for years. Barnicle remains a popular Boston broadcast personality. In 2000, Smith was hired as a columnist by *Ms. Magazine*.

As media companies continue to merge and the bottom line veers away from investigative reporting and toward commercial "synergy" with the parent company's related holdings, questions about ethics, accuracy, and intent are going to be raised more often. Or maybe not. Or heck, just wait for the movie.

The Smack

Buck Boatwright, a train conductor on the Kansas-Missouri run in the late 1880s, was a clever conniver who discovered he could make a better living from the passengers than he could from the railroad. He had become so adept at cons that, by 1900, he gathered all his schemes under one roof in a big store operation in Webb City, Missouri.

His con involved luring a fellow commuter from the waiting room of the train station into a street corner coin-matching game run by a third party. But first Boatwright connived with the commuter to "fix" the game against the third party. What the commuter didn't know was that Boatwright had already fixed the game with the third party. By the end of the scam, the commuter left town with two thoughts: (1) he was lucky to get out with his life, and (2) his friend Boatwright would join him on the train to split their winnings. He was wrong on the second count.

The con was called the "smack" because of the sound the coins made when they were clapped onto the backs of the players' hands.

REALITY CHECK

The Tear-Up

A simple technique involving sleight of hand, the Tear-Up is a short con in which a con man relents and agrees to give you back your check, tearing it up in front of you or even burning the pieces, to prove his or her honesty. When you get your next bank statement you realize that the con switched your check for a fake one of the same color (they come prepared) and cashed yours on the way home.

Melvin Dummar

When billionaire Howard Hughes died intestate in 1976, an unlikely man came forward to claim a bequest. Melvin Dummar (pronounced duMAR) was just a working guy who, one night in the desert, happened to give an old hitchhiker a lift and a few coins to help him out. Some time later, Hughes's handwritten "Last Will and Testament" showed up naming Dummar among 16 beneficiaries. The "Mormon Will," as it came to be known, was successfully contested by Hughes's all-powerful Summa Corporation, and all that the hapless Dummar got out of it was a painful lesson: the American dream is not a firm promise. His rags-to-rags story was told in

✓ REALITY CHECK

Fakus

Never judge a book by its cover, or even its contents! *Fakus* is the term for an old-time con practiced by book-sellers and newsdealers. They slip a $5 or $10 bill not-so-subtly between the pages of a book or magazine they are trying to get rid of. As the customer buys it, thinking she has found free money, the con man pulls the bill out before handing the merchandise back. This is like not telling the cashier when you get too much change at the supermarket, then counting it and realizing he gave you too little!

Jonathan Demme's award-winning 1980 movie *Melvin and Howard*, for which Dummar—played by Paul LeMat with Jason Robards as Hughes—had these thoughts (in an interview with the author):

Does the American dream work? Sometimes. The American dream is the ability to work and earn, to work for what you get out of life. I'd never expected in my life to have anything handed to me. When I picked up Howard Hughes I didn't ask him for anything, I didn't expect anything—and, as it turned out, I didn't get anything!

The dreams that I want out of life, I'm gonna have to earn them. I've been aware of that since I've been a small child. I think that if someone has something handed to them, they don't appreciate it as much as if they have to work for it and earn it.

I've had a lot of ups and downs. I've had a few cars repossessed and lost my wife and I've been, you know, milkman of the month. It's all part of life. I don't really look at it as being a loser. I wrote a song once called "A Dream Can Become a Reality" and they even used that against me in court. The opposing side got hold of it and twisted it around to say that you can rise from a beggar into a king, but the main point of the song was basically how I feel and look at life. It's the working hard and having faith and courage that makes your dreams come true.

It hurts to have people doubt me, but, of course, I've done a couple of stupid things in my life. To keep your name and credibility you have to be honest. It's frustrating, but if people want to believe it, okay, if they don't—well, you can't please everybody all the time. I'd like for everybody to believe me, but I have to live with it and face it.

One footnote: Among the provisions of the Hughes will—if it is ever verified—are the dissolution of Summa Corporation and the distribution of its holdings to the Boy Scouts of America, the Mormon Church, the Miami Medical Research Center, the family of Hughes's longtime operative Noah Dietrich. And, of course, Melvin Dummar.

The Handkerchief Switch

In the fortunetelling racket there's only one prediction that always comes true: *You will get ripped off.* One way this happens is the "handkerchief switch," traditionally pulled on people from unsophisticated, deeply religious, and superstitious cultures. This con is also called "the wipe."

Like shrinks and Internet chat rooms, fortunetellers work with whatever their customers tell them. Years of chicanery—and laws against quackery—have made most of them change the name of their profession to "spiritual advisers," but there are still some who reportedly continue to prey on the gullible, the vulnerable, the sick, and the lonely.

First, the victim is seduced into trusting the fortuneteller who informally asks a number of questions designed to probe his or her trust, susceptibility, and, of course, wealth. In most cases, it's all harmless smoke and mirrors, but if the client is deemed worthy of becoming a "mark," the fortuneteller will get around to convincing her that her cash is making her evil, and the best way to exorcise her demons is to bury or destroy the filthy lucre.

On a subsequent visit the wad of cash is produced and, in plain sight, is folded into a handkerchief. While distracting the victim, the fortuneteller switches the money-filled handkerchief with one holding plain paper. The "wrong" handkerchief is then buried in the woods, flushed down the toilet, or burned in the oven to release its evil spirits while the "real" handkerchief is stashed in the fortuneteller's safe.

If it sounds simple, it is. The simple tricks always work the best.

Phineas T. Barnum

The man who lived and thrived by the motto, "There's a sucker born every minute" (which, as it turned out, he never said) was born July 5, 1810. In the approximately 42,995,520 minutes until he died on April 7, 1891 (counting leap years), he might easily have conned that many suckers into one or more of his fantastic schemes. It is estimated that he made no less than $2 million

during his 80 years. Despite his reputation for success, however, Phineas T. (Taylor) Barnum went through three fortunes, two wives, and a veritable catalog of how to give the public just what it wanted—for a price.

His life itself was a circus. Born in the small town of Bethel, Connecticut, P. T. took off for the city, first Bridgeport, then Brooklyn. By age 19, he was married to a woman named Charity Hallett and already scouting around for something to promote. At first he became associated with Chang and Eng Bunker, two conjoined twins, whose Asian heritage introduced the term *Siamese twins* to the lexicon. But it was when he paid a hard-earned $1,000 in 1835 for the services of Miss Joice Heth that his career as a huckster truly began. At the time, Barnum was 25. Heth was 161, and she had been George Washington's slave/nurse. Or so the two of them insisted in the many handbills that the budding showman spread across New York City. It was a success. Barnum toured Heth throughout New England and took in $1,500 a week. (When Heth died in 1836, it came to light that she was actually only 70 years old.)

But Barnum never looked back. In 1841 he purchased Scudder's American Museum in New York City and discovered that he could speed the foot traffic through the exhibits with a sign that exhorted, "This Way to the Egress!" Only when the customers got there did they discover that *egress* was another word for "exit," and they would have to pay another 50¢ to get back in.

It was at Scudder's in 1842 that Barnum met the man who would make him famous: a four-year-old little person (called a midget in those days) named Charles Sherwood Stratton from Bridgeport, Connecticut. Barnum renamed him "Tom Thumb" (after the Grimm's fairy tale) and toured him around the world. By the time he was in his teens, Thumb stood 25 inches tall; at maturity he was still under 40 inches and weighed 70 pounds. In 1863 was given the title "General" Tom Thumb by Queen Victoria, the diminutive regent. Thumb and Barnum became close friends. When Thumb married Lavinia Warren (32 inches tall) in 1863 in New York City's Grace Church, Barnum promoted the union, standing the wedding party atop a grand piano to receive guests at the Metropolitan Hotel.

Tom Thumb was the genuine article, but the 1842 Feejee Mermaid was a fish of a different color, and Barnum apparently had no misgivings deceiving the public about her origins. In the same year he met Tom Thumb, Barnum encountered the preserved body of a mermaid from the Feejee (now Fiji) Islands. To get coverage, Barnum wrote letters under false names to New York newspapers and mailed them from a variety of far-flung locations so that they wouldn't be traced back to him. The ruse worked, and press curiosity attracted thousands of people to the American Museum at 25¢ a pop to see the withered specimen. Only later in his life did Barnum admit that the creature was merely the top of a monkey and the bottom of a fish. Meanwhile, he had firmly established his museum as a showplace.

Not content to be merely a promoter, Barnum then decided to be a producer. In 1844 he bought the touring rights to *The Drunkard, or the Fallen Saved,* a temperance play by William H. Smith, and presented it in major eastern cities. But it wasn't until he signed Swedish coloratura Johanna Maria "Jenny" Lind in 1850 that he became known as a theatrical impresario. Lind, 30, was called "the Swedish Nightingale." Barnum paid her $1,000 per night plus all expenses for her American concert tour. Her opening engagement at New York's Castle Garden grossed nearly $18,000 and kicked off a two-year tour that would bring her $130,000 (most of which she gave to charity) and untold more for Barnum himself. More than money, it gave him respectability.

Surprisingly, Barnum did not begin his most famous enterprise until 1870 when he was 60 years old: the Grand Traveling Museum, Menagerie, Caravan and Circus—or, as it has come to be known and loved, "The Greatest Show on Earth." Its first year, in Brooklyn, the circus grossed $400,000. In 1872 Barnum had the brainstorm to make it the first circus to tour the country by rail. With 65 cars, covering five acres, and seating 10,000 patrons per show at 50¢ per ticket, two shows a day, it made twice its $5,000 per day operating costs every day.

✓ REALITY CHECK

Jumbo

One of P. T. Barnum's biggest attractions, literally, lumbered along in 1882. Jumbo was acquired from London's Royal Zoological Gardens (they had swapped him with the Jardin des Plantes in Paris in 1865 for a rhinoceros). "The largest elephant in or out of captivity," Jumbo stood 11 feet high at the shoulders and weighed 6.5 tons.

Nevertheless, Barnum claimed he stood 12 feet high, measured 26 feet in length including the trunk, and weighed 10.5 tons. Jumbo proved so popular that his name became synonymous with bigness. Even after he was killed by a freight train on the Grand Trunk Railway (no kidding) in 1885, his skeleton continued to be a perennial attraction.

When Barnum had a notion, truth or falsehood meant nothing to him. The most notorious example is the Cardiff Giant. The story begins in 1866, when a Binghamton, New York, cigar maker named George Hull was visiting his sister in Ackley, Iowa. As a northerner, Hull had little patience with ignorance and superstition, so when he encountered both in the form of a revivalist minister named the Reverend Mr. Turk, he began concocting a scheme. Turk was a biblical literalist who believed that everything in Scripture should be taken exactly as stated. Thus, when he quoted Genesis 6:4 as saying, "There were giants on the earth in those days . . . mighty men which were of old, men of renown," the Reverend insisted that "giants" meant actual physical size, not intellectual and spiritual stature.

REALITY CHECK

The Gold Plug

Also called the "gold brick" short con, the gold plug was practiced widely during a bygone era. The victim is sold a gold ingot, which is actually a lead brick painted gold and stamped with official looking symbols. When the mark demands to test the brick, the con artist digs out a plug of real gold (which he planted earlier). Then runs like heck.

To teach Turk and his brethren a lesson, Hull obtained a 3,000-pound block of gypsum (a crystalline substance used in fertilizer, which turned out to be highly symbolic) from a quarry in Fort Dodge, Iowa. He then hired Chicago sculptors Edward Burghardt, Fred Mohrmann, and Henry Salle to chisel it into the rough-hewn shape of a 12-foot-tall man, taking great pains to make it look like a million-year-old fossil. They used acid to age the statue, and poked needles into its skin to simulate pores. Hull then had it shipped to the farm of his cousin, William Newell, near Cardiff, New York, where it was buried under the barn.

Hull and Newell waited a year before contriving to have workmen "discover" their fossilized friend in the ground behind Newell's barn on October 16, 1869. First, the workers uncovered a stone leg, then a foot, then the rest of what quickly became known as the Cardiff Giant. Before long, word leaked out (which was the whole idea). When a local newspaper headline heralded it "A Wonderful Discovery," Hull erected a tent over his "find" and reluctantly permitted visitors to view the specimen—first at 25¢ each, then at 50¢, and finally a dollar—watching in amusement as the crowds arrived by horse and wagon to the tune of 3,000 a day.

Estimates of Hull's initial investment range from $2,200 to $2,600, but he was well into profits—if, indeed, that had been his intention. By this time, Hull was in too deep to set the record straight even if he had wanted to. Besides, several scientists and public figures pronounced the discovery to be genuine, although others pointed out that human soft tissue would not petrify and began to debate whether it was merely an ancient statue or a modern hoax.

Meanwhile, the Giant's fame drew the attention of financial speculators, leading to one of the more contorted tales of legal irony to play out in the courts. Some time in late October or early November 1869, Hull sold three-quarters of his interest in the Giant to a consortium of Syracuse businessmen for $37,500. The trio may not have recognized a hoax, but they certainly recognized a good investment, and they began booking a tour of the Giant so that others might marvel at its magnificence. While they were making travel arrangements, none other than P. T. Barnum approached the cartel with an offer of $60,000 for a three-month license. Speaking for his partners, Hull refused and continued with plans to carry the Giant to Syracuse, where a temporary train station was built near the Barnstable Arcade to house the exhibit. Among the earlier visitors were Andrew White, president of Cornell University, and paleontologist O. C. Marsh of Yale University, both of whom rejected the Cardiff Giant as a hoax. White even reported seeing chisel marks.

But Barnum was not to be snubbed. He commissioned his own sculptor to fabricate a copy of the Giant and boldly displayed it in his American Museum in New York City. Not only that, the showman announced that his Giant was the *real* one, and that Hull was showing off a copy!

While the public eagerly waited for Hull's Giant to arrive in New York in December 1869 (where it was scheduled to be displayed near Barnum's Giant), the press finally got around to asking questions. Reporters tracked down Hull's neighbors in upstate New York who recalled him hauling around a large wooden crate. People in the quarry region of Ford Dodge, Iowa, remembered seeing him there supervising the excavation of a large block of gypsum.

✓ REALITY CHECK

Hot Merchandise

"Check it out" may not be the most descriptive sales pitch, but it is often heard on New York City streets and in parking lots of suburban shopping malls. Men offer to sell new, brand-name merchandise off the back of a truck. The seller winks and says it's surplus, the victim is supposed to think it's stolen, but usually it's just real-looking boxes filled with worthless weights. This also works with hot videotapes sold off blankets on streets in midtown Manhattan.

✓ REALITY CHECK

Laying the Flue

When money is plainly put into an envelope which has a false seal, it is called "laying the flue." The mark thinks his money is being safely sealed away in front of his eyes, but the con has slipped the bills through a slit in the bottom of the envelope and into her own pocket.

At the same time, David Hannum, one of Hull's investors, brought suit against Barnum for fraud. In a New York court in 1870, Hull was forced to confess that his Giant was a fake. Hannum's lawsuit against Barnum was dismissed on the grounds that Barnum could not have defrauded something that was already fraudulent. The twisted logic of the victory was not lost on Hannum, who said, "There's a sucker born every minute." Whether he was speaking of himself or the court is not certain, but the quote has been inaccurately attributed to Barnum ever since and has been taken to reflect his cynical attitude toward the public.

Oh, and there's an interesting epilogue to the story. Recent biblical study has led scholars to wonder if Goliath the Philistine—the big galute who took on David of the Israelites in the Books of Samuel—was one of a family of giants who lived in Gath in those days.

If Barnum knew how to make money, he also knew how to lose it. In 1855 he invested $500,000 in what turned out to be a stock fraud, but he managed to turn his loss into a gain by embarking on an editorial campaign against swindlers (always being careful to keep his name in front of the public).

Even though he suffered a stroke in 1890, Barnum continued to look to the future, particularly his own. He mused to a friend that he wanted to know what people would say about him after he died. The friend told the editor of New York's *Evening Sun*, and, on March 24, 1891, the paper ran: "Great and Only Barnum. He Wanted to Read His Obituary: Here It Is." There followed four columns of praise, for which, presumably, Barnum sent in a few changes. Two weeks later, he died for real.

In his will, he left his daughter, Helen, a "valuable property" in Colorado. It was a sick joke. Barnum was angry at Helen for abandoning her husband to shack up with a doctor in Chicago and wanted to teach her a lesson by giving her a tract of worthless land. Not long after he died, however, minerals were discovered on the property that made Helen richer than all of Barnum's heirs combined. Only in death could P. T. Barnum be beaten at his own game.

Charles K. Ponzi

Pyramid scheme is a highly charged term that is applied to any investment scheme where the early investors make money by selling to more investors, and those investors sell to still more investors, until there are eventually too many investors to ever return a profit on the investment. It has been used in chain letters, stock offerings, and other swindles, and remains among the most persistent cons because it works—but only if you're on board at the beginning. But whatever you call these schemes, they all have their roots with the same man: Charles Ponzi, inventor of the "Ponzi Scheme."

According to Mark C. Knutson's *The Remarkable Criminal Financial Career of Charles K. Ponzi,* in 1920, Ponzi collected upward of $9.5 million from as many as 10,000 investors by promising to pay them "fifty percent profit in forty-five days." His strategy was to use their money to buy Italian postal coupons, which he would sell at a 400 percent profit through the miracle of international currency exchange rates. Sure enough, he paid off his investors, at least in the beginning. The catch was that there were no postal coupons and no exchange rates. Ponzi was using new money to pay off old debts until there was so much new money coming in that he just stopped paying anybody, and kept everything.

Technically, pyramid schemes involve misclassifying "income" as "dividends"; that is, paying off early investors with money paid by later investors by telling the early investors that they are receiving profits. Or, as they say on the streets, "robbing Peter to pay Paul."

And the streets are where Charles Ponzi started—the streets of Parma, Italy—as Carlo Ponsi. Some sources place his birth in 1877; Ponzi himself said it was 1882. He seems to have emigrated to America in 1903, and then headed for Canada, where, six years later, he managed to get convicted of forgery in a scandal involving the collapse of a Montreal bank. Immediately upon his release in 1910, Ponzi returned to the States, where, almost as quickly, he violated immigration laws by smuggling five Italians into the country and was sent to federal prison in Atlanta. When he was released in 1912, he migrated to Boston and kept a low profile while the rest of the world fought the Great War.

The treaties that grew out of the Armistice shifted the lines of international finance in favor of the winners, and by 1920 Ponzi had discovered a way to work them to his advantage. Boston, with its tight Brahmin money, Ivy League schools, and old-line banks, offered him the shroud of legitimacy. At the same time, the city, with its sudden influx of European immigrants, delivered a financial feast. Forming the Securities Exchange Company, Ponzi devised his postal coupon scheme and, in December 1919, started offering ground-level shares at $100 each, promising a return of $150 in 90 days. To fan the flames of greed, he purposely repaid the notes in 45 days. In order to deter counterfeiters, he issued his certificates in varying colors, depending on the amount. The notes read:

> The Securities Exchange Company, for and in consideration of the sum of exactly $1,000 of which receipt is hereby acknowledged, agree to pay to the order of _____, upon presentation of this voucher at ninety days from date, the sum of exactly $1,500 at the company's office, 27 School Street, room 227, or at any bank.
>
> The Securities Exchange Company,
> (signed)
> Per Charles Ponzi

When challenged about the legitimacy of his operation, Ponzi would always explain that the transactions were carried out in Europe, outside of U.S. jurisdiction. In this way he deflected inquiries from the postal inspector, Chamber of Commerce, and anybody else who stopped by his offices (furnished with a $200 loan from a furniture dealer). Before long, he had collected enough investments, and rolled later notes over to pay off earlier ones, to buy a house in upscale Lexington, Massachusetts, and to acquire the services of the Hanover Trust Company to handle his financial deposits. Hanover's involvement with Ponzi would ultimately cost them their charter.

By July 1920, Ponzi was taking in $1 million a week, and had opened offices throughout the Northeast. There were stories about cash flowing in so quickly that he and his associates had to stash it in closets because they couldn't carry it to the bank fast enough. Of course, it sounded too good to be true, but what kept state and federal authorities at a distance was that all of Ponzi's investors were being paid off as promised, even though Ponzi himself never declared a profit.

In late July, the writ hit the fan. Massachusetts District Attorney Joseph C. Pelletier convinced Ponzi to stop accepting investors until a state auditor could authenticate his system. The agreement—and to this day nobody knows why Ponzi consented to it—effectively shut off the stream of cash, and with it Ponzi's ability to pay off his notes. His pyramid collapsed.

Why did Ponzi agree to pull his own financial plug? Even more curiously, why did he not pack his bags and flee in the dead of night? Instead, he stayed in Lexington and waited for the D.A.'s ax to fall. It did, in September 1920, but the trial was held off until 1922 while constitutional issues were argued. When proceedings finally began, the extent of Ponzi's scam became known. According to the auditor's testimony (as researched by Ponzi scholar Mark C. Knutson), he had collected $9,582,591 on notes with a face value of $14,374,755. When the business closed, $4,263,652 in notes were outstanding, carrying a pay-out value of $6,396,353. In 1925, Ponzi was handed a seven- to nine-year sentence; he was ultimately released in 1934.

What did Ponzi do while awaiting trial? According to some reports, he spent some time in Florida in the mid-1920s, right about the time that a Mr. and Mrs. Calcandonio Alviati began purchasing real estate in Duval County and started making money as land prices skyrocketed with the expansion of the state economy. By dividing and subdividing the lots, early investors could recognize huge returns with each subsequent transaction. There was only one problem: the land was under water.

Ponzi's connection was established and warrants were issued, beginning a freewheeling manhunt for the elusive investment

✓ REALITY CHECK

Fake Rocks

Confidence games are so named because they play upon a victim's misplaced confidence in the scam artist. Sometimes, when the victim demands a second opinion, the grifter cleverly uses a third party who won't know he's assisting a rip-off. That's how "the rocks" works: a mark is offered "stolen" gems and is accompanied to a legitimate jeweler who appraises them. The ones the victim then buys, of course, are fakes that have been switched.

schemer. He was eventually located in Port Houston, Texas, where the ship he had boarded in Tampa, Florida, was stopping before sailing for Italy. Ponzi was summarily apprehended by authorities and extradited to Massachusetts for the continuation of his fraud trial.

And what was Charles Ponzi's life like after prison? Most chronicles say that he returned to Italy, where he became a financial adviser to Benito Mussolini when the fascist dictator was rising to power. But even that didn't last, and Il Duce eventually asked Ponzi to leave his home country. By the time Ponzi died in January 1949, he was living in poverty in Brazil, and a collection had to be taken up to give him a proper burial.

It is not known whether the people who took up the collection promised a return on the investment.

The Pigeon Drop

Like the "drop swindle," the "pigeon drop" involves a "found" wallet, a sucker, and helpful strangers—in this case, two helpful strangers working in cahoots.

Stranger #1 discovers a fat wallet on the street in front of the chosen victim. Stranger #2 then appears and demands to share in the find. Strangers #1 and #2 argue over whether to keep the booty until one of them offers to phone his boss, who just happens to be a lawyer, a cop, or an "expert" in such things. The call is made (not!) and the advice is, "My lawyer will hold onto this money until it cools off, but in the meantime, we should all post cash bonds to make sure we won't blab about it."

By now the earnestness of Strangers #1 and #2 has convinced the victim to post his bond like the others, and off they go to the lawyer to entrust him with their money. Of course, the lawyer is in on the scam, and she disappears—along with Strangers #1 and #2— right after the hapless victim antes his share.

"Dropping the leather," as the pigeon drop is also called, works when the bankroll is big enough to compromise the victim's honesty, but it still needs a trio of truly convincing con artists to pull it off.

Hey Rube!

Rube is time-honored slang for an unsophisticated person generally hailing from a rural area. When it is preceded by the word *hey*, however, the combination becomes one of the most electric phrases in the American idiom: *Hey rube!*

At first glance, this looks like somebody's trying to get a farmer's attention. In practice, "Hey rube!" is the 911 call that carnival barkers yell to summon support when a fight breaks out with the townspeople.

Before American circuses were consolidated into the handful of reputable, high profile Big Tops that now tour the country (Ringling Bros. and Barnum & Bailey, Clyde Beatty, Shrine Circus, Cirque du Soleil, etc.), numerous small-time carnivals made their way along the back roads. Accompanying the acrobats, clowns, and bareback riders were a cadre of folks whose expertise lay in a particular kind of magic: that is, making customers' money disappear. The carnival midway was lined with booths where locals could test their strength by swinging a hammer to ring a bell (along a guide wire that could be loosened or tightened depending on the wager); knock a pile of six pins completely off a tabletop (with the bottom pins weighted so they never clear the surface); shoot a line of duck targets (with uncalibrated rifles); and participate in other "gaffs." Occasionally someone would be allowed to win, which always attracted a crowd. That's when the pickpockets went to work. If the picking was slow, a helpful barker would yell, "Watch out! There's a pickpocket in the crowd!" The warning was certain to make every man reach around to pat his wallet, helpfully identifying to the nearest "dip" (pickpocket) exactly where he was hiding his money.

Mounting complaints about the honesty of traveling carnivals led to municipal crackdowns whenever the circus came to town. When the circus owners couldn't cough up enough money for local licenses (which sometimes meant that they couldn't or wouldn't meet the bribery demands of the town fathers), the elephant kept walking, so to speak.

✓ REALITY CHECK

"Optimism: The doctrine, or belief, that everything is beautiful, including what is ugly; everything good, especially the bad, and everything right that is wrong. It is held with greatest tenacity by those most accustomed to the mischance of falling into adversity."

—Ambrose Bierce, *The Devil's Dictionary*

"Optimism is the madness of maintaining that everything is right when it is wrong."

—Voltaire

"I'm so pessimistic, I don't even buy green bananas."

—Tom Lehrer

"In this best of all possible worlds . . . everything is for the best . . . .. If this is the best of all possible worlds, what are the others like?

—Francois Marie Arouet Voltaire

The Great Impostor

Not all frauds involve money; sometimes they're just for thrills. At least, that seems to be the motive behind the incredible life of Ferdinand Waldo Demara Jr., popularly known as "The Great Impostor." Throughout an improbable career which he spent impersonating other people, Demara successfully posed as a law student, a hospital orderly, a Trappist monk, a Navy surgeon, a zoologist, a professor of philosophy, and a law student. Not bad for a high school dropout!

Demara was in his 20s when he pulled off most of his impersonations. Born in 1921, his career of chicanery flourished during World War II when those men who were not in the service found themselves highly sought after for work on the home front, no questions asked. At least, nothing else can explain the giddy combination of opportunity and cheek that kept Demara going. His most audacious gig as a *poseur* was during the Korean War when he pretended to be a surgeon with the Canadian Navy. In this capacity he did everything from pull teeth to amputate limbs, staying one step ahead of disaster by cramming from medical books before each operation. His ruse was uncovered not because he lost a patient (he never did), but because the Canadian Navy wanted to give him a commendation, and a search of their enlistment records revealed that he didn't exist. Incredibly, all they could do was discharge him with full back pay and "suggest" that he return to America. He lasted in the States until 1956 when, at last, he was busted while posing as a schoolteacher in Maine. At only one point in his incredible "career" did he ever spend any time in jail, and then it was not as a prisoner but as a prison official!

In 1961 Tony Curtis appeared as the peripatetic Demara in the motion picture *The Great Impostor*. For once a Hollywood movie couldn't be accused of distorting the truth.

The Gas Line Scam

During the United States gasoline shortage of the mid-1970s, when prices at the pump topped a buck a gallon (it seemed high then!),

✓ **REALITY CHECK**

The Shake

I may sound like a soda fountain drink, but in this scam the jerk is the guy with the money. In "the shake," a mark is lured into a street corner game (dice, coin matching, three-card monte, etc.). The game is then busted by cops, who turn out to be corruptible when they demand a payoff to drop the charges. Of course, the cops are in league with the con artists. All the players hand over a bribe, and the cops generously allow them to escape. After the relieved mark scurries away, the "cops" and the con artists get back together to distribute the spoils.

filling station lines backed up around the block. That's when good old American enterprise went to work. To be helpful, gas station attendants (they had them in those days) walked down the waiting line collecting cash so that impatient motorists could pay in advance. Only when the drivers finally arrived at the pump did they realize that the man who collected their money didn't work for the gas station.

Only the replacement of service stations by credit cards and self-serve filling stations kept this same scam from popping up during the gas crisis of 2000.

Frank Norfleet

Very seldom did the victim of a confidence game ever get to turn the tables on those who had bilked him. But Frank Norfleet, a Texas rancher, not only got even with the con men who cheated him of his fortune, he also led a one-man antiswindler crusade that became the last great manhunt of the Old West. It reads like an epic, and it's all true:

It is 1919 and four years of world war have forever changed civilization. Soldiers return to their homes hardened by the horrors of battle. European society has been bled of the last vestige of its innocence, not to mention an entire generation of manhood. Nations have formed international alliances that will forever realign political and economic power.

America, too, has grown up. The frontier has been settled, and the Old West is fast becoming a colorful memory. Even criminals are transforming; instead of the brutal rustlers and gunfighters who once struck terror into decent folk, a new kind of scoundrel is starting to appear: the confidence artist.

Texas rancher Frank Norfleet was marked for swindle by Joe Furey, W. B. Spencer, Bill Trumbull, and two confederates. Norfleet entered their big store by finding (ahem, being allowed to find) a

REALITY CHECK

The Single-Hand Con

Here we have an example of rich people who never have to spend money, except they're not really rich, and the money is yours. A "single-hand con" starts as a con artist strikes up a conversation with a traveler, shows him a large check to establish his legitimacy, borrows cash from the man while leaving the worthless check as security, and absconds. A pointed version of this is the basis of Mark Twain's classic short story, "The Man with the Million-Pound Note."

✓ REALITY CHECK

Dishonor among Thieves

Italian sculptor Alceo Dossena made a tidy living selling copies of Renaissance statues to a New York art dealer for $200 each, which wasn't anything to sneer at in 1918 when he started. What he didn't learn until 1928, however, was that his work was so good that the dealer had been selling his sculptures at grossly inflated fees as the genuine article. Dossena brought suit against the duplicitous art dealer and got so much publicity that, at an auction of his work in 1933, the Italian government decided to give each buyer a document that specified that the sculpture they had just bought was a genuine Dossena fake.

wallet on the carpet of a Dallas hotel. The tumblers clicked into place with precision: A passerby told Norfleet that the wallet belonged to a "very rich man" who sat on the Dallas Cotton Exchange. The "very rich man" offered Norfleet a $100 reward, which he graciously declined, so the wallet's owner offered to invest the money for him in cotton futures. After a short while the futures grew to $73,000, but Norfleet was told he could only collect it if he posted a $45,000 bond.

Enticed by his own opportunism, Norfleet withdrew his life savings, mortgaged his ranch, and turned the cash over to the rich investor. That was the last he saw of him, not to mention the other men who pulled off the scam. Or so the con men thought. When Texas authorities refused to enforce the law, Norfleet himself vowed revenge. He raised an additional $30,000 and spent the next four years on his own private manhunt looking for the scoundrels.

Each leg of his quest became a separate adventure as he pursued his prey with zeal. To infiltrate the myriad cons who were plying their trade across the territory, he learned the tricks of the trade and became a grifter himself, always alerting police at the last minute and leaving town like the Lone Ranger to continue his campaign.

In Denver while on W. B. Spencer's trail, Norfleet wormed his way into a phony stock exchange operation and exposed some three dozen con men, including local cops who were being paid to let it thrive. Spencer, however, slipped through his fingers. But Norfleet persisted, and finally cornered Spencer in Salt Lake City. It was his first capture, and it strengthened his determination. Four years and 40,000 miles later, he finally wrangled all five of the original gang members, including their leader, Joe Furey. Along the way he had spent $30,000 of his own money and recovered none of the $45,000 that inspired his vendetta. He appealed to the State of Texas for compensation, and in 1923 the Texas legislature voted him token expense money and thanked him for "assisting the cause of justice." When a court subsequently ruled the reimbursement of a private citizen (and a vigilante at that) to have been illegal, the offer was withdrawn. Nevertheless, the governor promised to take it "under advisement." By 1960, having survived to the age of 95, Frank Norfleet was still being told that the expense money was "under advisement."

The Norfleet story plays like something out of a movie, and several people (including the author) have tried to get it going. One who almost succeeded is Oscar-winning actor Robert Duvall, who would have been the perfect Norfleet—charming, steely, obsessive. Unfortunately, the media conglomerate that was developing the film with him decided that Norfleet was too old a character to attract the 16- to 24-year-old movie audience. They put Duvall's project "under advisement."

Green Goods

Imagine buying counterfeit money only to discover that it's fake. That's the racket that surfaced in America around 1869, shortly after the U.S. Treasury consolidated the outdated Union and Confederate bills after the Civil War. The trick was simply to show the mark some real U.S. currency and insist that it represented the high quality of the fakes. The con man then accepted the mark's money to purchase a stash of counterfeit bills, and delivered a bag of blank green paper. (Why green paper? No one knows for sure, but there are several theories: It was cheaper than bleached, fine white paper; the counterfeiters had a ready supply; or it was just a way to add insult to injury.)

In a forerunner to today's bothersome junk mail, bilk-worthy victims (such as bank presidents and recent lottery winners) were actually solicited by letter. The offer was blatant: Pay $100 and receive $1,200 in perfect counterfeit bills. Anybody who was venal enough to respond stepped into the first phase of the swindle, namely, coming to the meeting where he was shown a wad of genuine greenbacks (posing as fakes). The bills had to be genuine; that way, even if the mark brought along the feds, the evidence would be its own exoneration. If, after seeing the "samples," he went through with his purchase—well, he was in line to receive a lifetime supply of green memo pads.

✓ **REALITY CHECK**

The Tat

The Tat is a twist upon a twist, in which the mark is allowed to find a pair of crooked dice and is lured into a dice game where he thinks he will clean out the other players. Before you can say "craps," his crooked dice are switched for the crooked dice game's crooked dice. Any questions?

✓ REALITY CHECK

Say It Ain't So, Wyatt

Today Wyatt Earp is known as a lawman who tamed the West and fought at the O. K. Corral. But in the 1870s when he and his brothers worked as a team, he was known as a thug, gunfighter, pimp, and everything else he could get away with. He had been involved in horse stealing, was known to pocket the fines he collected as a lawman rather than turn them over to the municipal treasury, had a financial interest in the Dodge City town brothel and saloon, and apparently goaded the Clanton family into a slaughter (and nearly got run in for murder). Perhaps significantly, when he retired from law enforcement, he found work in Hollywood as technical adviser on Westerns.

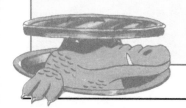

Cassie Chadwick

Cassie didn't resort to violence to break the law; she used her so-called feminine wiles to break the bank. In the 1890s, when other women were getting used to such labor-saving home devices as electric lights and washing machines, the fetching Miss Chadwick left home and arrived in Cleveland, Ohio, not to be a housewife, but to embark on one of the most astonishing cleanups in history.

Claiming to be the illegitimate daughter of steel magnate Andrew Carnegie, she flashed enough forged papers to secure a loan from the president of Cleveland's biggest bank. She then sealed her con with a stroke of genius. Cassie begged the man not to breathe a word of her secret, which was that a relative of Carnegie needed money. Of course, this tactic insured that, by the next day, the news was all over town; and Cassie Chadwick was immediately established in Cleveland society.

She began her swindle by borrowing a few tens of thousands of dollars from the local swells and quickly repaying it, thus assuring her credibility. Reasoning (accurately, as it turned out) that no one would dare approach Mr. Carnegie to confirm or deny her genealogy, Cassie kept escalating her loans until she was into various banks and individual lenders for hundreds of thousands of dollars.

Cassie's steel structure collapsed in 1904 when the *Cleveland Press* revealed, after a long investigation, that her real name was Elizabeth Bigley and that she was of Canadian birth. More than that, she was also a convicted forger who had been pardoned in 1893 by the governor of Ohio (later president), William McKinley. When the news broke, Charles T. Beckwith, president of the Citizens National Bank of Oberlin, immediately died of heart failure; she owed him a fortune. There was a run on Beckwith's and other banks that were discovered to have made loans to her.

But Mrs. Chadwick was nowhere near Ohio; she was in New York enjoying her spoils. She was brought back to Ohio, tried, and ended her spree in prison, where she died in 1907 living out her 10-year sentence.

Even at the time of her death, there were people who still thought she was the illegitimate daughter of Andrew Carnegie. But nobody ever said she wasn't a lady.

The Shell Game

Interestingly, this oldest of human swindles—the shell game—demands skill on the part of the swindler. According to crime expert Carl Sifakis (in *The Encyclopedia of American Crime*), a forerunner of the shell game is on record as far back as the second century A.D. in the writings left by Alciphron of Athens.

"Thimble riggers," as practitioners are also known, challenge the mark to guess which shell (clam, walnut, opaque shot glass, or piece of carved wood) is hiding the pea. The skill comes in making sure, through sleight of hand, that the pea isn't under any of the shells. Instead, it is pinched between the thumb and fore-finger. Thus, no matter which shell the mark pays to upturn, it will be empty, and yet the operator can easily slip the pea under either of the remaining two shells if challenged.

According to the knowledgeable Sifakis, a victim once turned the tables on a shell game operator by placing his loaded and cocked gun on the gaming table and announcing he would wager which two shells the pea was *not* under. Knowing that they were all empty, he pointed to two shells and flipped them over. "I guess there's no sense turning over the last one, is there?" he sneered, sweeping the winnings into his hat.

The Spanish Prisoner

It is a constant irritation to Amnesty International, whose work to free political prisoners and other wrongly held men and women is known worldwide, that scams like this exploit such situations. But that's the sad truth that keeps "the Spanish prisoner" alive.

Award-winning playwright David Mamet, who wrote and directed the film *House of Games*, found ample fodder in this enduring swindle to similarly dramatize it in his 1998 motion picture of the same name starring Steve Martin and Campbell Scott.

This scam takes the form of a personal letter that advises the recipient that a wealthy man has shipped a fortune in cash to a secure storage location in America but was captured by (fill in the name of the dictator) before he could escape his revolution-torn country. Alas, he now languishes in jail in (fill in the name of the country), but could probably bribe his way out if only, say, $5,000 could be sent to this post office box in (fill in name of the U.S. city), where the dictator's corrupt jailer can receive it. As an inducement, the letter promises, the wealthy man will repay the $5,000 plus a huge reward once he is released. Naturally, anyone who falls for this confidence game learns too late that there is no prisoner, no fortune, no reimbursement, and certainly no reward. But there is a post office box. Of course, by the time the postal authorities are informed about it, the owner and his fake name have vanished.

Although the scam is called "the Spanish prisoner," it has been used to prey on members of Miami's fervent anti-Castro Cuban community, Boston's IRA-supporting Irish community, American Jews who were desperate to liberate Europe's endangered Jews during Hitler's rise, and other diasporic peoples. Twists may include a sister, wife, or daughter of the prisoner who will deliver the bribe to the appropriate corrupt official, an organization that is fronting a collection for a liberation movement, and anything that encourages reckless donations. Historians have traced this routine back to the American Civil War, and the U.S. Post Office considers it to be a constantly resurfacing threat. The advent of computer-generated mailing lists and, more recently, Internet e-mail hoaxes, has only spread the influence of "the Spanish prisoner."

Chapter 4

Mass Hysteria: Historic Hoaxes and Classic Urban Legends

✓ REALITY CHECK

Public Versus Private Figure

Criminal notoriety and victimization are separate items when it comes to privacy, and hoaxers would do well to mind the distinction. The difference between a "public figure" and a "limited public figure" is that a public figure seeks notoriety, whereas a limited public figure becomes well known because of something that happens to him or her involuntarily. A movie star, therefore, is a public figure, and, by desiring fame, forsakes much of her privacy. A robbery victim, however, hardly sought the spotlight, and thus recovers his privacy once the news value of the crime has passed.

If it sounds too good to be true, it probably is.
—public service slogan used by
The Advertising Council

There is no such thing as a government conspiracy; the government says so. Despite such assurances—or maybe because of them—some people will fall for anything (if you need proof, look at the Macarena).

Abraham Lincoln may have said that you can't fool all of the people all of the time, but the way some things keep popping up, even the most harebrained rumors start to sound real. In more sinister times, the Nazis called this technique "the big lie"—repeat something often enough and it takes on the power of Truth. Of course, it's silly to apply their motives to UFOs, Elvis sightings, the Cardiff Giant, Piltdown Man, Bigfoot, or other persistent legends. Nevertheless, the longer a fabrication persists, and the less credible its denials, the harder it is to debunk (just ask the cheerful folks at Disney if Walt is really frozen). Call it human nature or mass hysteria, but the result is the same thing.

Sometimes the mere existence of a myth can mean more than the myth itself. Why do people believe that JFK, Elvis, James Dean, and Marilyn Monroe are comatose in a secret hospital? Do we share a need to believe in the permanence of our cultural icons beyond all reason? Nurturing such rumors is a tabloid press industry that has grown up not only around Elvis and his imaginary ilk but around such tragedies as JFK Jr., Princess Diana, and JonBenet Ramsey. And, when you stop to think about it, we know these people only through their publicity.

What is publicity? It is information that has been created, shaped, and distributed by the people who can benefit the most from it. Publicity isn't necessarily false, it just ain't necessarily so. But it is necessarily deliberate. There must always be a kernel of truth behind publicity, yet only in the past few decades have people begun to question that truth. Was Ricky Martin really that good, or was he just booked on so many TV shows, magazines, and radio playlists that the public couldn't avoid him? How did the media hear about him before the public did? Or did he become famous because he was famous?

Publicity eventually becomes reality; and in seeking both, the media have rewritten the rules of privacy. A century ago, "decent" folks were in the paper only four times: at birth, at debut, at marriage, and at death. Nowadays—Andy Warhol's 15-minute quota notwithstanding—it's hard to get a city newspaper to run a wedding notice unless you pay for it. And fame? Legacies are now measured not by what people do for others but by how often they are bleeped on a TV talk show. In other words, some seek greatness, others achieve greatness, others have greatness thrust upon them. But if you really want to make it in Mudville, go on Jerry Springer and slug somebody.

Fame used to require something special. A guy had to dig up a petrified giant in the back forty to make a tidy living showing it off in circus sideshows. Or he had to claim he found the crash site of a UFO, or the "missing link" connecting humans to the apes. Then people would come for miles around to gawk. Was it true? Was it entertainment? Was it worth two bits? This chapter features some of the classic all-time great hokums, cons, myths, and disinformation conspiracies. Lincoln was right. You can't fool all of the people all of the time. But if you can do it once in a while, you can make a pretty good living.

Piltdown Man

Half man, half ape, and all fake, Piltdown Man is a classic case of the exception that proves the rule—as long as the exception is phony. Piltdown Man doesn't prove anything except that the Cardiff Giant didn't stand alone.

For years, scientists sought a fossil specimen that would somehow connect prehumans and humans on the paleological timeline. To anyone who knows anything about evolution, however, that would be impossible. Human beings didn't go to sleep as apes on a Monday night and wake up Tuesday morning doing the *New York*

✎ **INTERVIEW**

From Aesop to AOL—Urban Legends as Sociology

In the olden days, fairy tales were told as though they had actually taken place, but the children who heard them knew they were make-believe. Today urban legends are told as though they are true, and the adults who hear them swallow the bait every time. What grownups need—if they're going to catch up with children, that is—are well researched, documented urban legend reference pages. It just so happens that, since 1995, amateur folklorists David and Barbara Mikkelson have run a snazzy, well written Web site that's so comprehensive that rumor-shaken companies link their own corporate Web sites to it (*www.snopes.simplenet.com*).

Nat Segaloff: How did you start the pages?

Barbara Mikkelson: Our hobby is researching urban legends. We dig into these stories for fun, and we finally got the idea of putting up what we were doing as Web pages. Part of what we were trying to do was create reference pages as opposed to just "here's a site that has a bunch of urban legends." We wanted to get into what we felt was fascinating: where they came from, the evolving history of the stories, whether they're true or not, and why we tell the tales we tell—why we're crazy about one story and we tell it to everyone we know, but we don't tell this other one. We came up with "Reference Pages," the idea being that not only would we provide our opinions, but we would also list the references so that people could check what we were doing and go back to the source documents themselves.

Segaloff: The odd thing is that a company can spend tens of millions of dollars in advertising and it doesn't have one-tenth the effect a good urban legend has about the same product.

Mikkelson: It probably doesn't. We love gossip, don't we? And so when somebody tell us something completely awful, that'll stick with us.

Segaloff: Like the schoolyard myths we heard; if you're eight years old and a nine-year-old tells you something, it's Gospel.

Mikkelson: You must remember, when we were kids in school, how we heard about Bubble Yum containing spider's eggs. That sounded like a lighthearted, stupid rumor, but that company had to battle that rumor like mad and never overcame it. It still makes the rounds.

Segaloff: What does it take to qualify for inclusion on your site?

Mikkelson: Very little. We list urban legends, but we also list wild bits of Net lore and rumors.

Segaloff: We used to tell stories face to face, and now we do it by machine. It's so much less personal.

Mikkelson: That's one way of looking at it. But let's look at a major change in how we're telling legends. At one time, storytellers would tell these stories. A storyteller, even though he might say, "This is a true story, it really happened," he didn't honestly believe it did. It's just one of those things you tell people, and the people listening to it knew that. Urban legends are also called "urban belief tales" because both the teller and the audience believe them. They're not presented as "once upon a time," they're presented as "this really happened in the town just over the hill to my cousin's hairdresser's sister." It comes with its own built-in credibility, or it comes to you as an e-mail that's signed by somebody who's a doctor or other credible authority figure.

Segaloff: Have you ever been tempted to start an urban legend on your own to see how far it goes?

Mikkelson: No, we never want to do that; however, we managed to do it anyway. If you look at a section of our site called "The Repository of Lost Legends" (TROLL), this was David's way of blowing off steam after having to be utterly factual about everything. He decided to write some wonderful pages, making the most outrageous claims possible, but doing it in a serious, scholarly manner. We came up with this wild claim that *Mr. Ed* on TV was a zebra, but since the show was filmed in black and white, no one could tell. A sensible person would have to know it's a joke, but people have mailed us pictures of zebras to show us we're wrong, or have told the story to others as if it were true. If we're doing anything, it's trying to teach people to think for themselves, to never suspend their common sense, and to quit looking for one authority to have all the answers.

✓ **REALITY CHECK**

Tielhard de Chardin

Pierre Teilhard de Chardin, S.J., was a maverick who embraced both the rigor of paleontology and the dedication of theology. At times the disciplines were at odds, and the conflict caused Father de Chardin to fall out of favor with the Catholic Church for promoting theories considered heretical. His spiritual tug-of-war proved so fascinating to a young theology student at Georgetown University in the late 1940s, however, that the student— William Peter Blatty—used de Chardin as the basis for the character of Lancaster Merrin in his novel, *The Exorcist.*

Times crossword puzzle. But the lure of finding the "missing link" was so seductive that, in 1912, Charles Dawson, an amateur archeologist, and Martin A. C. Hinton, a zoologist, sparked one of the most controversial discoveries in scientific history—or, as it turned out, unscientific history.

The story of Piltdown Man should have begun hundreds of thousands of years ago. Instead, it began in 1856, the year that fossil remains of the legitimate Neanderthal Man were discovered in the Neander Valley of the German Rhineland by Johann C. Fuhlrott. Three years later, Charles Darwin published *Origin of Species*, suggesting that Asia was the cradle of civilization. This was followed in 1852 by Édouard Lartet's finding Cro-Magnon remains in a French cave near Périgueux, France, in rock strata dating back nearly 40,000 years. The excitement generated by these events inspired further research, and at least one hoax: *Eoanthropus dawsonii.*

On December 18, 1912, at a meeting of the Geological Society of London, Charles Dawson and Arthur Smith Woodward presented fossil remains they had found in a gravel pit in the village of Piltdown in Sussex, England. The evidence was compelling, if inconclusive: a jaw (mandible) and a portion of a skull. Further excavation at the site yielded several animal teeth, part of another skull, and a tool carved from an elephant tusk. Although French and U.S. paleontologists questioned the authenticity of the bones, their British colleagues seemed convinced. There may have been some national pride involved, as well as an undercurrent of support for the theory that brain size was directly proportional to intelligence.

Remember, at the time, the exact chronological placement of antiquities was based on educated guesswork. The carbon-14 system of dating organic artifacts by computing atomic degeneration was not introduced until 1947.

But Dawson and Hinton swore they had found the real thing and convinced an impressive number of scientists. Sir Arthur Smith Woodward of the British Museum's Natural History Department, and his colleague, W. P. Pycraft, were among the first to give their support. The fact that Woodward's specialty was fish and Pycraft's was birds meant little. Jesuit paleontologist and theologian Pierre Teilhard de Chardin was also brought on board, as were Sir Arthur Keith, anatomist at the Royal College of Surgeons, and Grafton Elliot Smith, a Fellow at the Royal Society. Even Sir Arthur Conan Doyle had a hand in the affair.

Over the next few decades, additional fossil discoveries broadened our knowledge of our ancestors. There was just one problem: Piltdown refused to fit into any logical scenario. "You can make sense of human evolution," sighed one researcher, "if you don't try to put Piltdown in it."

It wasn't until 1953 that Piltdown was conclusively invalidated by Kenneth Page Oakley. By means of a fluorine test, Oakley and his team of scientists showed not only that there were no fossils in the Piltdown dig, but that those that had been found had been purposely placed. The bones had been chemically aged and altered with a mixture of chromium, iron, and manganese. In the end, the Piltdown skulls were revealed as a 620-year-old human skull, while the jaw belonged to an orangutan dating back about 500 years. The only genuine fossils were the teeth, but they were from an elephant, a hippopotamus, and a chimpanzee, respectively. The ivory tool was dismissed summarily.

There has been continued speculation over the years whether Dawson and Hinton had confederates in their ruse. Fingers have been pointed at Venus Hargreaves, a workman who would certainly have been needed to "salt" the dig site; and of course Woodward, Pycraft, Keith, and Smith. Charles Dawson had the good fortune to die in 1916 while he was still being celebrated. Unlike many hoaxes, Piltdown Man was not perpetrated to make money. The sole motivation seems to have been Dawson's fondness for practical jokes. The fact that he may have derailed legitimate paleontology for 40 years had nothing to do with it.

The Bayou Banshee

According to Irish folklore, a banshee is a spectral woman whose howling presence becomes visible to a family when one of its members is about to die. How an Irish apparition made her way to French Louisiana is anybody's guess, but she was reported to have revealed herself in 1899 in the town of St. Francisville, a picturesque ante-bellum community 40 miles north of Baton Rouge.

It was on February 2 of that year that—according to the 107-year-old *St. Francisville Democrat* newspaper—what became known as the Bayou Banshee appeared to a group of astonished townspeople as they were returning from church after evening services.

"She took form out of the clouds on a full moon-lit night," explains Colin Criminger, a folklorist who has made a study of the legend, "and followed the congregants down what is now Commercial Street, hovering above them and making terrifying wailing noises." Only the presence of the minister is believed to have kept the banshee from descending to the ground. As to her physical state, Criminger adds that "she was described as being transparent except for her face. Oddly, most witnesses said she had a blank face, while two others—a Mr. and Mrs. R. Langan— insisted that she resembled their teenage daughter, who was sick in bed and waiting for them at home. Alarmed, they rushed to the their house at the edge of the Myrtles Plantation and discovered to their horror that their daughter was dead. No cause was ever determined."

According to the *Democrat*, the Langan family had emigrated to agricultural St. Francisville from Ireland three years earlier. Gossip, says Criminger, sprung up almost immediately to the effect that the banshee had followed the Langans from the "Ould Sod," and the still-grieving parents were shortly driven from town by superstitious locals. The Bayou Banshee, however, stayed behind, took up residence, and is rumored to have appeared to others over the years, although "she" never again made the pages of the town newspaper.

The Hitler Diaries

One of the particular perversions of our times is that Nazi memorabilia continue to captivate even those people who are repulsed by their philosophy. Whether it's the "forbidden fruit" aspect of Lugers, SS insignia, Luftwaffe jackets, Panzer helmets, or place settings from Berchtesgaden, or the fact that the Third Reich did not survive the Second Millennium, Hitler sells.

Perhaps that's why the Führer's personal diaries—that is, the ones that Konrad Kujau painstakingly forged—held such fascination when they "surfaced" in 1983. A dealer in Nazi and other military regalia, Kujau said he found them in an East German hayloft. Apparently, the diaries had been stashed there in 1945 after being salvaged from an airplane that had crashed there while carrying Hitler's archives to safety. Among the supposed disclosures in the 60 volumes were that Hitler had encouraged his deputy Rudolf Hess to fly to Britain on a peace mission, and that the British Expeditionary Forces were deliberately allowed to escape from Dunkirk in 1940.

The diaries were purchased by the German magazine *Stern* for $3.3 million in a deal arranged by one of *Stern*'s writers, Gerd Heidemann. Shortly after the diaries were announced in April 1983, a reporter from the competing magazine *Der Spiegel* asked revisionist historian David Irving, whose biographies of Hitler favored the Nazi leader, for his opinion. Irving got right to the point with *Der Spiegel* just as he had with *Reuters, Newsweek*, the BBC, the *New York Times*, and others who had asked: The diaries were a fraud.

Not long afterward, Irving was invited to examine the diaries at Germany's ZDF television studios, and something clicked—or, rather, slanted. Irving was aware that Hitler had begun suffering from Parkinson's disease during the last weeks of the war, and, sure enough, the handwriting in the diaries for that period leaned to the right, a sign of the illness. There was also, to Irving's inspection, no evidence that Hitler had known about the Holocaust, exactly the position Irving had taken in his own writing, which blamed the Final Solution on Adolf Eichmann, not Hitler. With that, Irving announced that he was changing his mind: now the diaries were real.

✓ **REALITY CHECK**

Melvin Purvis, G-Man

Although Melvin Purvis is credited with capturing John Dillinger, no one knows to this day whose bullets pierced the gangster's body when he walked into an FBI trap. Purvis, the G-man heading the task force, would not allow the Bureau's highly respected ballistics department to render identification. From the moment of the kill in 1934, however, Purvis himself became a hunted man—not by organized crime, but by FBI Director J. Edgar Hoover, who was jealous of the media attention his underling was receiving. In 1960, Melvin Purvis took his own life with the nickel-plated, pearl-handled .45 that he used to catch Dillinger. His survivors have said that Hoover's tactics contributed to Purvis's decline.

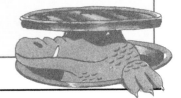

Early in May, after they had heard Irving's authentication, *Der Spiegel* revealed that it had found an SS soldier who knew about the 1945 plane crash, and he had denied the presence of diaries on board. A few days later, it was reported that a scientific analysis of the paper used in the diaries revealed a mixture of wood, grass, and leaves, all bleached with a whitener that had not existed at the time the books were supposedly written.

The Führer furor went off in a more bizarre direction when, astonishingly, *Newsweek* took the position that the authenticity of the Hitler diaries "almost doesn't matter" because of the larger issues that had risen around them; namely, the existence of neo-Nazi groups and Holocaust deniers. Although *Newsweek* was ridiculed for standing firmly on both sides of the issue, the point was made. In August 1984, Konrad Kujau and Gerd Heidemann went on trial in Hamburg. Also named, but not tried, was Kujau's girlfriend, Edith Lieblang. Heidemann was exonerated of forgery, but both he and Kujau were imprisoned for defrauding *Stern*, whose advance money was never recovered.

In a related story, on April 11, 2000, David Irving was defeated in a libel suit he had brought in England against Deborah Lipstadt whose book, *Denying the Holocaust*, portrayed Irving as "one of the most dangerous spokespersons for Holocaust denial." In his verdict against Irving, Justice Charles Gray called Irving a "Hitler partisan, a racist, and an anti-Semite," and he also refused permission for Irving to appeal to a higher court. Under British law, Irving now must pay Lipstadt's $3 million court costs. After the trial, the 62-year-old Irving declared himself financially ruined and lamented that "no publisher will touch me now."

Everything Old Is New Again: Prehistoric Monsters

Yeti. Sasquatch. Mapinguari. Yowie. Bigfoot. Chupacabra. Nessie. To some people, these names conjure images of legendary beasts, mysterious encounters, and direct links to our primordial origins. To others, the words *In Search of . . .* in front of these names qualifies them for a pseudoscientific TV show.

The pursuit of prehistoric monsters is not necessarily a scam; other than maybe a haggis restaurant on Loch Ness, nobody is really making money out of them. The belief in these creatures, or at least the hope that there are still worlds left to explore, is a tribute to human curiosity, as well as an enduring fascination with what preceded us on the planet (and therefore may still be around waiting to dine on us).

That having been said, do they really exist? The principal cast includes:

1. *The Abominable Snowman.* Specifics vary, but in general this is a primate-like creature with an ape's body and a human face. It is more commonly known as "Yeti" to the Sherpas of Nepal, who have described the creature as being reddish brown in color, having feet that point backward, and smelling as bad as he sounds. *The National Geographic* wrote that Sir Edmund Hillary (who "conquered" Everest) sought Yeti and, indeed, followed tracks in the snow. The magazine later determined, however, that the prints were simple animal tracks that had become enlarged by the melting process. A sample of Yeti fur turned out to be from the Tibetan blue bear. "Abominable Snowman," incidentally, is a mistranslation of the term *metoh-kangmi*, which is what Sherpas call Yeti.

2. *Bigfoot/Sasquatch.* According to eyewitness reports dating back to 1884, this visitor stands 6½ to 8 feet tall, weighs between 500 and 1,000 pounds, walks upright, and is covered with hair. The American name is Bigfoot, but when

✓ REALITY CHECK

The Burbank Bigfoot

An ersatz Bigfoot is said to have been the work of John Chambers, the Oscar-winning makeup artist who designed the ground-breaking *Planet of the Apes* facial appliances. Supposedly, Chambers and John Landis (gorilla fancier and director of movies such as *Animal House* and *Schlock*, a comedy about an ape-like missing link) dressed a guy in a Sasquatch suit and sent him through a California residential community to see what would happen. Both men, when asked by Those Who Care, denied having anything to do with the "Burbank Bigfoot."

the creature crosses into Canada, it becomes Sasquatch. Native American and Native Canadian legends describe a "hairy man" and were-creatures who stalk the woods and make huge footprints, yet never seem to leave any scientific evidence of their presence. The image the public knows best of this reclusive wilderness denizen comes from a 1967 color home movie taken by Roger Patterson and Robert Gimlin near Bluff Creek in the Six Rivers National Forest near the California/Oregon border. It shows a husky, fur-covered creature lumbering left-to-right on the edge of a stream. The film has never been proved to be a fake, but that's not the point, since it has never been authenticated either. Where Bigfeet have been seen in the Amazon they are called *Mapinguari*, and in Australia they are called *Yowie*.

3. *The Loch Ness Monster.* Probably the world's most beloved surviving prehistoric beast, the Loch Ness monster has played hard-to-get in the Scottish Highlands for at least 1,500 years. As far back as A.D. 565, St. Columba was reported to have seen "a large beast" in the loch (lake). Among the oldest legends is that the "beast" sticks a horse's head out of the water and lures children onto its back for a ride. Their hands stick to its skin, and it pulls them under, their livers washing ashore the next day.

But it took urban development to make Nessie a modern hero. In 1933 a roadway was constructed along the loch, and (according to the *Inverness Courier*) a young couple driving past happened to notice "an enormous animal rolling and plunging on the surface." By the end of the year a £20,000 reward had been offered for its capture. The money has frequently been claimed but never awarded. The closest anyone has come was when footprints were presented as evidence, but they turned out to be those of a hippopotamus. All sightings (some 4,000 of them according to the record books) have been chalked up to ducks, otters, logs, boat wakes, and a swimming deer, as in the classic, widely circulated, back-lit photo. Rather than scaring people, camera-shy Nessie has actually been embraced by the loch community, who politely endure visitors' curiosity. But the best thing about Nessie might be that she can't leave the water; as with so much else in the United Kingdom, even monsters know their place.

4. *Chupacabras.* The chupacabra is a mysterious force, or a demon, that preys on cows, sucking their blood. Of fairly recent note (reports only surfaced in 1996) and apparently indigenous to Hispanic countries such as Mexico and Puerto Rico, chupacabras have been described as compact tailless creatures with quills running up their backs, sharp teeth, and curved claws. The May 12, 1996, *Houston Chronicle* reported that a chupacabra raided a farmhouse in Zapotal, Mexico, punctured the throats of sheep, and was chased off by dogs. According to the owner of the farm, it could not have been the work of the region's customary predator, the coyote. There were also separate rumors that the U.S. and Puerto Rican governments had captured two specimens and were going to perform an "alien autopsy." If such an event transpired, the results were never released. Meanwhile, lock up your goats.

So what are we to make of animals appearing in modern times that supposedly vanished before humans were a twinkle in Darwin's eye? In light of the way species become extinct in the normal course of events, who's to say that some might not reappear, or might still survive in some uncharted region?

For example, in 1938, fishermen off the South African coast netted a 5-foot-long fish that was unlike anything they had ever seen. Through fossil records, scientists identified it as a coelacanth, a prehistoric fish thought to have become extinct 70 million years ago. Since 1972, almost a hundred others have been caught around Comoros in the Indian Ocean. So you never know . . .

There's a Phone in Mary Baker Eddy's Tomb

Mary Baker Eddy (1821–1910), the Discoverer and Founder of Christian Science, came to her belief in the healing power of prayer after reading about Jesus' healings in the New Testament. Among her other achievements, she wrote and published *Science and Health with Key to the Scriptures* (1875), the textbook of Christian Science, and founded the respected newspaper *The Christian Science Monitor* in 1908.

Despite Eddy's religious teachings, Christian Science has frequently been scorned by doctors and lawyers, among others in the general public, who are skeptical of the power of prayer alone over the science of medicine. Possibly it was this attitude that led to a wild rumor that Mary Baker Eddy has a telephone in her tomb, presumably to "phone home" to the living. "So far," the legend goes, "it hasn't rung."

The truth, as usual, is more prosaic. There is no telephone in Ms. Eddy's tomb—but there once was. When she passed in 1910 at the age of 89, her body was held at the Mount Auburn Cemetery in Cambridge, Massachusetts, until a burial crypt could be built on the grounds. Because of her prominence, a guard was stationed at the construction site instead of at the cemetery's office, and an extension telephone was installed so he could be reached in the course of his normal duties. Once Ms. Eddy was entombed, the phone line was removed, but the rumor that the phone is still there has persisted for almost a century. It isn't, but she is.

The Dinosaur Formerly Known as Prince

There is no such dinosaur as the brontosaurus. The reptilian herbivore that everybody thinks of as the brontosaurus is really the apatosaurus, which lived in the late Jurassic period around 140 million years ago. It was 80 feet long and weighed 30 tons.

The confusion apparently stems from the late 1890s when a team of paleontologists from the American Museum of Natural History in New York, led by Henry Fairfield Osborn, unearthed a sauropod skeleton, nearly complete except for its skull. For its 1905 unveiling, scientists fabricated a skull based on the known proportions of a related reptile, the camarasaur. And that's the way it stood for nearly a century. In 1992, the museum's brontosaurus was remounted to reflect knowledge that had been acquired in the previous decades, including its ability to move rather quickly and lift its tail into the air (the evidence: its fossil footprints were spaced apart, and there were no tail-drags between them). Why they had to name it *apatosaurus* instead of just changing the specs for the beloved brontosaurus is not known.

Operation Blue Book

One of the reasons that Unidentified Flying Objects (UFOs) carry the taint of a hoax is the very program that the U.S. government set up to see that they wouldn't: Operation Blue Book. "Blue Book," as UFOlogists call it, raised more questions than it ever answered, the most intriguing of which has always been, "If aliens are so smart, why do they show themselves only to people whom society is least likely to believe?"

It started not in another galaxy but 11 miles above Earth. In the 1950s, the U.S. military experimented with a highly classified aircraft called the U-2, which could cruise at altitudes of 60,000 feet and secretly photograph the ground installations of foreign armies. But the U-2 created an unexpected side effect. At the time, commercial airliners operated at altitudes between 10,000 and 20,000 feet. When these commercial flights accidentally shared air space (albeit at greatly different heights) with testing U-2s, sunlight would occasionally reflect off the U-2s' wings (or so the explanation went). Since commercial pilots didn't know that anybody else was up there, they began reporting UFOs. And rather than admit they were testing spy planes, the Air Force unit at Wright-Patterson Command in Dayton, Ohio, formulated Operation Blue Book. Because they couldn't

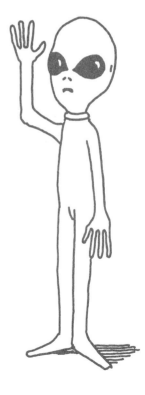

acknowledge the existence of U-2s, they were forced to invent all kinds of natural phenomena and ask the public to swallow them. When explanations such as "swamp gas," "meteor showers," and "stray weather balloons" didn't cut it, the Air Force could only shrug its epauletted shoulders.

UFO matters cleared up a little in 1960 (but muddied the waters of international diplomacy) when a U-2 flown by Francis Gary Powers was shot down over Soviet soil. Soviet Premier Nikita Khrushchev became so incensed over the incident that he walked out of a U.S.–U.S.S.R. Peace Summit. Suddenly the U-2 was no longer classified, but there was still a credibility chasm between Operation Blue Book and the numerous citizens who saw *something* in the sky. In later years Operation Blue Book staffers such as J. Allen Hynek (who inspired the film *Close Encounters of the Third Kind* after leaving O.B.B.) admitted that there were, indeed, some UFO sightings that no one could explain.

Roswell

If it was a hoax, which side pulled it? And why are people still talking about it—and not talking about it—half a century later? The Roswell "incident" is the first major encounter with UFOs, and the way the matter was handled set in motion a process of curiosity, secrecy, and skepticism that has tainted the incident ever since it occurred on July 4, 1947.

Roswell, New Mexico. Independence Day weekend in the hometown of the 509th Heavy Bombardment Group at the Roswell Army Base is threatened by a sudden thunderstorm that sweeps across the desert. Roswell citizens are used to sounds in the sky; the Air Force conducts test flights nearby.

The next day, when sheep rancher Mac Brazel comes across the remains of a failed test flight, he summons the military authorities. Later, Brazel is joined by Jim Ragsdale, who says he saw a plane crash while he and his girlfriend were camping. Another local, Barney Barnett, reports seeing crash debris—and bodies.

Major Jesse Marcel makes the initial inspection and fields the first barrage of questions when he reports finding thousands of pieces of metal scattered about the ground. Marcel describes the metal shards as being almost without weight, possessing remarkable strength, and capable of restoring themselves once they were crumbled or scratched.

The headlines scream UFO and offer speculation that an alien spacecraft crashed in Roswell, spreading wreckage over three-quarters of a mile. Just as quickly, Air Force General Roger Ramey calls a second press conference to retract the first one and to denounce Major Marcel as having been fooled by a downed weather balloon. Skeptics demand to know how a weather balloon could have crashed when the Air Force has no record of having launched one. Finally, Major Marcel agrees he must have been mistaken and holds up a shredded weather balloon that has just been recovered. *Mea culpa.*

Within days, though, reports begin circulating that a local undertaker delivered four child-size coffins to the base hospital. He adds that they were used to bury four alien creatures, three of whom died in the crash and were subjected to medical autopsy. A fourth, however, supposedly survived. How long? No one knows; perhaps it's still alive—but all files remain heavily classified.

In 1947, President Truman announced that the government had determined that UFOs and extraterrestrials did not exist. Nevertheless, over 350 witnesses to the Roswell incident, which began America's fascination with UFOs, insist that their testimony was ignored or declared top secret. In 1994, Rep. Stephen Schiff requested an investigation by the Government Accounting Office of the Roswell investigation. The conclusion was that no UFO crash took place.

Major Jesse Marcel died in 1986. But skepticism about the Roswell incident, fueled by books, documentary films, and a steady curiosity, survives.

✓ REALITY CHECK

No "Beaming" in Star Trek

Regarding Captain Kirk and his fellow *Enterprise* crew members, nowhere in any of the *Star Trek* feature films does anyone say, "Beam me up, Scotty." But then there's the bumper sticker that says, "Very funny, Scotty. Now beam me up my clothes."

✓ **REALITY CHECK**

View From Space

Crop circles shouldn't appear strange to anyone who has ever flown high enough in a commercial airliner to note the varying patterns of farmland below. The precision of the squares and circles are, of course, the result of surveying and agricultural planning. In any event, as astronaut Alan Bean reported in *More Misinformation* (by Tom Burnham), there are no manmade objects visible from beyond earth orbit (including the Great Wall of China). But, of course, whoever is making crop circles isn't human, is it?

Tulipmania!

It's hard to imagine that a simple flower could hold the fortunes of Europe hostage, but it did. The place was Holland, the date was the early 1600s, and the unlikely cause of the speculative investing frenzy was the tulip. Before it withered, half of Europe had been deflowered.

The object of desire was a botanical object that is thought to have originated in central Asia around A.D. 1,000. The tulip arrived in Holland during the 1500s courtesy of Carolus Clusius, director of the Royal Medicinal Garden in Vienna. His experimentation with the simple tulip caught the fancy of the public, particularly aristocrats, who sought ever more ornate cross-bred versions of tulip bulbs, and heavily invested in crop futures. By 1630, tulip traders were earning as much as $44,000 a month, causing concern in government and economic circles.

The market became blighted in 1637 when a cartel of bulb merchants failed to get their inflated price for their crop. As rumors of ruin spread, thousands of Dutch businessmen saw their investments plummet. The flower that had been all the rage in 1636 became a failure on the market a year later. In retrospect, the boom and bust became known as Tulipmania, and came to symbolize the lengths to which greed and ignorance could combine to invent, and then destroy, a financial movement.

Four hundred years later, the eloquent tulip is viewed as the national symbol of Holland. Few remember that it was once the lure, and the ruin, of an economy.

Crop Circles

At first they looked like a game of intergalactic Tic-Tac-Toe. The difference was that there were no Xs, only circles, and they weren't played on a piece of scratch paper in the back of a classroom, they mysteriously appeared over acres of farmland. Who or what had made them, and how, no one knew.

They are the infamous crop circles which, since 1966, have appeared all over the world, but mostly in England. Despite revelations that they are a hoax, crop circles have continued to show up. Some insist they may even have appeared as far back as 1678.

Crop circles look like the pressed-down dents that heavy furniture legs make on pile carpet; that is, if the legs are 40 feet across. Moreover, the crushed plants inside the precise perimeters aren't cut away or flattened to the ground, they are bent over at a point a couple of inches above the base.

Scientists have offered explanations ever since the phenomenon was first reported in Tully, England, in 1966. In the 1970s, the occurrence spread to the Wiltshire/Hampshire area where swirls appeared in fields of grass. Some circles were accompanied by reports of UFO sightings, leading to the belief that the turbulence of hovering alien spacecraft had done the work. By the summer of 1980, British meteorologist Terence Meaden offered the name *plasma vortex* (a.k.a. "Meaden Vortex") to describe a weather phenomenon that might explain their existence. Meaden was bested by Pat Delgado and Colin Andrews, who insisted that only intelligent beings could have caused them. Only when the formations began to take more complex shapes such as spirals, concentric circles, boxes, keys, and a Celtic cross did the public-at-large become aware of them; that was around 1990.

Conveniently, in September 1991, two Brits—Doug Bower and David Chorley—stepped forward and admitted they were behind the circles, demonstrating their technique to a hungry media. "Doug and Dave," as they soon came to be affectionately known, showed how the depressions could be made with a spike, a ball of twine, a plank of wood, a sense of playfulness, and perhaps a pint or two. The media lost interest when Doug and Dave admitted that they were unable to use their method to make the more complex designs. Soon afterward, whispers started that they had been hired to pose as hoaxers to throw suspicion off the real cause, namely, space aliens.

But the notion of farm visitation has been kept alive, not only by the artistry of the crop wheels, but by more disturbing reports from the American Southwest that involve cattle mutilation. Ranchers have discovered their livestock dead, with their lips,

✓ REALITY CHECK

Cattle Mutilations

Over 8,000 cattle mutilations have been reported since 1963, when the first spree was noted in Gallipolis, Oklahoma. Most happened in the mid-1970s and have been blamed on satanic cults, the CIA, mining interests trying to drive down land values, and, of course, UFOs. Lights have been seen in the sky around such mutilations, but they could be helicopters hoisting the cattle away, operating on them elsewhere, and then returning them, thereby explaining the lack of footprints or other evidence on the ground. In 1979, FBI investigator Kenneth Rommel issued a report blaming it on predators. The mutilations continue.

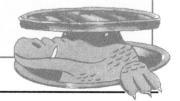

eyelids, udders, and/or genitals surgically removed. Some incidents have been ascribed to human cruelty; many have not.

In any event, the benign crop designs have long since stopped being merely circles: a 10-petaled mandala formation (a square within a circle) was found in 1993; a purported map of the solar system was found in 1995; and a 648-foot DNA double helix popped up in 1996, all in England. The Web site *http://indigo.ie/ ~dcd/intro.htm* explores crop circles and their origins. Devotees have reported finding related crop formations in Japan, Hungary, Brazil, Australia, Romania, Germany, and Canada.

There is vigorous debate about whether natural conditions can produce these designs, or whether they are the work of intelligent beings trying to communicate something to us obviously less intelligent beings. The one thing that people seem to be able to agree on is that nothing—other than the cows—has been damaged.

Fairies and Sir Arthur Conan Doyle

They were called the Cottingley Fairies, and the little girls who invented them managed to fool everybody, including the most skeptical mind in all of England—Sherlock Holmes.

In November 1918, 10-year-old Frances Griffiths and her 16-year-old cousin, Elsie Wright, took snapshots of each other in the Griffiths's backyard. When Mr. Wright developed the film, he noticed little white flecks near the girls. At first he imagined them to be birds or pieces of paper, but his daughter insisted they were fairies. When Elsie showed up with a picture of herself standing with a gnome, her parents became concerned. Unable to get a satisfactory explanation from Elsie, they circulated prints of the photograph to friends seeking an explanation. That's when the pixie dust hit the fan.

Elsie's mother, who was interested in the occult, showed the photos to friends at a meeting of the Theosophical Society, a group interested in religious mysticism. The photos were copied and examined, yet accepted with little or no challenge.

By coincidence, Sir Arthur Conan Doyle, the creator of the scrupulously precise sleuth Sherlock Holmes, was preparing to write an article on mysticism for *Strand* magazine. Doyle, whose son had been killed in World War I, had become involved with the movement in an effort to contact his boy in the spirit world. When Conan Doyle heard of the photographs he dispatched an associate, Edward Gardner, to visit the Cottingley location and produce new photographs. Rather than take them personally, however, Gardner trustingly left the equipment with Elsie and Frances and asked them to do the job themselves.

The November 1920 *Strand* sold out, and so did Doyle. By January 1921, he was being denounced from Wales to Scotland. According to Tom Huntington's article "The Man Who Believed in Fairies" in *Smithsonian Magazine,* one newspaper stated, "What is wanted is not a knowledge of occult phenomena but a knowledge of children." As if to counter the skepticism, Frances and Elsie took three more fairy photos that spring. Up to his death in 1930, Doyle remained convinced, but he was virtually alone. His conviction strained his friendship with magician Harry Houdini, who had made a career out of exposing fake spiritualists.

In August 1921, clairvoyant Geoffrey Hodson was summoned to Cottingley to verify the fairies. Hodson appeared but the fairies did not. The matter was put to a rest—until 1966 when reporter Peter Chambers of the London *Daily Express* discovered grown-up Elsie's address and quoted her as admitting that the fairies were "figments of my imagination." Ten years later, Yorkshire Television's Austin Mitchell found Frances, who challenged him to explain how two children could engage in a photographic hoax. Mitchell took up the challenge and, using a variety of cardboard cut-outs, showed in a television studio how it could have been done.

In 1983, both girls—by then grandmothers—admitted that they had fabricated the fairy pictures based on Arthur Shepperson's illustrations in *Princess Mary's Gift Book*. They did it, they said, because they were tired of not being taken seriously by grownups.

✓ REALITY CHECK

Anything but Elementary

Nowhere in any of Arthur Conan Doyle's Sherlock Holmes stories does the famous sleuth say, "Elementary, my dear Watson." The line is an invention used in the popular motion picture series starring Basil Rathbone and Nigel Bruce.

The Curse of King Tut's Tomb

Although the curse of King Tut's tomb sounds like something out of a Boris Karloff movie, it's absolutely true, though not for the reasons people think. There is a curse of the mummy's tomb, but it isn't supernatural; it's bacteriological. Before you start chanting "Imhotep," harken unto the tale of King Tut.

We know Tutankhamen—the celebrated boy Pharaoh who lived from perhaps 1367–44 B.C.*—through the splendid golden sarcophagus in which he was interred after having ruled Egypt from around 1358 to 1350 B.C. For a young man of either 18 or 23, he didn't do too badly. He changed the worship rites of his country from Ra, the sun king, to the religion of the priests of Amen and relocated the capital from Akhetaton to Thebes. Whatever rumbling the people or the court may have had over these radical changes evaporated in 1344 B.C when Tut went to dwell with his ancestors. They erected a pyramid in his honor at Luxor in the Valley of the Kings in his beloved Thebes.

And there he lay undisturbed for over 32 centuries, until November 1922 when archeologist Howard Carter, leading an expedition financed by George Edward Stanhope Molyneux, the Earl of Carnarvon, opened Tut's tomb. Bad idea.

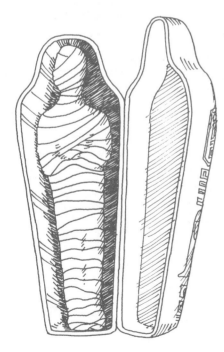

When Carnarvon, the first to enter the tomb, died five months later on April 23, 1923, at age 57, in a Cairo hospital, word flew around the world with the speed of a biblical plague that there was a pharaoh's curse at work. According to Gil Kewzer's *King Tut's Curse Due to Fatal Spores?*, over the following decade, while archaeologists (read: looters) rummaged through the 5,000 objects that had been packed away to keep Tut amused in the next life, people kept on dying, by some reports upward of 21.

Was there a curse?

According to some reports (never proved, but it makes great reading), chiseled over the doorway to Tut's inner tomb chamber was the hieroglyphic warning: "Death shall come on swift wings to

*Eight separate references were consulted for this, and no two of them agree on the years of Tut's life or reign.

MASS HYSTERIA

him who disturbs the peace of the King." But more to the provable point, a 1998 item by Gil Kewzer in the *Canadian Medical Association Journal* quotes the French scientist Dr. Sylvain Gandon as suggesting that the raiders may have fallen prey to microscopic spores that had lain dormant inside the tomb after it was sealed. Not only did Lord Carnarvon die of "complications" from an infected insect bite, but American archaeologists Arthur Mace and George Jay Gould both died within 24 hours of entering the tomb. Blame has been laid on a fungus that may have survived the 3,200 years of entombment, bursting to life when the chamber was invaded in 1923 and fresh air poured into the tomb. The curse, therefore, may not have been planned, only exploited. James McSherry, a professor of family medicine at the University of Western Ontario, Lonlow, Ontario, offered—in response to Dr. Gandon's hypothesis in the *Canadian Medical Association Journal* (May 4, 1999; 160:1289)—that the spores present in the tomb may have been the hearty anthrax.

Over the years, with the airing out of the tomb, no further deaths have been reported. Carter himself died of natural causes on March 2, 1939, in his home in London at the decent age of 64.

Nostradamus

Jeanne Dixon had nothing on Nostradamus. The venerable tabloid supermarket sage only predicts the future a month at a time. Michel de Notredame (that's his full name) wrote upwards of 1,000 quatrains that told exactly what was going to happen from 1552 to the Apocalypse with baffling—no, make that disturbing—accuracy. Or is any guy who makes a bunch of predictions gonna hit at least a couple of them over 450 years?

For the record, Nostradamus was a 16th-century physician and astrologer praised for ministering to the afflicted during the plagues. It was for his writing, however, that he has become venerated. Nostradamus composed *The Prognostications* and *The Centuries* around 1552. The former was the *Farmer's Almanac* of its day and

✓ **REALITY CHECK**

The Way the Fortune Cookie Crumbles

Reality Check: The more vague the prediction, the more chance it has of coming true. Whether it's Nostradamus, the *Twilight Zone* episode with William Shatner ("Nick of Time," where honeymooners become addicted to a penny machine), or a humble fortune cookie, you take from a prophesy what you bring to it. Just for fun, the next time you're at a Chinese restaurant with a group of friends, read the words " . . . in bed" at the end of whatever the fortune says.

applied to the immediate future. The latter was his 10-part epic of 1,000 four-line quatrains and an assortment of six-line "sixains," which contain predictions for the distant future. His visions gained early credibility when he predicted the specific manner of death of French King Henri II. "He will pierce his eyes in a golden cage," wrote Nostradamus, which actually happened when Henri was stabbed through his metal visor in a joust in 1559.

What most often frustrates literalists about the predictions is that they are enigmatic to the point of confusion. The reason usually given is that Nostradamus was writing during the time of the Inquisition ("Nobody expects the Spanish Inquisition") and, had he been more explicit, he would have been toast. Additionally, he was foretelling the future with 16th-century French, which didn't have words for "computer" or "A-bomb." Nevertheless, some of his predictions are startling (note: the following are out-of-context translations). Numerical references are to quatrains:

1. "Beasts ferocious with hunger will swim across rivers, the greater part of the army will be against Hister. The great one will cause him to be dragged in a cage of iron when the German infant observes no law" (2–24). This has been taken to predict the rise of Nazism and World War II and has stunned people by naming Hitler, almost.

2. "The Antichrist will start uniting the monetary systems of his region to help merge them into a single political entity. His ambition to rule the world will be advanced by instituting a single currency with others going defunct" (1–40). What does this say about the Eurodollar and the consolidation of the European Union?

3. "Man will upset the balance of the earth and cause great changes in the climate and seasons, causing much hardship and famine" (2–95).

4. "A weapon detonated at night will cause victims to think they have seen the sun at night. The weapon produces a large explosion of light. In addition to vast climactic

damage the weapon will produce monstrous birth defects in babies" (1–64). Sounds like thermonuclear weapons.

5. "The ransacking of the Vatican library by the Antichrist will bring to light and open to the world information, facts, and knowledge that had been suppressed for several centuries" (1–62). This Antichrist cuts both ways, however, revealing Nostradamus's suspicion of the Catholic Church.

Nostradamus also made references in his quatrains to events that have been interpreted as the discoveries of microorganisms by Pasteur and of microchips. The advent of Watergate, AIDS, and even the *Challenger* shuttle disaster are also counted among the predictions.

Nostradamus died on July 2, 1566. It would be a cheap shot to say that he died unexpectedly.

The Jersey Devil

There are so many versions of the Jersey Devil story, why settle for only one? Here's your chance to invent your own. The following is a multiple-choice collection of twists, turns, and permutations, most of which have arisen at one time or another, and any of which have been applied to the J.D. (Some assembly is required):

1. Start here:
   a. Once upon a time
   b. In the beginning
   c. A guy walks into a bar
   d. Call me Ishmael
2. In the year 1735 (which is fairly consistently cited), there was a woman named:
   a. Mrs. Leeds
   b. Mother Leeds
   c. Mrs. Shrouds
   d. Lucy Leeds
   e. Jane Leeds Johnson

✓ **REALITY CHECK**

The Battle of Los Angeles

On February 23, 1942—10 weeks after the bombing of Pearl Harbor—panic spread through Southern California with the rumor that a Japanese submarine had been sighted just off Santa Barbara. Air raid sirens sounded, people went nuts, and before the city relaxed, "The Battle of Los Angeles" entered local lore.

What was not a hoax, however, was Executive Order 9066, which President Franklin Delano Roosevelt signed on December 19, 1941, seizing the property of Japanese-Americans and confining them to domestic POW camps. Fifty years later, the U.S. government finally apologized and offered restitution to the survivors. Meanwhile, in 1979, the Battle of Los Angeles inspired the movie *1941*, the most disappointing film that Steven Spielberg ever directed.

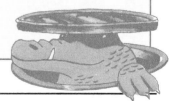

3. She was:
   a. A witch
   b. The town slut
   c. A normal woman who already had 12 kids
   d. A woman who had refused food to a traveling Gypsy
   e. The wife of a British soldier during the Revolutionary War

4. She lived in:
   a. Leeds Point, New Jersey
   b. Estelville, New Jersey
   c. The New Jersey Pinelands
   d. The New Jersey Pine Barrens
   e. The Vince Lombardi exit area

5. She gave birth to a child who had:
   a. A serpent's tail
   b. The head of a collie
   c. Cloven feet
   d. The wings of a bat
   e. The head of a horse
   f. Horns
   g. All of the above
   h. None of the above (it was deformed)

6. On seeing her child, the woman said:
   a. "May the Devil take this one!"
   b. "I hope it's a devil."
   c. "Shoo!"
   d. "Who ordered the pepperoni?"

7. On hearing its mother's rejection, the Devil:
   a. Ate the family and flew out the window
   b. Looked normal at first, then changed into #5
   c. Was kept out of sight by the family
   d. Flew away, but visited its mother every day
   e. Said, "I'm going to Disney World!"

8. Since then, appearances of the Jersey Devil have predicted:
   a. The Civil war
   b. The Spanish-American War
   c. Pearl Harbor

d. The Vietnam conflict

e. The Knicks making the playoffs

9. Evidence of the Jersey Devil's existence over the last 260 years includes:

   a. Raids on crops and the slaughter of livestock

   b. Hoofprints that suddenly stop, as if it flew away

   c. The screeching and flapping of wings

   d. Hoofprints on house and car rooftops

   e. Someone leaves the toilet seat up

10. This story sounds suspiciously like:

    a. an *X Files* episode

    b. "The New Adventures of Johnny Quest"

    c. *The Blair Witch Project*

    d. None of the above

    e. All of the above

In trying to codify the Jersey Devil legend, researcher Dave Juliano walks a fine line, suggesting that the creature is actually a sandhill crane, a bird that thrived in the New Jersey wildlands until its habitat was destroyed by development. Its stature (4 feet tall, 80-inch wingspan) and squawking song, plus its diet of crops, could explain some of the reports. Typical public hysteria that surrounds urban legends can account for the rest. Juliano also notes that, despite spurts of sightings throughout the years, especially since 1909, the occurrences have tapered off. However, interest in the legend has not.

Significantly, although the Jersey Devil has been branded as the scion of Satan, there are no reports that it ever attacked humans, only their credibility.

The Curse of the Hope Diamond

As the saying goes, if you're struck by lightning once, it's an accident; twice is a coincidence; the third time, it's a curse. So far, no one who has owned the Hope Diamond has been struck by lightning, but that's about the only thing that hasn't happened in the fabulous gem's gruesome history.

Alternately, the Hope Diamond is a remarkably well documented stone, and the truth about it supports none of the tales of mayhem that have followed. You decide.

Like the geologic forces that formed it, the origins of the Hope Diamond are murky. Believed to have been mined in India and weighing a remarkable 112 carats uncut, the gem was obtained by French merchant Jean-Baptiste Tavernier in 1666. Tavernier is most frequently cited as the cause of the curse that followed the gem throughout its 350-year history. He is alleged to have either stolen the jewel, or hired someone else to steal it, from the eye of a statue of the Hindu deity Sita near Mandalay. According to legend, Tavernier died a horrible death (this has been disputed). But it gets better.

In 1668 the jewel was sold to King Louis XIV of France. He had it cut into a heart-shaped 67-carat stone, which he named the Blue Diamond of the Crown. Apparently the curse went into hibernation for the next 121 years. But in 1793, it emerged with a vengeance, sending its owners, Louis XVI and Marie Antoinette, to the guillotine during the French Revolution. The royal jewels were then stolen and recovered—all but the great diamond, which was at the time called the French Blue.

In 1830, a 44.5-carat deep blue, oval-cut diamond appeared in London. It had no papers, but gem experts at the time believed it to have been the fabled French Blue, recut to disguise its origins possibly by Wilhelm Fals of Holland. For his part in defiling the stone, as well as for his son's part in purloining it, Fals is supposed to have died of grief, followed by his son, who took his own life. In any event, millionaire Henry Hope bought the French Blue and gave it its present name. Hope didn't own it long, however, although the record dims as to just who bought it from him. An Eastern prince, a Russian royal, a dancer at the Folies-Bergère, a Greek trader, and a Turkish sultan are all variously mentioned, each stalked by tragedy. But wait, there's more.

By 1911 the Hope Diamond came into the possession of the renowned jeweler Pierre Cartier, and the record became more concrete. Cartier sold it to Mrs. Evalyn Walsh McLean, a Washington, D.C. socialite. During her ownership, McLean's husband died in a

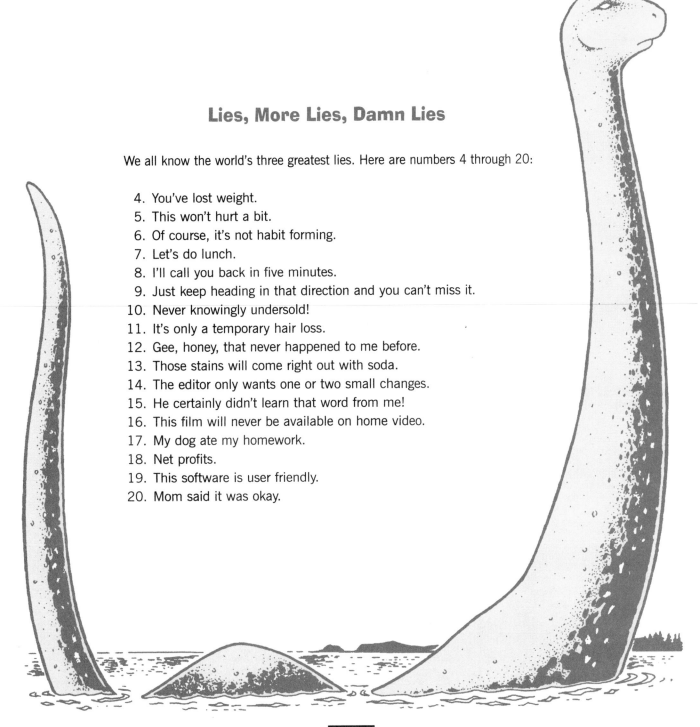

Lies, More Lies, Damn Lies

We all know the world's three greatest lies. Here are numbers 4 through 20:

4. You've lost weight.
5. This won't hurt a bit.
6. Of course, it's not habit forming.
7. Let's do lunch.
8. I'll call you back in five minutes.
9. Just keep heading in that direction and you can't miss it.
10. Never knowingly undersold!
11. It's only a temporary hair loss.
12. Gee, honey, that never happened to me before.
13. Those stains will come right out with soda.
14. The editor only wants one or two small changes.
15. He certainly didn't learn that word from me!
16. This film will never be available on home video.
17. My dog ate my homework.
18. Net profits.
19. This software is user friendly.
20. Mom said it was okay.

mental hospital, her daughter overdosed on sleeping pills, and her son died in a car accident. She even pawned the gem in 1932 to raise ransom money for the kidnapped Lindbergh baby, but it turned out to be a con engineered by Gaston Means. When the stone was recovered and Means was sent to prison, the misadventure was blamed not on the curse, but on the gullibility of a rich lady.

After Mrs. McLean died in 1947, her estate accepted the offer of New York jeweler Harry Winston to buy the Hope Diamond. The price was not disclosed, but its last appraised value, when McLean hocked it in 1932, was $100,000. In a move that will astonish anyone who ever had to wait in line at the post office, when Harry Winston agreed to present the Hope Diamond to the Smithsonian Institution, he mailed it to them. "It's the safest way to mail gems," he told the *Washington Star,* on November 8, 1958, just before shipping it. "I've sent gems all over the world that way."

According to the tapes and receipts, which he saved, Winston entered it as a 61-ounce registered package in New York on November 8, 1958, for $2.44 postage, plus another $142.85 for $1 million indemnity (total: $145.29). The diamond was delivered on Monday, November 11, by postal worker James G. Todd of Washington, DC.

Now for the Official Version, courtesy of the Smithsonian Institution: Jean Baptiste Tavernier purchased a 112 carat diamond, probably in 1666, and most likely from the Kollur mine in Golconda, India. He sold it to King Louis XIV of France in 1668, who had it recut by Sieur Pitau into a $67\frac{1}{8}$-carat stone in 1673. King Louis XV had it reset by Andre Jacquemin in 1749. In the height of the French Revolution in 1792, the crown jewels were stolen, including the diamond.

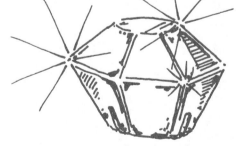

Its fate was unclear until 1812 when London diamond merchant Daniel Eliason was recorded as its possessor. It was later acquired by King George IV of England. In 1830, after his death, the diamond was sold privately to pay off royal debts. By 1839 it entered the possession of Henry Philip Hope, whose death that same year threw its ownership into legal turmoil. In 1902 Hope's distant heir, Lord Francis Hope, sold it to a London dealer to pay off his debts. The jewel found its way to Joseph Frankels and Sons in New York City, then to Selim Habib, then to C. H. Rosenau, then to gem dealer Pierre Cartier. In 1912, Cartier sold it to Mrs. Evalyn Walsh McLean. On her death in 1947, it was bought by Harry Winston, Inc. The firm toured it for 10 years before donating it to the Smithsonian.

Whether you believe that the Hope Diamond carries a curse, or that, statistically, any large group of people is going to encounter tragedy over three and a half centuries, it's still a compelling chronicle. One final note on the "curse": Not long after he delivered it to the museum, postal carrier Todd's dog strangled on its leash, Todd's house burned, he hurt his head in a car accident, and one of his legs was crushed by a truck. When the *Washington Post* asked him if he felt like a victim of the Hope curse, Todd told them, "I don't believe in any of that stuff."

The Hope Diamond now resides in the newly redesigned Janet Annenberg Hooker Hall of Geology, Gems, and Minerals at the Smithsonian Institution. It is not the largest diamond in the world—the Star of Africa that graces the British crown jewels dwarfs it at 530 carats—but it is certainly the most mysterious.

Chapter 5

Internet Hoaxes

The Internet is the worlds' biggest public library, except there's no card catalog. It's also the world's biggest gossip mill, bathroom wall, bulletin board, activist broadsheet, and, oh yes, open wallet.

Unlike the printing press (which presupposed literacy), radio (which needed electricity), or television (which cost a lot of money when it debuted), the Internet exploded into homes with no requirement beyond a telephone line, for those people who already owned computers. Unfortunately, its record penetration proved to be faster than society's ability to adapt to its unprecedented power. When radio started, there were only two networks; TV had four. But when the world went online, anybody and everybody could build a Web page. Abbott Joseph Liebling's famous comment that "freedom of the press is guaranteed only to those who own one" became instantly outdated. And scary.

The U.S. Department of Defense created the Internet in 1969 as a way for colleges and government agencies to communicate should traditional lines ever be cut (meaning: nuclear attack). In the 1980s, its scope was broadened when the National Science Foundation devised equipment that could connect civilian computers to the system. The World Wide Web was created in 1989 by the European Particle Physics Lab in Geneva, Switzerland, and debuted in 1991. Within five years, some 50 million people worldwide were online.

What were they watching? Internet technology radiates legitimacy, but looks can be deceiving in a world where even the youngest hacker is more hip than a *Fortune* 500 webmaster. Add to that the weak laws against "cyber-squatting"—that is, people who register somebody else's trademark as their own domain—and even familiar names are no longer what they seem.

The capability for deception make this still nascent medium the 21st century's loaded gun. The analogy is hauntingly consistent: Guns and computers are both marvels of technology. They level the playing field for anybody who owns one. They're constitutional unless used in crime, and the people who wield them can be trained or untrained, malicious or benign, or jerks who screw it up for the rest of us.

The potential of the Internet as a tool for democracy even has its hypocritical side. In 1999 Time-Warner's CNN celebrated the way the Internet was being used by rebel forces in other countries to overcome their government's censorship, yet the same corporation threw a hissy fit when cyber-fans posted video downloads of a *Buffy the Vampire Slayer* episode that Time-Warner's WB Network had censored. Such incidents will only get worse—or better, depending who owns the copyright. (By the way, this book is copyrighted!)

Digital technology has made it possible for any enterprising hoaxer to fabricate an alternate reality. In a world where Web sites can be devoted to morphing the faces of TV and movie actors onto the bodies of porno stars, what's to stop the FBI from cleaning up that famous backyard photo of Lee Harvey Oswald holding his rifle. You know, the one the conspiracists insist is a fake because the shadows don't match? Well, with Photoshop, they can!

Online commerce is also changing the way the world does business. Figures produced by Forrester Research in Cambridge, Massachusetts, show that Internet sales were $518 million in 1997; by 2001, they were projected to reach $6 billion. There were, of course, glitches. The 1999–2000 Christmas buying season was a watershed year for "e-tailers," but, too often, either their Web sites crashed, they didn't have the inventory, or the carrier (FedEx, UPS, U.S. Postal Service) couldn't get the merchandise to the buyer on time. Customer reluctance to give out credit card numbers also limits online sales activity. And there is growing opposition, even anger, at Web sites that collect, store, share, and sell personal information about the people who browse their pages. Despite this, the government and the industry have been reluctant to resolve issues about privacy and personal safety.

> ✓ **REALITY CHECK**
>
> ### Don't Give Out Your Password
>
> Remember how your parents always told you not to give out your name or phone number to anyone who calls and says, "Who is this?" or who says they've dialed a wrong number? The same wisdom holds true for the Internet. Never, ever give out your password to anyone, either online or on the phone, even if he or she poses as a representative of your computer service provider. For that matter, don't give out your Social Security number, either (by law, it is not supposed to be used for identification, even if everybody does anyway). Giving out your password is the same as handing somebody your wallet and a blank checkbook, all presigned.

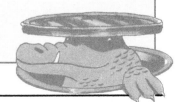

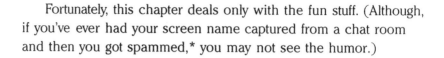

✓ **REALITY CHECK**

Death Ray Hoax

For every mother who ever told her son or daughter not to sit so close to the TV set, there existed the Death Ray Virus. A complete hoax (not just digitally but physically), this dastardly rumor—spread through an e-mail chain in the late 1990s—supposedly caused home computers to explode "in a hellish blast of glass fragments and flame" that "has injured at least 47 people since August 15." Blindness and death were thereby visited upon PC owners, not to mention gullibility. The virus was invisible, undetectable, and, ultimately, completely fake. It was identified by "a computer expert" who fastidiously reported that (an unnamed) college student in England was blinded when his 15-inch color monitor went up in his face. The reporter's sage advice: Stop using the Internet.

Fortunately, this chapter deals only with the fun stuff. (Although, if you've ever had your screen name captured from a chat room and then you got spammed,* you may not see the humor.)

The Internet Playing Field

Although the scientific, educational, and government communities were the first served by the Internet (with special operating systems enabling their access), the civilian community now makes the greatest use of this exciting communication technology. Despite its enormous potential, though, most people still depend on the Internet for three basic services:

1. Visiting chat rooms
2. Sending and receiving e-mail (in late 1999 the number of e-mails processed each day finally overtook the number of letters processed daily by the post office)
3. Browsing the World Wide Web (including news, e-commerce, entertainment, and research)

Taken in this order, number 1 is akin to talking, either on the phone or in the dark, with people whose identities are most likely not known to each other. If two people decide that they want to talk privately, they exchange e-mail addresses and leave the chat room "together." Of course, one of them may turn out to be a stalker, a pervert, a police officer, or some combination thereof.

Number 2 is very close to writing a traditional letter, except that stamps and carbons are free. (No, the Post Office is not going to charge 5¢ per e-mail to make up for lost stamps!) But there is also a qualitative difference. In the communications industry, one letter is

---

Spam is slang for unsolicited junk e-mail. It is not related to SPAM luncheon meat, which is the registered trademark of the Hormel Foods Corporation.

worth a hundred phone calls, and one phone call is worth a hundred people who thought the same thing, but didn't take the time to express it. In other words, when you take the trouble to write a letter and sign your name, it means something. E-mail is different. Although it's in writing, it involves none of the effort. Here's how big companies regard e-mail: they ignore yours, but they use their own to save interoffice paper costs.

And then there's "forwarding." Forwarding is the equivalent of sending a newspaper clipping to one or more friends without having to buy extra newspapers. If it is an item of interest, it can provide a common basis for discussion. Instead, people forward lists of jokes, homilies, virus hoaxes, and urban legends, usually accompanied by a page of server codes that gets longer each time. The exponential forwarding of documents taxes the capacity of servers, but that may be the point.

Browsing the Web (number 3) is by far the most intriguing capability that the Internet has over traditional publishing. It also returns freedom of the press to the people. With the change of Federal Communications Commission (FCC) licensing requirements in the 1980s, it became as difficult to get an opposing point of view onto a TV station as it was to buy one. But now any damn fool can post something on a Web page. What's more, those pages are frequently better designed and more interesting to read than so-called official media sources. On the downside, accuracy sometimes suffers. In the past, the sheer expense of running a reputable publishing house demanded that the material they issued was accurate, or at least spelled correctly. The Web changed all that. Now even lies can look legitimate (try visiting white suprema-cist sites some time), and the marketplace no longer equates credibility with polish. In 1989 a single online voice from Tiananmen Square spoke more truth than the entire Beijing government; at the same time, there are guys out there who say they just saw Elvis at Burger King.

The Internet is a triumph of rumor over reality. As with traditional commerce, brand names continue to dominate. That is why

✓ REALITY CHECK

The "Or Else" Virus

Here's the virus hoax equivalent of a spoiled brat saying, "I'm gonna hold my breath till I turn blue!" It's something that can only be called an "or else" virus—one that will activate itself in your computer and delete one file per day unless, quick, you e-mail it to 20 friends! Aside from the fact that no virus (even a real one) knows how to track e-mail (or probably cares), this is more like a virtual hot potato that lets you know who your friends are—or aren't.

Variations of this scam threaten to cancel your AOL account if you don't forward X number of e-mails, publish your Social Security number . . .

those Internet companies that establish a high public profile are bought and sold with such vigor (though seldom, if ever, at a profit).

Moral: Never invest in any enterprise that uses the word *cool* in its stock offering.

The Basics of Cyber-Terrorism

Viruses aren't the only way to vandalize a computer system. In February 1999, cyber-terrorists launched a jamming assault that shut down Yahoo!, CNN, eBay, and other Web sites with "attack software." They hacked (gained unauthorized access) into other people's personal computers and programmed them to request repeated searches from the sites, each time demanding a monstrous amount of data. The result of these DDOS (Distributed Denial of Service) requests was to overwhelm and ultimately shut down the servers.

The FBI made some arrests, but the problem will only get worse. A computer can only be hacked into when it is online. Thus, the growing popularity of Broadband, T-1, and DSL (Digital Subscriber Line), which allow subscribers to be online 24/7, by definition places tens of millions of home PCs in jeopardy. The only solution is to buy and install a "firewall" (hardware/software blocking device) from an antivirus company at a cost of $50 to as much as $2,000 for the UNIX units. The FBI is developing a firewall for public use, but after a litany of domestic spying revelations, who in her right mind would turn over her privacy to the FBI!

The other problem is that hackers view themselves as outlaws waging guerrilla war against evil multinational business overlords, sort of like Jesse James versus the bank. This comparison between the newness of the Internet and the American Wild West is appropriate only to the extent that both offer immense riches and little protection. The difference is that outlaws went in with their six-guns blazing and everybody knew who they were, whereas Internet hackers skulk around using counterfeit names and fake electronic addresses.

Ten Things to Know about the Internet

1. None of the *Fortune* 500 companies will give you money to forward their e-mail because they don't send any. Bill Gates's philanthropy does not include giving you $1,000 even if you send him the name of 10 friends (if you have any after doing that).

2. The Ritz-Carlton, Famous Amos, Neiman-Marcus, and Bloomingdale's don't have a cookie recipe that's any better than the one on the back of the bag of Hershey's chocolate chips. Even if they did, they wouldn't charge you $200 for it.

3. Neither you nor your computer can get a virus from reading an e-mail. You can possibly get a virus from opening an attachment to an e-mail if that attachment carries an "execute" (.exe) file. The problem is that many e-mail systems, except those like AOL, automatically download attachments to your hard drive before you even ask to open them, putting you in jeopardy. The only way to avoid this is to disable the automatic attachment downloading. Unless you know who is sending you an attachment, don't open it. If you're not sure, download it to a floppy disk and scan the disk with your latest antivirus utility program before opening it.

4. If you enter a chat room, you will probably start getting spam, the equivalent of junk e-mail. Spam is like being on a mailing list, and is just as impossible to get off.

5. You cannot get a virus from responding to an Instant Message (if you're an America Online customer).

6. Contrary to a popular e-mail myth, no one has ever stolen anyone else's kidney, even if the person sending you the e-mail tells you, "We checked this out."

7. Chain letters are not benign. If you forward one to 10 friends, you are conspiring in an act of cyber-vandalism designed to overload servers and spread spam.

8. NEVER NEVER NEVER tell a spammer that you want to be removed from its list. Never click the "click here to remove your name" box. All that does is confirm that they have found an active account. Either block their Web site or report them to your server for disciplinary action.

9. If you write e-mail from the office, remember that your employer owns the computer and therefore has the legal right to look at anything you put into it. Also, did you ever think that computer solitaire was an alien plot to make office workers waste time?

10. Even if you are online from home, never put anything in an e-mail or on your hard drive that you wouldn't want the police to read. There is no privacy in cyberspace, and there is no such thing as completely erasing files. A good cyber detective can recover nearly anything—so far.

The National Education Association (NEA) Funding Hoax

Given the way Senator Jesse Helms of North Carolina and Governor Jesse Ventura of Minnesota, among other elected officials (some of whom aren't even named Jesse), have attacked public funding of the arts, it's no wonder that the online community has launched "Save the NEA" or "Save PBS" e-mail campaigns. Unfortunately, cyber-griping does no good because the funding bills were safely passed years ago. Inundating a congressional representative's office with outdated protests only shows how ill-informed the squawkers are, and that hardly speaks well for their opinion. Besides, as anybody who works on Capitol Hill will admit, if pressed, no one takes e-mail as seriously as real letters, which are answered as a matter of policy.

Surprisingly, the NEA/PBS hoax did not begin life as a hoax, but as an actual call-to-arms when public broadcasting was, indeed, on the ropes. The CIAC (Computer Incident Advisory Capability) relates that David Brumley, network administrator at the University of Northern Colorado, reported to them that "in 1995 a couple of students wrote a letter and sent it out to support funding for PBS and NPR. This letter was not intended to be a hoax, but instead was only a misguided attempt by some students of ours to do some good." He added that the students "have been reprimanded."

When in doubt about the status of federal legislation, log on to the following Web sites and read the postings before angrily contacting an elected official:

U.S. Senate: *www.senate.gov*
U.S. House of Representatives: *www.house.gov*
Thomas Legislative Information on the Internet:
    http://thomas.loc.gov/
Directory of Senators and Representatives:
    http://congress.org.capdir.html

The Telephone and Internet Access Tax

Contrary to the rumors that periodically saturate the Web, there is no law "now pending" to charge an additional "connection fee" to the Internet. The fee that you pay to your normal telephone company to connect you to your server is all there is. The hoax apparently started in 1998 when legislation was filed that would effect a connection fee between telephone companies. A news organization misunderstood the terminology and thought it applied between phone companies and their customers. Before the story could be corrected, it spread across the Net like spilled coffee.

All bills that are filed in Washington carry identifying numbers beginning with "S" for Senate bills and "H" for House bills. Get it?

Forwarded e-mail urging action for an unspecified bill, or one without "S" or "H," is probably a hoax.

The E-mail Tax Hoax

As if the Internet connection fee hoax wasn't scary enough, another hoax emerged in May 1999 claiming that "the government of the United States" was attempting to tax e-mail at a nickel apiece. The logic behind the rumor was that the U.S. Postal Service was losing so much money as e-mail replaced letters that they needed a stipend to make ends meet. (This ignores the fact that the U.S.P.S. has been making a profit for years). Thus the legislation, "Bill 602P," would set up a nickel-per-message "alternative postage fee." But don't worry! They named an attorney in a Virginia law firm who was working without pay to kill the bill, as well as a Republican congressman (who didn't exist) who was behind it. That, in itself, should have quashed the rumor; a Republican favoring a tax?

No senatorial or congressional legislation has the letter "P" in it. Perhaps the hoaxer meant to blame the British Parliament.

The Trojan Horse

The fear of an Internet virus is a palpable one, since such things do exist and can do a tremendous amount of damage. Most viruses come disguised. They ride camouflaged within a program found on a contaminated disk, in faulty software, or in an infected download. For this reason, they are sometimes called "Trojan horse" viruses. Not all Trojan horses are viruses; some do not crash a whole operating system, but they may make a nag screen pop up now and then saying "Peace on Earth" or "Wazoo" or some similar nuisance. Generally speaking, a Trojan horse is aimed at specific users (*e.g.*, AOL subscribers, people who bought particular software, etc.) Small consolation, right?

Trojan horses are named after the ersatz peace offering given to the City of Troy by the Greeks during the 1184 B.C. Trojan War.

According to the legend, while the Trojans slept, Greek soldiers hidden inside the hollow wooden statue opened the city gates from within and let in the Greek army. The trick gave rise to the saying, "Beware of Greeks bearing gifts," although writer Jack Douglas suggested that it could also go, "Beware of gifts bearing Greeks."

The incident led to an unusual Internet warning, which appeared on the CIAC Web site in March 1999, about a Trojan horse virus:

> WARNING! WARNING! WARNING! WARNING! If you receive a gift in the shape of a large wooden horse do not download it! It is extremely destructive and will overwrite your entire city! The "gift" is disguised as a large wooden horse about two stories tall. It tends to show up outside city gates and appears to be abandoned. DO NOT LET IT THROUGH THE GATES! It contains hardware that is incompatible with Trojan programs, including a crowd of heavily armed Greek warriors who will destroy your army, sack your town, and kill your women and children. If you have already received such a gift DO NOT OPEN IT! Take it back out of the city unopened and set fire to it. Forward this message to everyone you know—(signed) The Oracle.

Unfortunately, in June 1995 an actual Trojan horse virus, PKZ300, made its way around the Internet. It has all but disappeared now and should not be the subject of any warnings. Information on it can be found at *www.pkware.com*.

The "Good Times" Virus Hoax

Not only is there no "Good Times" virus, but even the hoax about its existence was a hoax. It first entered the national scene in November 1994 when e-mails contained the alert:

> Here is some important information. Beware of a file called Goodtimes. Happy Chanukkah everyone, and be

---

✓ REALITY CHECK

Let's Crash AOL Virus Hoax

As the biggest Internet access provider (40 million subscribers at this writing), America Online is a prime target for hoaxers. That's why the 1998 "AOL RIOT" campaign could have been a nuisance, albeit not a disaster. "There will be a virus upload on AOL's main server," the advance e-mail warned. "Because of the outrage of AOL's increasing prices ($19.95 to $21.95 per month), [we have] decided to create a riot on May 1 that will cause havoc on AOL. There will be no AOL staff— just complete pandemonium!" It was officially identified as a hoax by AOL's VP of Integrity Assurance, and life went on . . . at $21.95 per month.

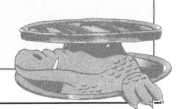

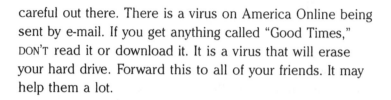

✓ REALITY CHECK

Virtual Greeting Cards Hoax

When you care so little to spend the very least, there are—*ta-DAA*—virtual greeting cards! The rumor persists that companies that send online birthday, Christmas, anniversary, Ramadan, greetings—animated, tuneful, personalized, and a little tacky—will cause people's systems to crash. They don't. At the worst (because somebody had to give them your address to send you the card), you get put on spam lists. In March 1999, one particular electronic greeting card company was the victim of an e-mail campaign purporting that their cards caused people's systems to crash (their name won't be used here so as not to perpetuate the lie). They don't.

careful out there. There is a virus on America Online being sent by e-mail. If you get anything called "Good Times," DON'T read it or download it. It is a virus that will erase your hard drive. Forward this to all of your friends. It may help them a lot.

Following this marginally literate warning, another one appeared that trumpeted the Federal Communications Commission's entry into the field spreading the word about Good Times. That, too, was false.

There is no Good Times virus. But a classic response to it, written and posted by Patrick J. Rothfuss in December 1996, has since earned a place in Internet lore. It is reprinted here from the CIAC hoax page:

READ THIS:

Goodtimes will re-write your hard drive. Not only that, but it will scramble any disks that are even close to your computer. It will recalibrate your refrigerator's coolness setting so all your ice cream goes melty. It will demagnetize the strips on all your credit cards, screw up the tracking on your television and use subspace field harmonics to scratch any CDs you try to play.

It will give your ex-girlfriend your new phone number. It will mix Kool-aid into your fish tank. It will drink all your beer and leave its socks out on the coffee table when there's company coming over. It will put a dead kitten in the back pocket of your good suit pants and hide your car keys when you are late for work.

Goodtimes will make you fall in love with a penguin. It will give you nightmares about circus midgets. It will pour sugar in your gas tank and shave off both your eyebrows while dating your girlfriend behind your back and billing the dinner and hotel room to your Discover card.

It will seduce your grandmother, It does not matter if she is dead, such is the power of Goodtimes, it reaches

out beyond the grave to sully those things we hold most dear.

It moves your car randomly around parking lots so you can't find it. It will kick your dog. It will leave libidinous messages on your boss's voice mail in your voice! It is insidious and subtle. It is dangerous and terrifying to behold. It is also a rather interesting shade of mauve.

Goodtimes will give you Dutch Elm disease. It will leave the toilet seat up. It will make a batch of Methamphetamine in your bathtub and then leave bacon cooking on the stove while it goes out to chase grade schoolers with your new snow blower.

Listen to me. Goodtimes does not exist.

It cannot do anything to you. But I can. I am sending this message to everyone in the world. Tell your friends, tell your family. If anyone else sends me another e-mail about this fake Goodtimes virus, I will turn hating them into a religion. I will do things to them that would make a horse head in your bed look like Easter Sunday brunch.

Health Alarms

There used to be a time when "epidemic" meant a disease, not just a warning about one that sent people into a panic. Yet that's an unfortunate side effect of the ease with which information, particularly false information, can be spread through electronic technology. Perhaps it has to do with our acquired willingness to believe anything we see in print (as opposed to something spray-painted on a wall, which has pretty much the same level of reality as these Internet disease hoaxes).

Worse, hoaxes may dissuade people from seeking timely, accurate medical treatment to stem the spread of an actual health problem. Genuine, up-to-date information about epidemics, pandemics, plagues, and maladies can be found at the Web site of the Centers for Disease Control and Prevention: *www.cdc.gov/ncidod/dbmd/diseaseinfo*.

Meanwhile, fallacious online medical alerts include:

1. *Flesh-eating bananas.* The dreaded (and extremely rare) "flesh-eating disease" that gets so much television coverage when it appears in humans is a Group A streptococcus bacteria called *necrotizing fasciitis.* It attacks and kills soft tissues under the skin and causes gangrene. A rumor started in early 2000 that it could be contracted by eating bananas. Rather than a disease warning, it sounded more like a scheme to damage Chiquita Brands International's controversial investments in Central America. This hoax was also maliciously attributed to an actual, but completely innocent, federal government worker whose phone starting ringing off its hook with inquiries.

   Now for the facts: The disease is real, but you can't get it from bananas, so the warning is a hoax. Group A strep is spread through direct contact with secretions from an infected person's nose or throat. So unless that's where you've been storing your banana, there is absolutely no chance of catching it from "the world's most perfect food."

2. *Ovarian/cervical cancer test warning.* As if the danger of ovarian and cervical cancer is not authentic enough, warnings pop up on the Web urging women to have "rare, additional" tests performed by their gynecologist "because I know someone who didn't do this, and she died." When this chain letter began, it was followed by back-and-forth e-mail between people who called it a hoax and those who argued that all available tests should be used in the fight against cancer in women. Both sides have valid arguments, but the only one that benefited directly was the health care industry. As with most medical advice, get it from your physician.

3. *How to survive a heart attack when you're alone.* Incorrectly attributed to an article in the Mended Hearts, Inc., newsletter, this chain letter suggested that, if your

heart stops beating, or if you're having a heart attack, you have 10 seconds to start coughing in order to provide oxygen and to restart your heart. The American Heart Association (AHA), with whom Mended Hearts is affiliated, does not recommend this technique. In fact, the AHA advises that no studies conclude that coughing is more reliable than calling 911 and administering CPR. The AHA also urges the public to know the early signs of heart attack, which may include pallor and chest pain that moves to the neck, shoulder, and arms. For current information, browse to *www.americanheart.org*.

4. *Antiperspirants cause breast cancer.* Coming out of the same left field as "the body breathes through pores in the skin," this rumor insists that blocking perspiration also prevents the body from purging itself of toxins, which leads to cancer. According to the Texas Department of Health, toxins are purged, in part, through the lymph system, not through perspiration. The American Cancer Society is not aware of any evidence that shows substances in deodorants or antiperspirants to be toxic or to cause DNA damage. The chief thing that happens when you use deodorants is that you smell like a strawberry.

5. *Aspartame lawsuit.* Aspartame is a chemical sweetener produced by the Monsanto Corporation. It is used as a sugar substitute under the name NutraSweet, Equal, and Spoonful. Activist Betty Martini, through an organization called Mission Possible, maintains that Aspartame, under certain circumstances, produces symptoms similar to multiple sclerosis, and thus may lead to a misdiagnosis in patients presenting those symptoms. An e-mail of an unsourced article written by "Nancy Markle" (who may or may not exist, according to Ms. Martini)

✓ REALITY CHECK

Flaming

Flaming is the practice of inundating someone with nasty e-mail messages until their system crashes. It is usually reserved for strategic displays of outrage over outlandish behavior, strong opinions, or just plain bad manners. It's fighting spam with spam, and it considered to be improper Netiquette, even if the slimy cuss deserves it. Under some circumstances, sending threatening e-mail messages is considered a criminal offense. Therefore, the best way to get back at a spammer is to block the Web site from your e-mail system and report it to the Community Action (or similar) address of your Internet access provider.

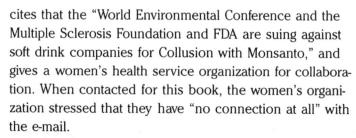

cites that the "World Environmental Conference and the Multiple Sclerosis Foundation and FDA are suing against soft drink companies for Collusion with Monsanto," and gives a women's health service organization for collaboration. When contacted for this book, the women's organization stressed that they have "no connection at all" with the e-mail.

What makes the e-mail so compelling is a line that says, "Even if this is only partially correct, I find this to be quite scary." Martini's Web site, which includes numerous links and endorsements, is at *www.dorway.com.*

Y2K

As the year 2000 approached, so did an awareness that most computers wouldn't be able to make the transition into it. Buried in most operating systems (the basic program that drives the computer) was something called the "Y2K bug."

How do most people abbreviate the year in writing? For the last century, people used '01 through '99 with the understanding that the first two digits were automatically "19" unless otherwise specified (*e.g.,* 1830, 1848). But that's just the content of the document; regardless of what may be in it, it was created on a date that fell in the 1900s. Thus, when a computer filed the document in its memory, it, too, abbreviated the year of filing to 96, 98, and so on. The reason it did this is that computers had not been programmed for the transition from the 1900s to the 2000s.

The people who developed computer systems unintentionally created this confusion. When computers were invented, they possessed so little memory that even those two seemingly insignificant digits would have taken up byte space that could have been better used to designate for other data. The inventors figured (wrongly, as it turned out) that better systems would be developed in later years, people would change over to them, and all would be well come Y2K.

✓ **REALITY CHECK**

BubbleBoy Virus

The *Seinfeld* TV series may have been "a show about nothing," but a virus named after one of its episodes turned out to be quite something indeed. This one is real. The episode and the virus are both "BubbleBoy," in which George Castanza accidentally infected an immunodeficient youth who was confined to a plastic bubble. The virus (which only infects Microsoft Outlook 98, Outlook 2000, and Outlook Express that comes with Internet Explorer 5) is a "worm" that creates files that reregister your operating system to "BubbleBoy/ Vandelay Industries." It then acts like the Melissa/Mailissa virus (see page 144) to send itself to everyone in the user's e-mail address book. The BubbleBoy can be spread when the e-mail

(continued on next page)

In some ways that was true. Home computers and software smoothly accommodated to Y2K somewhere in the mid- to late-1990s. It was the government and the business community that had problems. They had invested so heavily in computers early on that retooling them for Y2K ran into billions and billions of dollars in fixes. Hence, the Y2K scare.

But nothing went wrong. The world didn't end, the economy didn't crumble, traffic lights kept working, and toilets still flushed.

Was it a hoax?

Virus Information

Any device as complicated as a computer is going to occasionally hiccup. Sometimes an inexperienced user upsets the balance and causes a system shutdown. Sometimes the dang thing just crashes. And sometimes a computer is infected by a virus.

Viruses must be deliberately written and introduced into a system. They do not spontaneously "evolve" from the gizmos that go into making a computer. The Internet has not only aided viruses, it has also spread information about them. When it is accurate, it is helpful. Most of the time, the information is a hoax. Hoaxes have been traced back to 1988.

Computer viruses can be destructive, but they are not predatory. You have to do something to activate them. Depending on their design, viruses can do anything from making your screen flash "hello!" every time the computer is turned on to distributing your e-mail address book to strangers to completely erasing your hard drive.

One, called the Y2K virus, even went through all the documents and changed the Ys to Ks. Get it? What's so disheartening about viruses is that the hackers who create them are so brilliant that it's sad to see their considerable talents wasted.

With more operating systems, viruses cannot be "caught" from reading e-mail or from browsing the Web. Even if you use somebody else's floppy disk, you have to open the document containing

✓ **REALITY CHECK**

BubbleBoy Virus

(continued from previous page)

recipient opens the message in Outlook. Microsoft provides a "patch" (a program that can be downloaded to mend a hole in the program they already sold you) at *www.microsoft.com/security/Bulletins/ms99-032.asp*, with more information available at *www. microsoft.com/Security/Bulletins/MS99-32faq.asp*. (This information is from F Secure Corporation.)

the virus for it to infect your system. Viruses are not released when your grandchildren's photo appears on the screen.

Viruses usually come embedded in "attachment" to e-mail. Programs that might carry viruses are those ending with the suffix ".exe" (executable programs). Zip files are also becoming a more popular way to infect. If there is a question about a downloaded program, save it to disk and scan the disk with an antivirus program, or scan the download file onto your hard drive.

The only vaccination against computer viruses is an antivirus utility that scans the computer and all incoming material specifically for them. Any antivirus program, however, is only as effective as its currency, so whichever one you use must be constantly updated. Two of the most popular antivirus utilities are Norton/Symantec (*www.norton.com*) and McAfee VirusScan (*www.macafee.com*).

The Michelangelo Virus

Michelangelo Buonarroti was born on March 6, 1475, and managed to create a couple of knickknacks (*Pietà, David*, the Sistine Chapel ceiling, etc.) before he died in 1565. However, he had absolutely nothing to do with a similarly named computer virus that appeared in 1991. Embedded in 500 PCs that were subsequently shipped to unwitting users, this virus was programmed to go off on March 6, 1992, and every March 6 thereafter, at which time it would erase their hard drives.

As antivirus companies scrambled to find a cure, reporters covered the phenomenon with the zeal of a political scandal. Meanwhile, most computer users simply temporarily advanced the date on their system setup to "March 7," sidestepped the virus, and kept right on typing. By the time Michelangelo's ghost had finished his birthday cake, between 10,000 and 20,000 PCs worldwide—not the 5 million that early reports had predicted—were affected. In subsequent years, as antivirus programs did their job, infection reports dwindled to a trickle, and Michelangelo was back in the Vatican where he belongs.

Internet Cleanup Day

There used to be a children's phone prank that involved calling an unsuspecting person and saying, "Hello, I'm with the phone company. We're trying to clean up our office and we'd appreciate it if you'd yank about six feet of phone wire in at your end so we could get the slack off our floor . . ."

Well, there's a counterpart to this patently stupid (but kind of charming) hoax called "Internet Cleanup Day." The CIAC explained it as (naturally) a chain-letter e-mail announcing that from 12:01 A.M. on a specified day until 12:01 A.M. the next day the Internet is going to be "cleaned up" by five powerful search engines that are going to "sweep the Internet and delete any data that they find. So be sure not to log on during that time, or your computer will be sucked dry. Furthermore, the hoax warning says, "disconnect all terminals . . . shut down Internet servers, (and) . . . disconnect all disks and hard drives."

Obviously, if nobody is on the Internet, there's nothing to be cleaned. In any event, this hoax is the cyber equivalent of asking, "Is your refrigerator running?"

The Bill Gates Hoax

If Bill Gates didn't exist, paranoid computer users would have to invent him. Instead, in 1997, they discovered the "Bill Gates Hoax" and sent it whizzing through cyberspace.

The hoax involved an "announcement" from the Microsoft chief executive that his company had implemented an e-mail tracking system that needed to be tested, and so would the recipient please forward the message to everybody he or she knows. When it reaches 1,000 people, everyone will get $1,000 and a free copy of Windows 98. The hoax exploited three rampant beliefs:

1. Everybody knows that Bill Gates is supernaturally rich.
2. Everybody hates Microsoft.
3. Microsoft hides tracking devices (cookies) in its software.

✓ REALITY CHECK

Name-Calling

Sticks and stones may break your bones, but names will never hurt you—unless you use them in a chat room. A sly practice of hate groups is to infiltrate chat rooms visited by people they hate. Nazis will visit Jewish chat rooms, homophobes will drop into gay chat rooms, racists will browse into African-American chat rooms, and pick verbal fights. When the offended party fights back, the hate-monger files an instant complaint against them with the access provider. Since Internet access providers like to think that they are upholding "community standards," they invariably wind up taking the side of the racist, homophobe, Nazi against the aggrieved minority group. So the next time you're in room where the chat turns to cat, pretend it's a game show and zap the hatemonger before he or she gets someone else.

Fortunately or unfortunately (depending on whether you're a Microsoft stockholder or a customer), the e-mail was, is, and will probably be, forever phony. Similar "giveaway" scams have been ascribed to Disney, Miller Brewing Company, Netscape-AOL, the Gap, IBM, and other major companies. All are false.

How to Identify a Hoax

Internet hoaxes don't have horns or stripes. However, if you see a forwarded message and it contains more than three of the following items, you should probably delete it and go about your business:

1. It says "pass this on to a friend."
2. It says "this is real" but offers no documentation.
3. It uses a lot of technical terms.
4. It contains misspellings and bad grammar (confusing *its* and *it's* is a dead giveaway).
5. It tries to be coy by vaguely mentioning "the government" or "a giant corporation" without naming either.
6. It has links to other people's Web sites.
7. It drops names of companies like AOL and Microsoft that are not in the virus detection business.
8. The threats described in the message defy logic.
9. It tells you to forward it to everybody you know.
10. You haven't seen it corroborated by other media.

Note: I asked Loren Rose, whose company, Rose Consulting, keeps many southern California systems up and running, to elaborate on some of these issues. Says Rose, "You'll never hear of a virus via a forwarded mail, but through attachments. It's a paradox. If the virus was so dangerous, and itself is spread by e-mail, what makes anyone think that a message casually forwarded after the fact would somehow reach them before this monstrous and life-threatening virus does?" Rose defends AOL's virus stance by noting that the Melissa virus (see page 144) was not spread by AOL users, but by people using Microsoft Network, Earthlink, Outlook, Eudora, and other systems that automatically open ".exe" files—something AOL does not do. In addition, he says, AOL regularly updates for Trojan horses. As for AOL scanning attachments for viruses, Rose reminds that, "Attachments are generally hundreds of times larger than the e-mails themselves, so scanning them would require more horsepower per day to do it effectively than any ISP could afford."

As to hackers being caught, Rose adds to Rosenberger's comments: "Everyone who's on the Web has a unique http address. 'Good' hackers use one address to connect to another to another to another, etc., so that the trail is very long. They also target places that don't keep logs for very long, so that by the time someone gets around to tracking them, the trail stops at some lame ISP that doesn't have the old data."

AOL4FREE Hoax

Now that America Online has merged with Time-Warner to create the largest production and distribution entity on the planet, it is doubtless going to be subjected to more of the kind of attacks that assailed it in 1997 when a hoax called "AOL4FREE" zoomed through cyberspace. At that time, it had three components:

1. AOL4FREE Macintosh program
2. AOL4FREE virus warning hoax
3. AOL4FREE.COM Trojan horse program

The AOL4FREE Mac program, exposed in the March 1997 issue of *CSI Computer Security Alert,* gave free, and illegal, access to America Online. It was traced to a Yale student who pleaded guilty to defrauding AOL of between $40,000 and $70,000 in service charges. Any use of the program would subject the user to similar criminal sanctions.

✓ **REALITY CHECK**

Forwarded Lists

There was a time when people who had nothing to say kept it to themselves. Nowadays when people have nothing to say, they forward you a list of what somebody else has said. The proliferation of joke lists, "did you know" lists, heartwarming parables, weird observations (mostly stolen from comedian Steven Wright), and the like is proof that silence is golden, but e-mail is irresistible.

People who can't tell jokes seem to think it's okay to forward them. That's like somebody who can't cook sending his friend groceries instead of taking him or her out to dinner.

Friends don't spam friends. But if they do, they remove the little marginal << marks when they do it!

✍ **INTERVIEW**

The False Authority Syndrome

Who is behind Internet hoaxes? Can the major Internet Service Providers do anything to stop them? Why would anybody want to hack into a Web site? These are questions I asked Rob Rosenberger, one of the industry's most authoritative hoax debunkers. He credits "False Authority Syndrome" as behind much Internet mythology; that is, someone says "this is real; it's from a newspaper" when forwarding a hoax, and people believe it. Rosenberger now consults for Vmyths.com, an online clearing house for virus myths.

Segaloff: Are there any legitimate viruses—that is, any that aren't hoaxes?

Rosenberger: Everything's pretty much hyped. You and I can count on a couple of hands the number of viruses. Michelangelo was one; Melissa was another.

Segaloff: Is it safe to say that you should never open up an ".exe" file unless you know what it is?

Rosenberger: Yes. One, beware of anything anybody sends you attached to an e-mail if you don't know them; and, two, beware of anything anybody sends you attached to an e-mail if you *do* know them. Competent computer people tell you not to open anything except from somebody you know.

Segaloff: Do you think spammers are behind internet hoaxes?

Rosenberger: I don't think that spammers are creating urban legends and hoaxes to increase their mailing lists. But I do think that the savvy spammer will get his name out there so he can get a mailbox that gets filled with these hoaxes so that he can pluck out what are known as "Golden E-mail Addresses." The people on those lists are one friend or family member writing to another, so we can assume that they are active names. So when somebody forwards a message to a hundred of his "bestest" friends, the chances are pretty good that everybody will wind up on some spammer's database sooner or later, and they'll all get more spam.

Segaloff: And this is why you should never respond to an e-mail that says "click here if you want to be deleted from our list."

Rosenberger: I never do that. They lie to you. Enough said.

Segaloff: Can you really shut down a server by spamming it too much?

Rosenberger: We do that all the time. I remember a really funny one back in 1998. In October the United States Postal Service shut down. They lost their national e-mail infrastructure because one guy forwarded a "Win a Holiday" alert to everybody in "usps.gov." It wasn't really him that nailed the network. What happened was,

fifty-five people all hit the "reply to all" button and there were millions of messages flying through the network trying to get to their destinations, and the whole infrastructure had to be taken down that night just so they could purge it of all the excessive e-mail.

Segaloff: When one is not sure about an e-mail attachment, what does one do?

Rosenberger: Just get rid of 'em. Throw the e-mail away. I might respond to the guy saying, "I'm sorry, but you sent me an attachment and I just don't trust it. Thanks." Leave it to them at that point; they can either send it back to me and tell me why they sent it, or . . .

Segaloff: How are hackers caught?

Rosenberger: A lot of them are just stupid; they leave trails and they brag about it in chat rooms. A lot of this stuff qualifies as a joyride; they hack first and then they figure out what to do: "Great! We broke into Yahoo! Now what?" One of the things that was really "stupid" in my opinion was the American Exchange/NASDAQ hack. They could have gone blitzoid with that and really messed up the Stock Market. Instead, all they did was screw up the Web page a little bit. On the other hand, the Aastrum hack where somebody put a press release up on their site announcing a merger with their archrival—that was planned. They could have prepared two press releases for whichever system they could hack into,

posted it, and then called their brokers to sell short or whatever they wanted to do. So there's a plot.

Segaloff: What do you think about hackers who break into a system and then say, in their defense, that they were doing a public service by showing how bad the security was?

Rosenberger: If you break into a Web site to prove a point, why not just go to the company and describe it in detail? You don't have to go out and do it.

Segaloff: The people who create antivirus software have to keep discovering viruses in order to survive.

Rosenberger: This is an important issue. There are a lot of guys out there who, in advancing the state-of-the-art in viruses, are, in turn, advancing the state-of-the-art in antivirus software. The antivirus vendors want to describe it as a parasitic relationship. In fact, it's symbiotic; but the antivirus vendors can't do anything to change the relationship. Besides, it would make for bad publicity if vendors went around saying, "Virus writers sometimes do useful research." Antivirus vendors don't deserve the negative publicity for this symbiotic relationship, and I defend them on this point.

Segaloff: How would you describe what you do for a living?

Rosenberger: I fight virus hysteria. I get paid to fight it full-time now. Ironically, all of my fame comes from the very hysteria I seek to destroy.

The AOL4FREE virus warning hoax was just that. It was another in the growing stockpile of supposed viruses that were allegedly embedded in e-mails, but meant nothing.

Conversely, the AOL4FREE.COM Trojan horse, if run, was actually capable of deleting all files in a directory, and then the subdirectories, and finally the directory itself, but only on the C: drive of a DOS. system. It was not a Macintosh program. It was not a virus, but it was a Trojan horse, meaning that it enters one program and does a specific—and separate—job.

The Mailissa Virus

She went by two names, both of them deadly: *Melissa* and *Mailissa*. She was a virus that attacked Microsoft Word 97 and Microsoft Word 2000 documents and then e-mailed a copy of herself, attached to the infected document, to up to 50 people on the victim's e-mail address book.

According to CNET News.com and Reuters, she was created by David L. Smith, then 31, of Aberdeen Township, New Jersey. He hacked into America Online on March 26, 1999, to implant the virus (crashing his own PC along the way). Melissa/Mailissa went on to cause an estimated $80 million in damage. She was designed to use Microsoft Outlook (contained in MS operating systems) to do her bidding, but she had a heart—of sorts. If the computer was already infected, she wouldn't send out a second set of 50 e-mails. Approximately once an hour she also displayed a screen message:

Twenty-two points, plus triple-word score, plus fifty points for using all my letters. Game's over. I'm outta here.

Smith was arrested on April 1 and pleaded guilty on December 9. He is one of the first people ever to be prosecuted for spreading a computer virus.

Get-Rich-Quick Hoaxes

There are, as of this writing, only three ways to get rich on the Internet:

1. Invent a Web site that everybody likes and at least one person will pay a lot to buy from you, or for which you can make an IPO (Initial Public Offering) that will turn you into an instant gazillionaire (in which case you will not make a profit, you will just make money).
2. Sell merchandise online. Assuming that you can find a carrier to get the wares from the supplier to the consumer in a timely manner, you'll rake it in.
3. Invent a porn site that people will subscribe to. Approximately 4 percent of Web sites are porn, but they receive as much as 20 percent of browser search requests. Why the disparity? It's like when the TV ratings service call up and, amazingly, nobody is watching *Wrestlemania*, they're all watching PBS.

Helpful Web Sites

Since the Internet does its part to circulate urban legends, it's only fitting that Web sites exist to quash them. As of this writing, these sites have proven unusually helpful (and frequently witty) in ferreting out Internet hoaxes. If you want additional sources, type the phrase "urban legend," "virus hoax," or "Internet hoax" (including quotation marks) into your Web browser.

Urban Legends Reference Pages:
www.snopes.com
Dead People Server:
http://dpsinfo.com
Urban legends in general:
www.urbanlegends.com

✓ **REALITY CHECK**

Bad Day

At first people thought it was from a security camera that caught an office worker one step from going postal. Turned out it was a staged test that was designed to see how well, and how fast, a video upload could travel around the net. The 1998 stunt broke popularity records. It was called "Bad Day," and the 25-second video shows a stocky man typing at his workstation. Something obviously goes wrong with his program once too often, so he picks up the keyboard and batters the monitor with it, stalking angrily out of his cubicle as another worker meekly peers over the partition to see what's up. As of this writing it was still available from at least one server, or you can browse the Net looking for "Bad Day Movie."

Stories censored by major news outlets:
www.projectcensored.org

About.Com's Urban Legend page:
http://urbanlegends.about.com/library/blhoax.htm?pid=2733&cob=home

U.S. Department of Energy Computer Incident Advisory Capability (CIAC) internet hoaxes and chain letters listing: *http://hoaxbusters.ciac.org*

Computer virus myths:
www.vmyths.com

Hoax warnings:
www.datafellows.com/news/hoax.htm

Don't spread that hoax:
www.nonprofit.net/hoax

The Darwin Awards Web Site:
www.darwinawards.cjb.net

U.S. Senate:
www.senate.gov

U.S. House of Representatives:
www.house.gov

Thomas Legislative Information on the Internet:
http://thomas.loc.gov

Directory of U.S. elected officials:
http://congress.org/congressorg/dbq/officials

Chapter 6

Hollywood and Bust

This ain't a business, it's a racket.
—Hollywood proverb

Incongruous as it sounds, Hollywood was born in Fort Lee, New Jersey. At least, that's were most of the early filmmakers hung out in the early 1900s when the "flickers" began to move from the peep shows to the Nickelodeons and money started to come in. Lots of it.

For those few years, thinly settled Fort Lee served its purpose. Its plentiful woods, easily traveled roads, and picturesque buildings lent themselves as locations for 1903's breakthrough narrative *The Great Train Robbery*, 10 minutes of blazing guns and cowboy action. But after a while the weather, the sunlight, and the terrain proved limiting. Even more limiting was the Motion Picture Patents Trust, which was headquartered in nearby East Orange, New Jersey, where Thomas A. Edison had built his Black Maria film studio. Together with George Eastman (who devised perforated film), importer George Kleine, producer Frank Marion, fellow inventor Thomas Armat, and others, Edison demanded royalties from the burgeoning number of fledgling independent production companies that were making movies with homemade (and sometimes purloined) equipment.

Rather than meet the Trust's demands to pay license fees, and refusing to stop making movies, these producers packed their bootlegged cameras and fled westward, eventually settling in the sleepy Southern California village of Hollywood. Once there, they discovered a temperate climate, constant sunshine, and wonderfully varied scenery. Better yet, they discovered that the Mexican border was only an hour's mad dash away if the Trust's lawyers showed up with subpoenas. Sometimes the Trust hired thugs to shoot the independents' cameras, and occasionally the independents themselves; frequently the independents (such as pioneer director Allan Dwan) shot back.

Thus did Hollywood become a land of fugitives, scoundrels, and misfits, creating an image that the town has sustained ever since. By 1915 the Justice Department had broken up the Trust, but by then the studio system was ensconced and no longer cared about it.

Hollywood didn't invent the movies, but it perfected their manufacture and presentation. More important, the studios raised the process of selling them to the level of art. Even today, although the old-line studios no longer exist as they once did, six or seven powerhouse companies continue to dominate the world marketplace through vertically integrated corporations that the U.S. government has consistently refused to examine (quite unlike their behavior toward the Patents Trust).

Since movies, at their essence, are built on fantasy, it stands to reason that Hollywood uses fantasy to attract audiences to see them. It hardly matters whether a particular title is actually "the greatest epic ever made" or so-and-so is really "the biggest star in the universe." Audiences long ago became immune to the hype. Over the years, ballyhoo has evolved into a cherished tradition; the only problem is when the ballies start to believe their own hoo.

"The tragedy of film history is that it is fabricated, falsified, by the very people who make film history," lamented silent movie actress–turned–historian Louise Brooks in *Lulu in Hollywood*. Brooks ought to know. She languished in flapper roles in the 1920s until she fled to Europe and enjoyed artistic stardom in two German classics, *Pandora's Box* and *Diary of a Lost Girl*, for director G. W. Pabst. Brooks later retired to Rochester, New York, where she installed herself at Eastman House to view, comment on, and write about movies and the town that made them.

"It is understandable," Brooks continued, "that in the early years of film production, when nobody believed there was going to be any film history, most film magazines and books printed trash . . . But since about 1950 film has been established as an art, and its history recognized as a serious matter. Yet film celebrities continue to cast themselves as stock types—nice or naughty girls, good or bad boys—whom their chroniclers spray with a shower of anecdotes."

The movies and the 20th century grew up together. At the beginning, they shared an excitement about technology, an optimism

---

✓ **REALITY CHECK**

A Vamp There Was

What was a nice Jewish girl from Cincinnati doing in Hollywood saying she was from the Middle East? Making a living as a movie star, that's what. Her name was Theodosia Goodman, but it was as Theda Bara that she gained fame as the "vamp" who lured men to death-by-romance in a series of films she made for William Fox beginning in 1916. A pure contrivance of press agentry, "vamp" was short for "vampire," but Theda Bara (whose name was an anagram for "Arab Death") didn't suck her beaux' blood, she emptied their hearts and wallets in such films as *A Fool There Was*. She found little work after 1919, when vamps were over, and died in 1955.

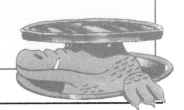

for the future, and even a certain clumsiness in getting down to business. Then came World War I and America shouldered its global responsibility. Likewise, moviemakers realized that they had become an international enterprise. As the century wore on, with America and Hollywood both becoming multinational, there was less room for fun, more chance for error, and a growing cynicism about both. Movie industry old-timers lament the end of the "old days," always forgetting that the "old days" were pretty tough at the time. But as we'll see, those moguls were also adventurous and creative; after all, they built legends that survived a hundred years. So what if they used fakery, legerdemain, and puffery? It's only a movie!

It isn't easy to separate the hype from the history, but that's what this chapter is about.

The IMP Girl

Mary Pickford may have been the first "movie star," but Florence Lawrence was the first screen performer whose name became known to the public. She was also the subject of the first movie publicity hoax. One fed the other.

Born in Canada in 1886, Lawrence toured in her mother's stage troupe until 1907 when she entered the infant movie industry as an actress with the Biograph company. At the time, producers kept the names of their performers secret for fear they would demand higher salaries, but Lawrence received so many fan letters addressed to "the Biograph Girl" that her rising fame was hard to ignore. When Biograph (whose star director was D. W. Griffith) staunchly refused to identify her on screen, Lawrence accepted an offer in 1910 from producer Carl Laemmle to come to his competing Independent Motion Picture (IMP) company.

To announce the move, Laemmle promptly had her killed by a streetcar. At least, that's what Laemmle's publicity manager, Robert Cochrane, planted in the newspapers, setting the stage for the feisty Laemmle to angrily denounce his own story the next day in an advertisement that implied the Patents Trust was behind it all:

We Nail a Lie!

The blackest and at the same time the silliest lie yet circulated by enemies of the "Imp" was the story foisted on the public of St. Louis last week to the effect that Miss Lawrence (the "Imp" girl, formerly known as the "Biograph" girl) had been killed by a street car. It is a black lie because so cowardly. It was a silly lie because so easily disproved. Miss Lawrence was not even in a street-car accident, is in the best of health, will continue to appear in "Imp" films, and very shortly some of the best work in her career is to be released. We now announce our next film:

"The Broken Bath"*
(Released March 14th. Length 950 feet.)

A powerful melodrama dealing with a young chap, his sweetheart, and a secret society. There's action from the first foot of film and keeps you five million miles up in the air until the happy finale. It is the kind of film dozens of our customs (sic) have been begging us to produce. Watch for it.

Laemmle cagily added an invitation for the public to greet Miss Lawrence and her costar, King Baggott, on her arrival in St. Louis, where the streetcar accident had supposedly happened. This first "personal appearance" resulted in a crowd of hundreds and a near-riot at the train station, but it did the job. Lawrence's popularity—under her own name this time—inspired other producers to relent, and the star system was born.

Alas, Miss Lawrence herself did not benefit from her own innovation. In 1914 she was seriously injured when a screen stunt backfired

---

*Some texts refer to this title as "The Broken Oath," which makes more sense, given the film's printed synopsis. The newspaper display ad, however, clearly shows "Bath." But it also shows *customs* rather than *customers*.

and, except for a small role in 1916, she disappeared from movies. A comeback failed in the 1920s, and in the 1930s Miss Lawrence was reduced to doing work as an extra. In 1938, depressed and impoverished, she swallowed ant paste and died (for real, this time) at age 52.

Ben Hecht's Script Scam

In 1937 prolific playwright, novelist, and screenwriter Ben Hecht (who, with Charles MacArthur, had written the classic newspaper play *The Front Page*) phoned Harry Cohn, the famously crude head of Columbia Pictures, to sell him a script idea.

"There are these three guys who all serve together in the British military," Hecht enthused. "But one of them wants to quit to go get married, and the others try to convince him to stay. When that doesn't work, they trick him into fighting a big battle, and by the end of the shooting he realizes that he prefers action to domestic life, and he re-enlists."

"That's a great story," the feisty Cohn supposedly told Hecht, "except I already own it."

"What do you mean you already own it?" said Hecht. "I just wrote it."

"You're damn right I own it!" yelled Cohn. "It's called *His Girl Friday* and you sold it to me ten years ago when it was called *The Front Page*."

"So I did, so I did," chuckled Hecht. He and Cohn swapped some pleasantries and hung up. So much for Harry Cohn being an illiterate mogul.

But that's not the end of the story.

Hecht sold his military-buddy idea to RKO Radio Pictures where it was made with Cary Grant, Victor McLaglen, and Douglas Fairbanks Jr. It became a classic called *Gunga Din.*

As for *The Front Page*, Columbia Pictures released it in 1941 as *His Girl Friday* after director Howard Hawks and screenwriter Charles Lederer performed a gender switch on the Hecht-MacArthur property about a conniving newspaper editor (Cary Grant) who tries to keep reporter Hildy Johnson (Rosalind Russell) from quitting the paper by tricking her into covering a prison escape.

Yes, Atlanta, There Is a Scarlett O'Hara

Frankly, all America gave a damn who played Rhett Butler when *Gone with the Wind* was made into a movie. It had to be Clark Gable. But the film's publicity-conscious producer, David O. Selznick, kept everyone guessing who would be Butler's screen inamorata, Scarlett O'Hara. As it developed, Selznick—more precisely, his masterful press agent Russell Birdwell—shrewdly milked the public interest for all it was worth.

From the time Margaret Mitchell's Civil War epic was published in 1936 to the date the casting of Vivien Leigh was announced in 1939, Selznick and Birdwell kept the world guessing. Hindsight, however, suggests that Selznick needed the publicity more than he needed Scarlett. Although it was a runaway bestseller, filming the story had been all uphill. Selznick was forced to pay a usurious amount of money to MGM for the services of Clark Gable (where he was under contract), a situation made even more painful because the head of MGM, Louis B. Mayer, was Selznick's father-in-law. Moreover, the producer was already paying a cadre of designers, costumers, researchers, writers, and rewriters to adapt the 1,037-page novel into a movie that could be seen in one evening. His choice to film it in the then costly Technicolor process demanded a firm start date in order to schedule the heavily booked cameras.

Everything cost money—and lots of it. As costs rose, Selznick was forced to ask the principal backer of Selznick International Pictures, John Hay "Jock" Whitney, for more and more. The only way to insure the investment seemed to be publicity.

Whether David O. Selznick found Scarlett O'Hara or Scarlett O'Hara found David O. Selznick is a Hollywood legend. Between September 28, 1936, and December 20, 1938, the studio screen-tested 30 actresses for the role and interviewed hundreds more. The front-runners were Paulette Goddard (nine days of testing), Anita Louise (five days), Doris Jordan and Margaret Tallichet (four each), Marcella Martin (three), and established female stars such as Talullah Bankhead, Frances Dee, Lana Turner, Jean Arthur, Joan Bennett, and

✓ **REALITY CHECK**

Oh Dear, Mr. Gable

For decades it has been taken as truth that when Clark Gable removed his shirt in *It Happened One Night* in 1934 and was seen to be bare-chested, undershirt sales dropped 50 percent. Certainly the movies have a powerful influence on fashion and styles (witness *Annie Hall* and *Bonnie and Clyde*), but there is just no way to track whether the undershirt trade was hurt by Gable's pecs or by the Great Depression, both of which were in full bloom at the time. Still, it made Gable look popular at a time when his MGM contract was up for renewal.

Edith Marrener (who later changed her name to Susan Hayward). Even Mrs. J. H. Whitney tried out, to no avail.

While Hollywood screen tests were being made, Selznick and Birdwell fed the nationwide frenzy. Selznick office secretary Lydia Schiller even kept a file of "Scarlett letters," what she called the hundreds of unsolicited suggestions from the public (one even mentioned Vivien Leigh). Among those mentioned most frequently were Margaret Sullavan, Katharine Hepburn, Bette Davis, and Miriam Hopkins.

Selznick's two problems were money and indecision. By December 1938, faced with mounting debts and closing deadlines, Selznick had no choice but to start filming *sans* Scarlett. His first logistical task was to clear the Culver City back lot of its old outdoor sets, which included the huge jungle fortress gate for *King Kong*. Since Atlanta had to burn anyway, the decision was made to shoot that harrowing sequence first. On the night of Saturday, December 10, stunt coordinator Yakima Canutt stood in for Gable, driving the buckboard that carried Scarlett, Prissy, Melanie, and her newborn baby (the latter three unseen on the floor of the wagon) through the flaming ruins. The male stunt performer playing "Scarlett" hid "her" face from the camera.

All of Hollywood—as well as several fire departments—showed up to watch the conflagration. In the crowd was David Selznick's brother, Myron, who was an agent. With him was a young British actress visiting America in the company of her fiance, actor Laurence Olivier. As the flames rose and the red light shone upon the face of Vivien Leigh, Myron introduced her to David, saying, "Here's your Scarlett." David said later, "I took one look and knew she was right . . . I'll never recover from that first look" (from *David O. Selznick's Hollywood* by Ronald Naiver).

Leigh screen-tested on December 21 and 22, 1938. She was the last actress to be considered. In the end, the "Scarlett O'Hara war" was won by a combatant with an inside track.

Hollywood's Only Honest Phony

America doesn't have royalty, it has Hollywood. When politicians want to grab headlines, they don't have to stand on a soapbox in London's Hyde Park and denounce Buckingham Palace, they go on Larry King and blast the movies.

Hollywood, on the other hand, loves royalty, especially the real thing. When Gloria Swanson married Marquis Henri de la Falaise de la Coudraye in 1925, she triumphantly returned from France as a "*marquess*." In 1948 Rita Hayworth met and married Aly Khan, a real prince; the only problem was that he wasn't single at the time, and there was a slight scandal until May 1949 when his divorce came through.

Swanson and Hayworth kept their careers, endearing them to audiences and the film community. When Grace Kelly married Prince Rainier of Monaco in 1956, however, she forsook Sunset Boulevard for Cote d'Azur. A characteristically unimpressed *Variety* ran the wedding announcement as if it were any other: "Bride's the actress, groom is a non-pro."

But the royalty Hollywood truly adores is the fake kind, especially when he was named (by himself, no less) "His Imperial Highness Prince Michael Alexandrovitch Dmitri Romanoff."

Mike Romanoff—actually born Harry Gerguson, some say in Brooklyn, possibly even Hungary, but who's counting—did just what everybody else did when he came to Hollywood: he reinvented himself. Burying a past that included bouncing checks, riding rails, and strong-arm loan collecting, Romanoff became a fake prince but a real restaurateur when he opened Romanoff's on Rodeo Drive in Beverly Hills in the late 1930s. It was not an elegant bistro, but it featured seven booths in the bar. As the place caught on, the assignment of those seats came to mean as much to status-conscious Hollywood as screen billing. Only Humphrey Bogart, who became Romanoff's close friend, was accorded a regular booth. Of course, it was Booth #1. When Romanoff's moved down Rodeo Drive in 1951, it was redesigned so that every seat was in a booth, and there were 24 booths.

✍ INTERVIEW

The Death of Superman

When George Reeves, the actor best known for playing the title role in *Superman*, committed suicide in 1959, the headlines screamed "Superman Kills Self." That would not be the final insult to the 45-year-old performer who, on TV, may have been the Man of Steel, but, in real life, had feet of clay. Almost immediately, the circumstances surrounding his death, augmented by family meddling and police bungling, gave birth to a morbid "Who murdered Superman?" cult that has not diminished in nearly half a century.

Gary H. Grossman, whose 1976 book *Superman from Serial to Cereal* is available on *www.supermanbook.com* and *www.georgereevesbook.com*, has had 25 years to put the mystery into cultural perspective. Now a highly successful television producer, Grossman feels that it has to do with the public's craving for heroes.

Grossman: We grew up in a time, in the fifies, when there were heroes. Clayton Moore was the Lone Ranger, we had Roy Rogers, we had Sky King, Gene Autry, and George Reeves as Superman. It hurt George as a serious actor, but he was also beloved. We were people, growing up, who had three channels, not two hundred channels. We could write our heroes and get a letter or picture back. We could go to a personal appearance in Boston or Albany or New York City or UCLA and twenty-five thousand or fifty thousand kids and parents would come in and see those folks. So when someone who plays a hero dies, you have a connection; when someone who plays an invincible hero dies, that's suddenly a different emotional reaction, and then when the headline screams "Superman Kills Self" you have an even different [and greater] emotional reaction. And I think,

for me in 1959, it was a seminal moment. It was the first contact I ever had with somebody dying, it was the first contact I had with a celebrity dying, and it was the first contact I had with a suicide. Or, an apparent suicide. To this day, it is still an astounding mystery.

Segaloff: The party guests heard two shots, but the police found five bullet holes.

Grossman: Lenore Lemmon claimed that he had been showing her the gun at some point earlier, and that the gun had gone off.

Segaloff: Was it one bullet to the head or two?

Grossman: I've heard different things. As I understand it, it is very difficult to shoot yourself twice in the head. The autopsy reports that there was one bullet in his head.

Segaloff: How do we explain the spent bullet shell under his body?

Grossman: That can't be explained if you're just shooting yourself. It can be explained if there's someone else in the room.

Segaloff: We have Marilyn Monroe, James Dean, JFK, and other cultural heroes who society cannot accept are dead. Why do we want to keep people alive when we know they're dead?

Grossman: People may not believe that George is alive, but people may want to have a sense of completion about his death. But let's just say that irrefutable evidence came out about his death. I think it would still be debated; people would still hold onto the myth of what they wanted to believe, sparked by people who keep those kind of things alive because it always makes good copy. Resolved endings don't make a good story.

Segaloff: There's an industry that has been built up around these dead people?

Grossman: Yes. Mysterious deaths sell.

"In order for a restaurant to be intimate, it has to be smaller," Romanoff told journalist Ezra Goodman. "Unless it is intimate, certain tables are undesirable. There is no use having tables people don't want to sit at. The arrangement in the old restaurant created a good deal of ill will. Now everyone is satisfied."

And Prince Michael made sure of it. Short, with gray, close-cropped hair, a bulbous nose, and a protruding lower lip, he would strut around his domain wielding a riding crop while deigning to visit select diners. Yet despite this veneer of nobility, the "little prince" could occasionally lose his aplomb. Producer Samuel Goldwyn repeatedly banned Romanoff for unsportsmanlike conduct at the croquet games that Goldwyn held on his perfectly groomed lawn. A diminutive scrapper, Romanoff could defuse and dispatch contretemps that took place in his restaurant. But nobody pushed Romanoff's buttons better than his pal Bogart, who knew that the restaurateur's pet hatred was writer-director Preston Sturges. According to Peter Lorre, one night Bogart and actor Robert Coote, who was staying at Romanoff's house, purposely got Sturges stinking drunk and deposited him in Romanoff's living room.

Screenwriter Herman Mankiewicz (*Citizen Kane*) once playfully threatened to ruin Romanoff by exposing him as a real prince trying to pass himself off as an impostor. But Mank knew it wouldn't matter in a place like Tinseltown where everybody used to be someone else. To this day, no one has an accurate record of Romanoff/Gurgeson's true past, which may have included up to 15 aliases. More significantly, people loved him too much to ask.

Fronts

When the Blacklist struck the film and television industry in the 1950s, it not only made a blot on freedom, it drove hundreds of talented men and women underground. Many were forced to change careers. More struggled along without ever realizing their potential. Some "cleared" themselves by turning against their friends and colleagues. But a few writers survived by turning the hypocrisy of the blacklist against itself. They used "fronts."

Reeves's Death

On the night of June 19, 1959, there was a party in the Benedict Canyon home of George Reeves. Reeves had just ended a 10-year affair with Toni Mannix, the estranged (but still married) wife of Eddie Mannix, vice president of Metro-Goldwyn-Mayer. Now engaged to marry Lenore Lemmon, Reeves had been forced to take out a restraining order against Toni, who had been pestering him with phone calls. Reeves, who was no stranger to drink, may also have been taking prescription painkillers as the result of injuries sustained in a minor traffic accident a week earlier. Lemmon was downstairs with friends but George, who was not in a partying mood, went upstairs to bed, to which Lemmon responded, "He's pissed off, and he's going to take a gun out of his dresser and shoot himself." Moments later there were two shots. Reeves's body was discovered on the bed, shot through the head. Then the mystery began:

1. There were five bullet holes in the bedroom wall, but only two shots.
2. Reeves was found on his back on the bed, his body covering the spent shell. How did it get there? Was it the shell from the bullet that killed him, or was it there from an earlier firing?
3. What possessed Lemmon to predict George's suicide? Or was it part of a cover story?
4. Why was Lemmon allowed to leave town and never questioned by police?
5. Why were people allowed to enter the roped-off murder scene to wash the bedsheets and retrieve liquor and other objects from the house?
6. Why was Reeves's body embalmed before a proper autopsy could be performed?
7. Why would Reeves kill himself when he had just landed a job in a "comeback" project?

A "front" was a real person who would allow his or her name to be attached to a script written by a blacklisted writer. It was important to ensure that when a producer demanded a meeting, an actual human being could show up. As long as the blacklisted writer paid taxes on the income, nobody cared. (The 1976 film *The Front*, starring Woody Allen and Zero Mostel, dramatizes the process. It was written by Walter Bernstein and directed by Martin Ritt, both of whom had, like Mostel, been blacklisted.)

For fifty years the existence of fronts was one of the biggest frauds in Hollywood. Most producers knew full well what was going on but feigned ignorance. After all, a blacklisted writer working through a front could be hired for a fraction of his or her former salary and, for once, couldn't complain when the script was butchered. Pre-blacklist writers who earned $2,500 a week learned to settle for $2,500 for an entire script, especially if they had a family to raise. The duplicity was suffocating and pervasive.

Some producers, like the notoriously cheap King brothers, paid rock-bottom prices for top-notch writers such as Dalton Trumbo who wrote the story for their 1956 film, *The Brave One*, under the name "Robert Rich." More prestigious producers such as Stanley Kramer (*Inherit the Wind, The Defiant Ones*) and Sam Spiegel had no qualms hiring blacklisted writers, albeit secretly. Spiegel paid Michael Wilson to write *Lawrence of Arabia*, which carried Robert Bolt's sole credit until it was revised by the Writers Guild of America in 1996. Spiegel also hired Wilson and writer Carl Foreman to script *The Bridge on the River Kwai* but allowed the credit and the Oscar to go to Pierre Boulle, who had written the novel. The fact that the French Boulle spoke no English didn't raise any eyebrows at the time. Dalton Trumbo and Ian McLellan Hunter worked on *Roman Holiday*, among other films, without credit; and when "Robert Rich" won an Oscar for *The Brave One*, it went unclaimed for 18 years.

Politically progressive producer Hannah Weinstein, working in England, hired blacklisted Ring Lardner, Jr. and Ian McLellan Hunter to write her TV series *The Adventures of Robin Hood* from 1955 to 1958, but their names weren't allowed on screen by the American TV industry. In New York, producer Charles W. Russell was similarly brave in hiring Abraham Polonsky, Walter Bernstein and Arnold

Manoff right under the nose—er, eye—of CBS to script their TV series *Danger* (1950–1954) and *You Are There* (1953–1955). Most of the episodes concerned people at a crisis of conscience, which was exactly the sort of humanitarian concern that got the writers blacklisted in the first place. Polonsky, Bernstein, and Manoff used front names, but Russell dealt with them directly, while keeping CBS in the dark.

In 1968, blacklisted writer/producer Paul Jarrico (*Salt of the Earth*) made it his life's work to help the Writers Guild of America (WGA) restore credit to blacklisted writers whose names were not allowed on screen. The WGA's ongoing announcements include the following (see *www.wga.org*):

Born Free—Screenplay by Lester Cole
Inherit the Wind—Screenplay by Nedrick Young and Harold Jacob Smith
Day of the Triffids—Screenplay by Bernard Gordon
The Robe—Screenplay by Albert Maltz and Philip Dunne, adaptation by Gina Kaus
The Young One—Written for the screen by Hugo Butler and Luis Buñuel
El Cid—Screenplay by Philip Yordan, Frederic M. Frank, and Ben Barzman, story by Frederic M. Frank
Cry, The Beloved Country—Screenplay by Alan Paton and John Howard Lawson
Friendly Persuasion—Screenplay by Michael Wilson
Odds Against Tomorrow—Screenplay by Abraham Polonsky and Nelson Gidding
Hellcats of the Navy—Screenplay by David Lang and Bernard Gordon, screen story by David Lang (This film is of interest because it was where actress Nancy Davis met her future husband, actor and blacklist supporter Ronald Reagan.)

Tragically, the 82-year-old Paul Jarrico was killed in a car accident on October 29, 1997, two days after taking part in an industry-wide apologia called "Hollywood Remembers the Blacklist." Among his last requests had been that his own screen credits, which included TV's *Sgt. Bilko* and *The Defenders*, be ignored until other writers had had theirs fully restored.

✓ REALITY CHECK

Million Dollar Hunt

When producer Dino DeLaurentiis made the feature movie *Million Dollar Mystery* in 1987, he promoted it with a $1 million prize that would be given away to the lucky ticket buyer who solved a mystery within the film. To ensure that the excitement carried over when the picture was released in home video, he announced a second $1 million prize for the home viewing audience. Unfortunately, not only did the film bomb at the box office, but the fabled producer's releasing company—DeLaurentiis Entertainment Group—likewise went bust. There is no record that either prize was ever awarded, or, for that matter, that anybody ever asked for them.

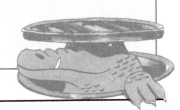

Political fronting of screenplays has disappeared, although a variation has surfaced as a few over-50 screenwriters supposedly hire younger people to pretend that they've written their script. In this way, the senior scribes hope to outwit Hollywood's "graylist." One 55-year-old writer recalled bringing his 28-year-old nephew with him to a studio "pitch" meeting, during which the 30-year-old production executive addressed his entire conversation to the nephew. The nephew was a dentist.

William Castle

He was half charlatan, half businessman, and all showman. He was producer William Castle.

Although he tried repeatedly to establish his name in the marketplace as forcefully as Alfred Hitchcock, Frank Capra, Cecil B. DeMille or, since then, George Lucas or Steven Spielberg, it was Castle's fate to reside in the bargain basement of the film pantheon. Even Roger Corman, whose filmography reads like the cult movie section at Blockbuster, managed to squeeze out a classic now and then. But Castle will forever be known for crass, crudely made, horror/exploitation schlock that was sold with promotional gimmicks, not production gloss:

- *Macabre* (1958). Gimmick: Each patron's life was insured by Lloyds of London in case they died of shock watching the movie (heart disease victims excepted).
- *The Tingler* (1959). Gimmick: "Percepto"—Select theater seats were wired (some say with electricity, some say with vibrators) that went off and made people scream at the right moment.
- *House on Haunted Hill* (1959). Gimmick: "Emergo"—A skeleton sailed out over the heads of the audience (yanked by some hapless usher at the right moment).
- *13 Ghosts* (1960). Gimmick: "Illusion-o"—Patrons received red and blue cellophane "viewers" with which they could either see, or not see, the film's special effect ghosts.

- *Homicidal* (1961). Gimmick: Just before the terrifying end of the movie there was a "Fright Break" where scairdy-cats could get a refund if they ran up a "yellow streak" and hid in the "Coward's Corner" of the theater.
- *Mr. Sardonicus* (1961). Gimmick: "Punishment Poll"— Audiences got to vote "thumbs up" or "thumbs down" on whether the villain got what he deserved (guess which always won).

Castle sometimes used respectable actors such as Barbara Stanwyck and Robert Taylor (*The Night Walker*), Joan Crawford (*Straight-Jacket*), Oscar Homolka (*Mr. Sardonicus*), and Vincent Price (*House on Haunted Hill*) and capped his career by producing (but not directing) the classic *Rosemary's Baby*. His star glows brightest, however, for audiences who fondly remember the way he gleefully picked their pockets on Saturday matinees.

None of this is meant as criticism. Castle personified the gusto, cheek, and creativity that made movies popular in the first place. Indeed, modern Hollywood now calls what he perfected "high concept"—in other words, hype.

And hype is what fueled New York–born Castle. Born in 1914, he won his first show business job at age 15 by claiming that he was related to studio mogul Samuel Goldwyn. He survived in Depression-era Hollywood by doing a number of studio jobs. By the late 1930s, he was directing low-budget Westerns. In the mid-1950s, he was smart enough to latch onto the emerging youth market. The rest of Hollywood took only 25 years to catch up.

"William Castle was my idol," says John Waters in his book *Crackpot*, who was inspired by Castle's marketing savvy to make such films as *Polyester* (Gimmick: Odorama scratch 'n' sniff cards) and *Pink Flamingos*. "What's the matter, Hollywood?" Waters challenges nostalgically. "People are getting bored with the theater going

✓ **REALITY CHECK**

Crawford's Christmas Film

In the late 1940s, Joan Crawford filmed a special Christmas announcement that was shown in movie theaters to encourage charity donations. The short begins as Ms. Crawford is standing at the top of a grand staircase saying good night to her children in their bedroom off-screen. One of them responds, "Good night, Mommie Dearest."

experience! Can't you come up with something? William Castle, where are you when we really need you?"

Castle was loved by audiences, hated by critics, and ignored by Hollywood. His films are hard to find nowadays, not only because their rights are sometimes as murky as their photography, but because they were a group experience and this is a home video age. What teenager is gonna rent *House on Haunted Hill* and pay his kid brother to run across the living room dressed as a skeleton? Maybe this is why 1999's fancy remake of that picture died at the box office; it was (shudder) respectable!

Castle, who admitted that he modeled his career on that of P. T. Barnum, was also quite the ham. He established his ebullient, cigar-smoking persona by hosting his own previews of coming attractions. In 1975, he even acted in *Shampoo* (for Hal Ashby) and *Day of the Locust* (for John Schlesinger). Castle died of a heart attack in 1977 while producing *200 Lakeview Drive*.

In 1993 director Joe Dante and screenwriter Charlie Haas painted a loving portrait of a William Castle-esque movie promoter in their film *Matinee*. Played by John Goodman, the promoter travels the country touting his cheapie horror film, *Mant*, with the ad line, "Half Man, Half Ant, All Terror!" It's just the sort of thing the real William Castle would have done if only he'd had twice the budget and half the gall.

Master of Ballyhoo

In 1920, a retired Levenworth, Washington, lumber salesman named Thomas R. Zann checked into a first-floor suite at the fancy Belleclaire Hotel at 77th and Broadway in New York City. A short while later, workers hoisted a large packing crate into his room from the street. Hotel management was told the crate contained a piano. Afterward, Mr. Zann phoned room service and calmly ordered a 15-pound steak. *Raw.*

It turned out that the crate belonging to Thomas R. Zann, who signed his name "T. R. Zann," contained a full-grown lion named

Jim. Within moments, newspaper reporters were alerted to the presence of the duo, and the ink started flowing:

Pet Lion Agitates Hotel*

Order for a 15-pound steak reveals his presence and excitement begins!

Jim, a full-grown bushy-haired lion of the breed that is often seen stalking majestically across the movie screen in jungle scenes caused more emotion and excitement yesterday in the Hotel Belleclaire, 77th Street and Broadway, where he is sharing a suite of rooms on the first floor with his owner, than that hostelry ever dreamed of experiencing. Jim is the pet of Thomas R. Zann, a retired lumber merchant of Levenworth, Washington, and both are on their way to Africa.

Zann and Jim checked out of the hotel soon afterward, followed by even more press coverage:

Beef-eating Lion Leaves Hotel

T. R. Zann and Jim, his pet lion, left the Hotel Belleclaire yesterday with moving picture cameras to record their going. Neither the man, represented to be a retired Washington lumber dealer, nor the lion, left a forwarding address beyond a hint that a kindly old man in Yonkers had offered the best asylum. However, those interested in the traveling fortunes are hopeful that Jim, at last, might reappear somewhere on the movie screen.

Of course, that was the whole point. Thomas R. Zann ("Tarzan") was the invention of Harry Reichenbach, one of Hollywood's first and still greatest press agents. He staged the

---

*Both extracts from *A Million and One Nights* by Terry Ramsaye. New York: Simon & Schuster, 1926, 1954.

✓ REALITY CHECK

Et Tu, Julius?

Twentieth Century Fox was almost put out of business when their 1965 epic, *Cleopatra*, ran so far over schedule that the studio had to sell off its back lot to pay the bills (the back lot, incidentally, became Century City in Los Angeles). Nevertheless, public interest in the film had been kept at a fever pitch because of the well-publicized romance between its two stars, Elizabeth Taylor and Richard Burton, each of whom was married to someone else at the time. The studio capitalized on this by erecting a billboard in Times Square featuring the glamorous Taylor reclining and Burton cooing into her ear. Only later did the lawyers realize that the film's other star, Rex Harrison, had to be included on the billboard. So Harrison's face was painted within a smaller square, giving the impression that he was peeping in a window at Taylor and Burton making out.

publicity stunt for the Samuel Goldwyn movie *The Return of Tarzan*, which starred Karla Schramm and Gene Pollar, making sure that the opening newspaper ads exploited every last bit of the brouhaha he had inspired:

Notice!
Mr. T. R. Zann
That daring adventurer who took his pet lion to the
Belleclaire Hotel
will appear personally next Sunday
in conjunction with the new film startler
The Return of Tarzan
at R. S. Moss's Broadway

On another occasion, Reichenbach, who helped Rudolph Valentino get his first job in 1919 opposite Clara Kimball Young in *Eyes of Youth*, was called on to rescue the Latin Lover's slipping career after his marriage to the domineering Natacha Rambova in 1923 sent it askew. Mindful that Valentino's masculinity was in question, Reichenbach had him grow a beard. Then he got a barber's association to threaten publicly to boycott Valentino's films unless he shaved off the offending hirsuteness, which he did, as newspapers and newsreels witnessed every stroke. Nevertheless, it wasn't until Valentino made *Son of the Sheik* in 1926 that his fame was completely restored. Unfortunately, it was because he died.

Was Reichenbach supremely gifted, or was it just all so new—and the press so naive—that he couldn't fail? Probably a little of both. He started his career early in the century with medicine shows, then he was hired by Sam Goldwyn, then by the Jesse L. Lasky Featured Players Company (arguably the first Hollywood studio) to thump their tub, and went on from there. It was Reichenbach's gift for knowing what would interest the press, and thereby the public, that made him so effective. He was also a master at working both sides of the street. According to historian Terry Ramsaye in *A Million and One*

Nights, Reichenbach was once hired to publicize the exhibition of a Paul Chabas painting called *September Morn*, which featured a partly clothed woman. He hired a gang of kids to razz the painting, called the police to razz the kids, and let the newspapers do the rest.

The thing about publicity, say old-timers who know how to generate it, is that nobody gets hurt and everybody wins. As entertainment has developed into a multibillion dollar industry, however, film companies have found it more efficient (albeit less creative) to spend tens of millions of dollars on television commercials to "buy a gross." And journalists now cover movies as what they are—hype—rather than as news events, although studio publicity departments valiantly try to blur the line.

Maybe it's more honest, but it sure is less colorful.

Elvis—the Man, the Myth, the Ghost

Presley, Elvis Aaron. Born: Tupelo, Mississippi, January 8, 1935. Died: Memphis, Tennessee, August 16, 1977. Are you sure? Really, really sure? Okay, then:

- Why did the Memphis medical examiner say his body was found in the bathroom in a state of rigor mortis, but the police homicide report said he was found in the bedroom merely "unconscious"?
- Why hasn't anyone claimed his life insurance policy?
- How could he be photographed in the pool house behind Graceland's Meditation Garden in December 1977?
- What about all the Elvis sightings?
- Were his last words really, "Honey, I'm going to the bathroom"?

Without rehashing the details of Elvis's death at the age of 42 from a heart attack brought on by drug intake, it is safe to say that if the King were certifiably alive, he could not be any more popular. His mansion, Graceland, continues to be visited by 500,000 people a year. His estate, valued at $4 million when he died, is worth 25 times that now. His licensed image can be found on T-shirts, ashtrays, cups, plates, and other items ranging from truly bad taste (a bourbon decanter) to the kind of patriotic approbation he always sought while he was alive (the 1987 29¢ U.S. postage stamp). The famous 1970 picture of the open-shirted Elvis shaking hands with President Richard Nixon in the Oval Office remains the National Archives's most requested photograph.

In her exhaustive 1990 exploration of the phenomenon, *The Elvis Files*, writer Gail Brewer-Giorgio suggests that the myth of Elvis's non-death has become its own "regenerating" entity.

There is much truth to this contention as theorists, in the book and elsewhere, claim to be able to prove that he is alive by the use of numerology, cross-referencing with biblical indices (Jesus' age versus Elvis's), and sightings by "credible" sources.

The most cynical reason is the most logical: Elvis would be of retirement age today, and—like Jim Morrison, James Dean, Charlie Parker, and others whose fame depends upon their youthful sex appeal—if Elvis were old, he wouldn't be worth the price of a Moon Pie and a Coke.

Yet Elvis Presley continues to sell records and influence singing styles. An entire subindustry of Elvis impersonators exists, which is bifurcated into "young Elvis" and "fat Elvis." The advantage is that when young Elvis impersonators grow up and put on a couple of pounds, they can still find work as fat Elvises. Elvis impersonation contests have their own self-contained appeal, like *Star Trek* conventions, with the entertainment value of the competition itself overshadowing whoever wins. Then there's the Las Vegas preacher who dresses like Elvis and performs marriages, and an even more obscure fetish culture in which both women and straight men find themselves sexually

✓ REALITY CHECK

One Last Elvis Note

When the U.S. Postal Service sought to issue its 29¢ Elvis Presley stamp, there was a minor controversy over which Elvis should be pictured—the sleek, sexy, 1950s Elvis; or the paunchy, troubled, yellowed, 1970s Elvis. The USPS finally went with the former, but still drew criticism from the people who argued that since Elvis is still alive, how can he be on a stamp?

attracted to the young Elvis with his swiveling hips, tight pants, and sensuous mouth.

The "Elvis lives" myth transcends those surrounding Dean, Monroe, Morrison, and even JFK (who, some insist, remains in a secret hospital connected to tubes). Several explanations exist, each feeding on a different human foible:

1. The power of Elvis's persona and the liberating effect he had on the lives of the baby boomers have created the need to keep him alive. If Elvis is dead, so is the defining icon of an entire generation.
2. The ease with which just about anybody can look like Elvis suggests that his popularity may be due to his representing something in each of us, and now it's working in the other direction.
3. A small group of devoted tricksters might very well be behind the Elvis sightings, much like the "crop circles" hoax or the mysterious "lady in black" who, for years, left flowers at Rudolph Valentino's tomb.
4. Elvis might, indeed, have faked his own death in an effort to escape the crushing scrutiny of fame.
5. His mentor/manager Colonel Parker, against whom Elvis was supposedly starting to rebel, might have opportunistically drawn mists around Elvis's death in order to exploit the value of his estate.
6. Elvis's involvement with Richard Nixon raises questions about a government conspiracy (inconceivable as it sounds, Elvis, a drug addict, applied for, and was granted, clearance as an undercover narcotics agent by the U.S. Drug Enforcement Agency).

But the most believable reason for the "Elvis Lives" myth has nothing to do with "facts," real or contrived. He simply was the greatest entertainer of his generation, and it's no wonder that his generation craves the reassurance of his company, even if it has to come from beyond the grave.

✓ **REALITY CHECK**

Rain Man

Film companies are scrupulous about extracting every dime possible from a film, and one of the most durable submarkets has been presenting them in airplanes. The only problem is that the airlines shy away from pictures that are too long, too racy, or too depressing. They also won't show anything that has to do with plane crashes. That's why, when they presented the 1988 Oscar-winning *Rain Man*, the airlines trimmed the scene in which Dustin Hoffman refuses to board a plane with his brother, Tom Cruise, unless they fly Qantas, which has the best safety record. Needless to say, the only airline company that left *Rain Man* intact when they showed it at 35,000 feet was Qantas.

Nyet Profits

They say that in Hollywood even the books have books. How else can a picture such as *Batman* (1989) cost $50 million, gross $1 billion, and still be $16 million in the hole as of 1995. Maybe that's why the studio had to make three—or is it four—sequels to retire the debt.

The answer is called "Hollywood bookkeeping," that rarified, Byzantine art that's more creative than any movie ever produced. From time to time, high-profile plaintiffs such as actors James Garner and George Clooney, producers Steven Bochco and Chris Carter, columnist Art Buchwald, or the estate of JFK assassination prosecutor Jim Garrison file suits demanding an accurate accounting. But in 100 years of movies, no Justice Department investigation has ever tried to untangle the Gordian knot slang-wise known as "nyet profits."

Given the tens of thousands of individual expenditures from salaries to petty cash that go into making a movie, it's expected that an occasional fake chit might be turned in. But it's bigger than that, as depositions have shown: Stars demand that their retinues be placed on salary; producers fill their homes with furniture bought on their film's budget; publicists take nonexistent reporters to lunch on the studio dime; directors lease their own land to the company for location shooting; you name it.

But the siphon that nobody talks about is the one that gushes into the pocket of the people who own movie theaters. What makes theaters so special is that they deal in cash. Movies are one of the few commodities that you pay for in advance, yet you can't get a refund if you don't like the product. By 10:00 P.M. every night, the day's box office kitty is safely locked away. Now multiply that by a week, and again by the number of screens in a multiplex, and multiply it yet again by the number of multiplexes in a theater chain's circuit. Finally, put this asterisk next to the answer: if the theater owner holds onto the money for 30, 60, or 90 days and doesn't turn it over to the film's producer, he or she amasses millions of dollars of interest-free investment capital.

"At least the exhibitors get to build nice, new theaters on the interest your money earns them," producer-director Roger Corman said, quoting his attorney. Over the years, theaters have devised several scams to separate the filmmaker from his profits. Ironically, the instinct runs so deep that even theater employees have discovered ways to cheat their theater-owner bosses. Here are five ways that *some* exhibitors *conceivably* do this (which is not to imply that anybody ever *has*):

1. **Advertising scam:** Theater owners demand to place the advertising for the films they show and submit the bills to the film's distributor for reimbursement. They may or may not share the agency commission with the distributor. They also may arrange to overpay for the advertising and submit the inflated bills for reimbursement while, in actuality, paying the lesser amount.

2. **Free passes:** Theater owners get to keep the entire service charge on their "free passes" while having to share the money they make on tickets. A typical exhibition contract calls for a 90/10 split; that is, the studio gets 90¢ on the dollar and the theater keeps 10¢. Thus, the most a theater owner can make on a $9.00 ticket is 90¢, but on a $2.00 pass they keep the whole thing. Because of this, exhibition contracts generally limit the number of passes to no more than 2 percent of any house, but it is seldom enforced.

3. **Bicycling a print:** Multiplex theaters move popular films into bigger auditoriums and bump unpopular films into smaller auditoriums. If you've ever left an auditorium to go to the lavatory and returned to find the name of another film over the door, you are already familiar with this trick. Technically, films are supposed to play in the auditorium for which they were contracted, but nobody ever complains. The term for this is

bicycling, a carry-over from the days when ushers were dispatched with individual reels of film to pedal from one theater to another across town. If the usher encountered heavy traffic, there was an intermission.

4. **Palming tickets:** If a cashier and ticket taker are in cahoots, the ticket taker may scoop torn stubs from the trash and secretly hand these back to the entering patron while palming the patron's untorn ticket to resell. The use of computer-generated tickets has greatly reduced this ruse.

5. **Re-using popcorn bags and boxes:** Theaters make their profits at the concession stand, and they don't have to share them with the filmmakers. Popcorn sales are computed by counting the containers sold. Sometimes ushers will dig through the trash after a show, retrieve uncrushed boxes, wipe them clean, and resell them. Remember that movie theaters are the only place where you buy food and eat it in the dark.

Marilyn Monroe

"There's been more written about Marilyn Monroe than about World War Two," filmmaker Billy Wilder once said, "and there are many similarities." Wilder, who directed her in *Some Like It Hot* and *The Seven Year Itch*, later added, "She was the meanest woman I have ever met around this town. I am appalled by this cult."

Yet as difficult as the great blond love goddess was for many of the people who worked with her (primarily the men), she was just as unforgettable to her friends and the public. Witness the public's thirst for anything it can learn about her since her apparent drug overdose on August 15, 1962.

And "apparent" is the fuel that keeps the Monroe saga alive. Born in 1926 in the charity ward of Los Angeles General Hospital to Gladys Baker Mortensen, "Norma Jean" was placed in the first of a succession of foster homes when she was less than a month old. Many moves, many schools, and many promises later, she married, began modeling, made her first two suicide attempts (pills, gas), and posed for her famous nude calendar by the time she was 23.

It was agent Johnny Hyde who brought her to public attention in October 1950. Hyde died two months later, but not before seeing that she was signed to Twentieth Century Fox, where she slowly developed into a star. It was said that she was the only starlet who did not have to "service" studio chief Darryl F. Zanuck during the notorious mogul's famous 4:00 P.M. liaisons. The reason? She was involved with Zanuck's silent partner, producer Joseph Schenck.

Her pictures, her marriages, her divorces, and her glamour are well known, as are her alleged dalliances, particularly with President John F. Kennedy and his brother, U.S. Attorney General Robert F. Kennedy. For years it has been rumored that the abortion she had in July 1962 was JFK's love-child. She was shooting the Fox comedy *Something's Got to Give* when it did, and she was fired for tardiness and incompetence. A month later she was dead.

Rumors, doubts, and questions circulated even before her body was in the ground of the Westwood Memorial Cemetery near UCLA. Why did she overdose on the Penergan and Nembutal she had been prescribed two days earlier? Did she try to make a phone call to actor Peter Lawford the night she died? Was she asking him to try to reach his brother-in-law Robert F. Kennedy on her behalf? Why were objects disturbed in her Brentwood house?

The circumstances of her burial were as noteworthy as her death. Despite her worldwide renown, Monroe's body lay unclaimed for days in the morgue until her former husband, Joe DiMaggio, arranged for its removal to a crypt. He sat beside her coffin all night before the funeral, and then decreed that it be closed for the services, from which he barred all but 20 people. Some years later an attempt was made to break into Monroe's crypt, but it was stymied by 2 feet of solid concrete that sealed her to the ages. From the date of her death until 1982, DiMaggio continued sending six red roses three times a week to her final resting place. DiMaggio died in 1999.

✓ **REALITY CHECK**

Dish Night

Even though the rest of the world was being caught in the Great Depression, the movies didn't feel the financial crunch right away. The public needed an escape, and they kept buying tickets. Eventually, though, the economy caught up with Hollywood. To lure customers back, theater owners instituted "dish night." Each week a different plate, cup, or saucer was given away with each ticket bought. If you and your family went to the movies enough times, pretty soon you'd have a place setting. When audiences had gathered enough place settings, theater owners started offering towels and washcloths, then raffles. Finally they hit on the idea of just making better movies.

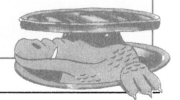

By dying at age 36, Marilyn Monroe never grew old. As to why her short but turbulent life has inspired so many books and such a fanatic following, just look at the nature of the star system itself, and the way it uses up people.

And then there's the political side: Could this breathy voiced nymph who seduced a president, and who ran with people who ran with mobsters, have been more than she seemed to be? Was she the airhead she portrayed, or the genius her friends swore she was? Did the White House have her killed? Did the Syndicate? If she was so valuable a star property, why didn't the studio have her hospitalized?

"A sex symbol becomes a thing," Monroe once said. "I just hate being a thing." Through a confluence of questions, mistakes, triumphs, and tragedies, she became more than a thing. She became a legend.

The Films That Ate Hollywood

You've got to love any movie that's called *I Spit on Your Grave*, or *Ilsa: She-Wolf of the SS*, or *I Dismember Mama*. These and a thousand others that sound just as tacky form the legacy of "exploitation" pictures that nurtured a whole generation of moviegoers. The era that sired these fringe dwellers has vanished, co-opted by the studios and cable TV, but the memories they conjure, and the dollars they made shaking down audiences, are part of Hollywood's colorful past. Unlike today's glossy studio fare, none of them was ever meant to be taken seriously; they were just an excuse for 500 screaming kids to get out of the house on a Saturday afternoon, or for 500 cars to park at a drive-in so that the 1,000 people in them could neck.

Exploitation films do not aspire to art; they exist solely to separate audiences from their money. At least they don't deplete the ozone layer. Here are some of the most notorious that have ever tickled the public's fancy:

1. *I Drink Your Blood* and *I Eat Your Skin*. This 1970 double feature from producer Jerry Gross (no kidding)

was billed as "two of the most horrifying Horror Shows ever presented." The first was about a kid who feeds hippies rabies-infected meat pies; the second (actually made in 1964) had something to do with zombies.

2. *2000 Maniacs.* A car caravan of northern vacationers is sidetracked into a southern town where ghosts of the Civil War dead slaughter them in ways that would make Andersonville look like Club Med. Famed sleazemeister Herschell Gordon Lewis had $80,000 to make this 1964 gorefest, which film historian Richard Meyers has called "Bloody Brigadoon." Although made before the movie rating system, this was self-labeled "Inadvisable for Children Under 16," which, of course, meant that every kid under 16 lined up to try to get past the cashier!

3. *Ilsa, She-Wolf of the SS.* Producer Herman Traeger and director Don Edmonds thoughtfully dedicated this 1974 romp "with the hope that these heinous crimes will never occur again." And what "heinous crimes" were they referring to? Well, in just 95 minutes, *Ilsa* told the story of a medical camp warden, played by Dyanne Thorne, who conducts pain experiments on female prisoners by day, and sex experiments on male prisoners by night.

4. *Faster Pussycat, Kill, Kill.* Russ Meyer, king of the nudies, created this truly subversive romp in 1966. Ostensibly an outdoor action picture in which a series of male thugs try to ravage a trio of cantilevered women, it turns into a prefeminist revenge movie in which the women vanquish the men in ways that defy physics (not to mention dramatic logic). Meyer is a curious case. He has been vilified by feminists for portraying women as sex objects, yet he empowers his female characters in ways that still make mainstream Hollywood uncomfortable. The fact that the sex is simulated, and that Meyer's snazzy editing was 20 years ahead of MTV, makes this a film that manages to exploit even itself.

5. *Ms. 45.* Home video has done for this 1981 quickie what no rumor campaign ever achieved: it has made it a film

classic, and given its director, Abel Ferrara, a reputable career (*Bad Lieutenant*, *Miami Vice*, and the 1993 re-remake *Body Snatchers*). Zoe Tamerlis stars as a rape victim who gets a gun and shoots any man who propositions her. Written by Nicholas St. John for Navaron Films, *Ms. 45* surprised audiences with its production polish, not to mention its message.

6. *Foxy Brown.* Does this sound like Quentin Tarantino's 1998 homage, *Jackie Brown*? It ought to; both starred Pam Grier as one tough lady, only this 1974 original—written and directed by Jack Hill—got there first. Foxy is a hooker who goes after bad white guys. Coming amid the blaxploitation films of the early 1970s, *Foxy Brown* struck a cord with audiences who appreciated an action hero who was black, female, and justified.

7. *Last House on the Left.* Remember when Lucy met Desi? When Laurel met Hardy? When Abbott met Costello? Similar film history was made in 1970 when producer Sean S. Cunningham met writer-director Wes Craven while making a documentary called *Together*. When that soft-core cheapie took in millions, the releasing company, Hallmark, re-paired Cunningham and Craven to make *Last House on the Left.* Released in 1972, the slasher movie was sold with the tag line "To avoid fainting keep repeating 'It's Only a Movie . . . Only a Movie . . . Only a Movie'." They also affixed a warning that said, "Not recommended for persons over 30!" Since then, Cunningham has begat a money-minting series called *Friday the 13th*, and Craven has become the screen's most respected interpreter of dreams with his *Nightmare on Elm Street* franchise. As for Hallmark Releasing, keep reading . . .

8. *Mark of the Devil.* It's loud, it's bloody, and it's sickening, but that's not what made this 1972 torture-fest (with Udo Kier, Herbert Lom, and cult actor Reggie Nalder) successful. It's the fact that Hallmark Releasing gave away a free vomit bag with every admission. The gimmick was both perverse and memorable, but here's

the kicker: original barf bags have been known to sell for $100 at collectors' shows!

9. *Night of the Living Dead* and *Texas Chainsaw Massacre*. It's a tossup which film is more famous, or did more to establish the trend of Midnight Screenings. Whether George A. Romero's 1968 zombie epic is gorier or more chilling than Tobe Hooper's 1974 horror fest is something for academics to debate. Suffice it to say that both films succeed because of their delicious aura of "forbidden fruit," which revved up audiences before the screenings even began. Like people waiting in line to see *The Exorcist* (in 1973) who got sick out of sheer anticipation, *Living Dead* and *Chainsaw* stand as the epitome of the exploitation film in which the group experience over- shadows the film itself.

10. *Snuff*. Whether this 1976 "event" was what everybody said it was, or was just a huge hoax, is something that hardly matters any more. The rumor started by entre- preneur Alan Shackleton was that *Snuff* was made in Argentina "where life is cheap." The imported film was a nominal murder mystery about a Charles Manson–like crime. The U.S. distributor filmed extra footage, how- ever, in which an actress, cast to resemble an actress in the South American original, was shown cleaning up the set while being secretly filmed. Suddenly people crash in on her! The girl is grabbed! Knives are pro- duced! They tear her apart! Blood flows everywhere! Or does it? Educated by two decades of anatomically real- istic gore effects, modern audiences would have no trouble seeing that *Snuff* was a fake. But in 1976 it was cutting edge, so to speak. It was also brilliantly exploited by Shackleton, who hired people to picket the film, then hired more people to play law enforcement authorities who hassled the pickets!

In a tragic example of life imitating schlock, in 1991 the Edgar award–winning mystery writer Gregory Mcdonald (*Fletch*) wrote a

---

✓ **REALITY CHECK**

Casino Royale Riot

For the 1967 James Bond comedy *Casino Royale*, Columbia Pictures' New England PR representative John Markle collaborated with the Boston exhibitor, Sack Theatres, to hold a midnight showing and admit anyone who showed up dressed as a spy. Who would show up for a midnight screening? they wondered. What they hadn't considered was that the stunt was held in late May, which was the pre-exam reading period for the 100,000 Boston area college students—10,000 of whom showed up at the 2,800-seat Savoy Theatre expecting to be admitted. When 7,200 weren't, the Boston Police were called in to disperse the crowd, and the event made headlines from Tokyo to Times Square.

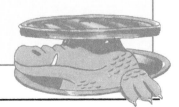

novel titled *The Brave* in which a Native American named Rafael sacrifices his life in a snuff film to raise money to save his tribe. The book was optioned for filming by a would-be producer named Aziz Ghazal. In late 1993, Ghazal killed himself, his wife, and their daughter after evidence emerged that he had sold the rights to two different companies: Jodie Foster's Egg Pictures and the Disney subsidiary Touchstone Pictures. In 1997 The Brave was eventually filmed starring, and directed by, Johnny Depp, but it has not been released as of this writing.

Urban Legends of the Stars

"There is only one thing in the world worse than being talked about," wrote Oscar Wilde in *The Picture of Dorian Gray*, "and that is not being talked about." For decades, this has been the *de facto* credo of movie stars such as Humphrey Bogart (among others) who said, "I don't care what you print about me as long as you spell my name right."

Good thing Bogie isn't alive today, because if he read what people write about modern stars, it would kill him. Either it's a rumor campaign to "out" allegedly gay and lesbian actors, or it's a whispered defamation against a romantic leading man who—according to the friend of someone's sister who works in a hospital emergency room—came in one night to have a gerbil removed.

But truth has never stopped a good story, as these enduring examples from Hollywood's past can attest (since you can't defame the dead, names are used where that qualification exists):

1. *Myth*: Before she was a star, Joan Crawford made a porno movie called *Ballin' the Jack*. Whenever Mommie Dearest acted temperamental on the set of *What Ever Happened to Baby Jane?* (1962), her costar, Bette Davis, would whistle the song of the same name to put Joan in her place.
   Truth: If such a movie exists, you'd think it would have turned up by now.

2. *Myth:* Clara Bow, the "It" Girl, once held an orgy with the entire USC Football Team.

   Truth: Not proved. The legend was started in the pages of a New York scream sheet called *The GraphiC* (sic) by Daisy DeVoe, a secretary whom Miss Bow fired for behavior that, today, would be labeled stalking. One of the Trojans (that's the name of the USC team) was Marion Michael Morrison, later to be rechristened John Wayne. Bow sued DeVoe and won, but by then the damage was done. It didn't help that, in 1931, Bow made her sound debut in a racy film called *The Wild Party.*

3. *Myth:* Jayne Mansfield was decapitated in the 1967 automobile accident that took her life and that of her dog.

   Truth: False. The rumor started because, in a well-known photograph of her totaled car, her blond wig is seen on the windshield, and early newspaper reproduction allowed people to confuse it with a severed head.

4. *Myth:* William Randolph Hearst murdered Thomas Ince aboard the Hearst yacht.

   Truth: It will never be known exactly what happened on November 15, 1924, as newspaper magnate William Randolph Hearst, his mistress Marian Davies, and guests such as Charles Chaplin, writer Elinor Glyn, producer Thomas H. Ince, Hearst reporter Louella Parsons, and others embarked from San Diego, California, on the Chief's 280-foot pleasure cruiser, the *Oneida.* By the time the ship put back ashore, Ince was dead. Hearst's own paper printed that he was felled from acute indigestion, and not on the yacht, but at the Hearst ranch. No official inquest into Ince's death was ever held. He was cremated on November 21 as his family, Davies, Chaplin, Mary Pickford, Douglas Fairbanks, and Harold Lloyd mourned. Finally, San Diego D.A. Chester Kemply held an inquest, but only Dr. Daniel

Carson Goodman, who worked for Hearst, agreed to testify, and he echoed the "acute indigestion" story.

So what really happened? Time has sifted the following: Hearst abhorred drinking, but Marian Davies (who was truly beloved within the film industry) could be counted on to sneak liquor to party guests without the Chief knowing about it. Thus, as the *Oneida* floated away, so did the party. A jealous lover, Hearst owned a diamond-studded revolver and was an expert shot, using it to pick off sea gulls for his own amusement. Somewhere in international waters he realized that Chaplin and Marian were missing. Knowing that Chaplin had a reputation as a satyr, he stalked off to find them. When he discovered both tramps *in flagrante delicto*, Hearst shot at Chaplin. Anger ruined his aim, however, and the bullet went out the porthole and into the forehead of Thomas Ince, who happened to be passing by. Hearst instantly swore everyone on the *Oneida* to secrecy, especially gossip columnist Parsons. By the time she stepped off the gangplank, Parsons had a lifetime contract with Hearst.

5. *Myth:* Fatty Arbuckle raped a girl with a Coke bottle.
   Truth: False, and this remains one of Hollywood's saddest scandals. Over Labor Day weekend, 1921, Roscoe "Fatty" Arbuckle, the screen's second most beloved comedian (after Chaplin), hosted a booze-drenched party in San Francisco's St. Francis Hotel. One of the many guests was an actress (and likely call girl) named Virginia Rappe. At some point, wearing nothing more than pajamas and a leer, Arbuckle took Rappe into the bedroom. According to witnesses, there ensued screaming, after which Arbuckle emerged and impatiently ordered those present to remove Rappe "to the Palace [Hotel]" where a satellite party was going on. Instead, the young woman was taken to the Pine Street Hospital where she later died.

   Arbuckle was picked apart in the newspapers, primarily by the Hearst press, which had just introduced the tabloid format in 1919 and needed a big story to establish it in the marketplace. Hearst later boasted that Arbuckle sold more papers than the sinking of the *Lusitania*. Somewhere along the way it was suggested that Arbuckle, too drunk to "perform," used a glass soft-drink bottle as his stand-in.

After three trials (two hung juries and a third that not only acquitted him but issued an unheard-of apology), Arbuckle was finished. Will H. Hays, Hollywood's newly appointed censor, cared only about cleansing the movies' reputation, and banned Arbuckle from the screen.

The truth behind the scandal has only gradually surfaced. Arbuckle's producer, Adolph Zukor, who had to absorb $1 million in shelved films, wrote in his 1953 memoir that the pressure to make feature films, rather than short comedies, killed most silent comedians, and implied that the official banning abrogated Arbuckle's expensive studio contract. Writer David Yallop (in *The Day the Laughter Stopped*) revealed that Rappe was not molested in any way, but a doctor's report to that effect was not allowed at trial. He also suggested that Rappe died from a bungled abortion, which was not her first. Historian Kevin Brownlow added that Pine Street was a maternity hospital.

Nevertheless, the mental image of the 300-pound Arbuckle and the tiny Miss Rappe swirls around the whole sordid affair more than 80 years later. In the late 1920s Arbuckle attempted a comeback as a director (using the names "William Goodrich" and "Will B. Goode"), but he died in 1933—some say of a broken heart.

The Men Who Never Were

Who are Alan Smithee and George Spelvin? The answer is no secret to people who work in the film, television, and stage arts, but they share a secret that is supposed to be kept from the audience.

Since 1968, "Alan Smithee" has been the pseudonym that the Directors Guild of America (DGA) applies to films and TV shows from which the original director has demanded that his name be

---

✓ **REALITY CHECK**

Invasion from Mars

The October 31, 1938, "Invasion from Mars" broadcast masterminded by Orson Welles and writer Howard Koch created a famous hoax, which everybody denied for insurance purposes, and several subsequent careers. What is less well known is that the drama, presented as though it were a series of news bulletins, inspired the Federal Communications Commission to pass an edict that no broadcaster could air anything that sounded like a news broadcast that was not, in fact, legitimate. That rule has been bent, if not erased, over the years by such films as 1983's *Special Bulletin* (about nuclear terrorism) and 1994's *Without Warning* (meteors hit earth during prime time) and by a glut of commercials and infomercials that ape newsroom locations.

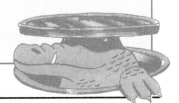

removed. Begun as a pressure tactic to force studios to stop meddling with the director's work, the idea was that, if the public saw the name "Alan Smithee," it would know that the film was a botch. Directors such as David Lynch (*Dune*), Martin Brest (*Scent of a Woman, Meet Joe Black*), Michael Mann (*Heat*), and others have subsequently refused to accept credit for the studio mangler's handiwork. The capper came in 1998 when screenwriter Joe Eszterhaus wrote a satire called *An Alan Smithee Film: Burn Hollywood Burn* about an actual director named Alan Smithee who wants to take his name off a movie, but the name they want to put on is . . . Alan Smithee. Eszterhaus's script was directed by Arthur Hiller (*Love Story, The Americanization of Emily*), and guess what? When Eszterhaus tampered with Hiller's edit, Hiller took his name off and had it replaced with (ta-DAA!) Alan Smithee! The DGA recently decided to use different pseudonyms because "Alan Smithee" has become too well known. But doesn't that defeat the purpose of using it to signal the public that tampering has taken place?

As for George Spelvin, he is a well-regarded (and apparently ageless) stage actor who has appeared in a number of productions, all of them quite unmemorably. Unlike Alan Smithee, however, the presence of George Spelvin is not a tip-off of incompetence. Rather, he is cast when a member of Actors Equity "doubles" two roles in a play and the production doesn't want to tip off the audience by having the same name appear twice in the program. The second appearance (for example, as a killer or long-lost brother) is listed as "George Spelvin," and the surprise is preserved, at least until the curtain call.

John Barrymore's Body

Actor-writer Paul Henreid swore the story was true. When he, Humphrey Bogart, and Peter Lorre were filming *Casablanca* in 1942, word came that John Barrymore had died. Barrymore had spent his waning days at fellow reprobate Errol Flynn's house in the Hollywood Hills. Although Henreid insists he didn't participate, Bogart and Lorre, along with two friends, bribed the mortuary attendant to lend them Barrymore's body. They carried him to Flynn's house, propped him in a chair, placed a whiskey in his hand, and waited for Flynn to return. According to Lorre, Flynn got home, nodded to Barrymore, and was three steps to the bar when he said, "Oh, my God!" followed by orders for everybody to show themselves. They did, more drinks were poured, and stories were told. But Flynn refused to help carry the body back. The Barrymore story, affectionately passed around Hollywood circles for years, was finally dramatized on screen by writer-director Blake Edwards in his 1981 black comedy, *S.O.B.*

Three Men, a Baby, and a Ghost

In a medium where special effects are designed to make people think they're seeing the real thing, it figures that someone would start a rumor about a real thing that looks like a special effect. Well, not exactly, but keep reading.

The 1987 Disney/Touchstone comedy, *Three Men and a Baby*, starred Tom Selleck, Ted Danson, and Steve Guttenberg, and was deftly directed by Leonard Nimoy. Based on a 1985 French film called *Three Men and a Cradle*, it concerned three carefree bachelors who gain an overdue sense of personal responsibility when somebody leaves an infant on their doorstep.

But it wasn't the infant on the doorstep that made people race to see the film again (and later rent the video); it was the "ghost" of a young boy standing in a window in the back of one of the rooms. Or was he?

"Let me tell you the story as I recall it," Leonard Nimoy explains, still amused and amazed at how the urban legend got started.

The film had been in release for several weeks and was quite a successful movie when I heard—and I don't remember exactly where or how—that a lady had contacted the press somewhere in the U.S. and said that she had lived in that apartment in which the movie took place, and that she had a son who had died in that apartment, and she was quite convinced that the ghost of that son appeared in one of the scenes in the film.

✓ REALITY CHECK

Moon Landing Hoax

Despite the success of the U.S. space program, some people are still not convinced that astronauts landed on the moon. They maintain that the whole thing was a special effect shot inside a Hollywood studio, probably directed by Stanley Kubrick, and that rocket ships still aren't capable of leaving Earth's atmosphere, let alone achieving interplanetary travel. (Given the recent funding cuts to NASA, it's possible that some of these people have been elected to Congress). Strange thing is, these are the same people who buy the supermarket tabloids and report alien abductions. Go figure.

It was an intriguing story, so I looked at the footage. To begin with, the apartment never existed. It was a totally fabricated set designed by Peter Larkin and built on a soundstage in a suburb of Toronto. The lady . . . could not have lived in that apartment, because it was not real. But it captured the look and feel of a New York apartment on the upper West Side facing Central Park West; we had a backing outside the window [showing] Fifth Avenue on the other side of the park. It worked.

The scene to which she refereed took place in the bedroom of the Ted Danson character. The character was developed to be a narcissistic actor, quite self-obsessed, and we decided to decorate his room with a lot of memorabilia from his own work. We had made for us, in Toronto, a standee cutout of Ted in a top hat and tails as though this were from a play that he had been in, and was used in the lobby of the theater. That standee, which was maybe five feet tall, was put [behind] the window that overlooks Central Park West and there was a gauzy curtain draped over it. In one particular shot, as the camera panned across the room, it looked as though there was a ghostly figure behind that drape. It was totally accidental. But the press had fun with it, I had a lot of inquiries about it, it was not a real apartment, it was not a real ghost, and that's the whole story.

No stranger to publicity after playing the role of "Spock" on the indestructible television and motion picture series *Star Trek*, Nimoy wonders where such rumors start, but dismisses the possibility that the ghost was a marketing stunt.

"I have to believe that this lady was serious," he says compassionately.

I think [she] really believed that this was an apartment that she had lived in, and in which her son had died. It wasn't a prank. It was somebody who was caught in this obsession and had to tell somebody about it.

I would suspect that somebody in publicity might have enjoyed the fact that it was out there, that some people who had already seen the film might be motivated to go back and see it again, or buy the video. [But] I've never run into anybody who had enough imagination to try to pull that off.

Riley Weston—I Was A Teenage Grownup

Movies and television thrive on make-believe, but woe be unto anyone who tries to turn make-believe to his—or in this case her—advantage. In 1998 a vivacious young woman named Riley Weston was hired by Touchstone Television and Imagine Television to write episodes for a TV show, *Felicity*, that they were coproducing for the WB Network. They were impressed with her energy, skill, and youth.

Her two-year, $50,000 writing agreement landed the 19-year-old Weston on *Entertainment Weekly*'s summer "It List" of the 100 most creative people in entertainment. Here was a bright girl who spoke the language of the target 14- to 19-year-old audience, dressed in the style of the coveted youth market, and presented herself with the kind of self-assurance that makes network executives feel that their jobs are secure.

The only problem was that Riley Weston wasn't 19, she was 32. She wasn't a writer, she was an actress. And her name wasn't Riley Weston, it was Kimberlee Elizabeth Kramer.

But the real problem wasn't that she had pulled off a deception (although that's the reason Touchstone and Imagine gave for canceling her deal when the truth surfaced), it was that a bright, personable outsider had made a lot of television executives look stupid.

Wait. Aren't these the same executives who routinely cast 20-somethings as teenage high school students? Who hire gay actors to play straight characters, and straight actors to play gay characters? Who publicize their own shows on the covers of their subsidiary's magazines and interview their own stars on their own networks' talk shows? Who's scamming whom, anyway?

Chapter 7

Modern Urban Legends

Think of the ten worst things that could happen to you, and I bet any one of them would make a great movie.
—Paul Schrader, writer, <u>Taxi Driver</u>

By definition, urban legends happen to other people. They are the morality tales of our time, and they grow, not from the minds of our most celebrated storytellers, but from the whispered rumors of average people. Like the slasher movies their plots often resemble, urban legends are easily visualized, are often grim, can be summed up in one sentence, and always, *always* happen to "a sister of a friend of this guy I know from work . . ."

Like most fables, their job is to teach, although the precise lesson can be obscure. If Aesop's classic "The Fox and the Grapes," for example, is about the excuses we make when we fail to get what we want, then surely "The Cockroach in the Hairdo," in which a schoolgirl doesn't shampoo her hair and gets a bug infestation is a warning about personal hygiene. But what are we to make of the gruesome urban legend about the police decoy:

A small town discovered that it could cut the money it was spending on traffic cops by parking an empty police car behind a highway billboard and propping a uniformed mannequin in the front seat. The appearance of a "hidden" policeman would scare speeders into slowing down. Before long the decoy was discovered and, like a road sign in rural areas, soon became a target for gun-toting joyriders. Intent on stopping this affront to the law, a young crusading state trooper stationed himself in the car to catch the shooter. Instead, he caught a bullet.

What does this urban legend teach? Not to shoot at police cars? Not to hire stupid state troopers? That radar is a better bet than a decoy? Although no specific message is forthcoming, one overriding impression remains: *Boy, I'm glad that wasn't me!*

This is why urban legends are never told in the first person. If they were, they could be verified. In a court of law, urban legends would be deemed hearsay, and therefore inadmissible. On the streets, however—as well at the water cooler, on the playground, at the poker table, in the laundromat, and especially on the Internet—they are not only admissible, they attain the power of truth.

Urban legends are subversive. At their most chilling, they paint a grotesque portrait of the social order in a nose dive. In such classics as "The Vanishing Hitchhiker," "The Choking Doberman," "The Organ Donor Baby," and "The Repentant Car Thief," our security systems fail us, our passions leave us vulnerable to harm, our fears cloud our minds, and no good deed goes unpunished. Even such (comparatively) fanciful tales as "The Poodle in the Microwave," "The Mexican Pet," "Alligators in the Sewers," and "The Broken Computer Cup-Holder" portray a level of stupidity that could only be found in someone else—right?

Urban legends may tell us more about the way we are than we want to realize. They cut straight to the heart of our yearnings, and no sponsor, ratings, corporate owner, or focus group can tack on a happy ending. Indeed, implicit in every urban lesson is an intense "whew!" And urban legends contradict every means of verification that civilization has devised to protect itself. They are born of vague parentage; like a virus, they are spread by mouth or (more recently) the Internet; and only later, if at all, do they appear in the mass media. Here is where they take on another life, because as much as people insist that they hate "the press," they still believe what they see in it. Interestingly— no, make that frighteningly—even when a newspaper debunks an urban legend *as an urban legend,* the only thing that people seem to remember is that it was in print, and therefore it's true. The mere appearance of something on talk radio or in a newspaper becomes its own validation.

But the sad truth about urban legends, particularly those that clog the Internet, is that they waste resources. When they happen online, they can crash or slow down systems. They invade our

---

✓ **REALITY CHECK**

My Cup Got a 404

A woman calls Gateway (or Dell or Apple) for customer service and says, "Help! I just broke the cup-holder on my computer! What should I do?" After a moment of confusion, the technical support person says, "But Ma'am, our computers don't have cup-holders."

"Of course they do," she insists. "You press a button and it pops out for you to rest your coffee cup on."

"Oh, that!" says the support person. "That's not a cup-holder, that's the CD-ROM drive."

Characteristically, when this story is told, it always involves a woman making the call, and a man answering it. Whether that says more about people who call support lines, or people who make up stories about people who do, is a whole other discussion.

privacy, harvest the data of our lives, and exploit what little compassion remains in the human condition. In the end, it boils down to where you place your trust: the media, the government, or some guy with a Web site. Consider this chapter before you decide.

Disneyana

Few American figures provoke more urban mythology than Walt Disney. Two reasons may explain this. First, Disney's imagination fuels our own fancies, just as he inspired his employees. Second, all he created is, and has always been, controlled with a sense of near-paranoia.

Remarkably, for a man whose genius had no antecedent, Disney and his successors left nothing to chance. Possessive to a fault, litigious to a fare-the-well, and as spontaneous as a mountain, Team Disney (as it is known) researches, tests, analyses, extrapolates, and lobbies every decision before they commit to it. It would follow, therefore, that anything connected with the Disney organization has to exist on purpose.

Or does it? Here are 10 urban legends that have been associated with the Walt Disney organization over the years. The point is not whether they are true or false, but the mindset that nurtured them both inside and outside the Magic Kingdom:

1. **Someone died at Videopolis—false.** Videopolis is the 5,000-square-foot high-tech amphitheater at the Anaheim, California, Disneyland where music events are held. In legend, which is false, a fight broke out when it first opened in 1985 and a boy was stabbed. Rather than risk a scandal by calling an ambulance, park security bundled the boy into a private car and drove him to a nearby hospital. Because it was not an official emergency vehicle, it had to stop for all the red lights. The boy bled to death before reaching the hospital. Disney supposedly made a large financial settlement with the boy's family to hush it up. Never proven, this rumor recently resurfaced

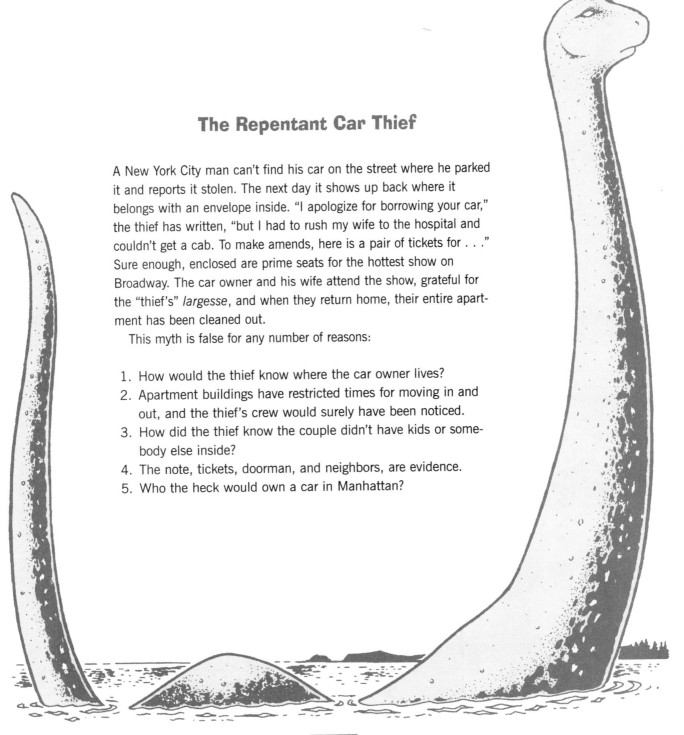

The Repentant Car Thief

A New York City man can't find his car on the street where he parked it and reports it stolen. The next day it shows up back where it belongs with an envelope inside. "I apologize for borrowing your car," the thief has written, "but I had to rush my wife to the hospital and couldn't get a cab. To make amends, here is a pair of tickets for . . ." Sure enough, enclosed are prime seats for the hottest show on Broadway. The car owner and his wife attend the show, grateful for the "thief's" *largesse*, and when they return home, their entire apartment has been cleaned out.

This myth is false for any number of reasons:

1. How would the thief know where the car owner lives?
2. Apartment buildings have restricted times for moving in and out, and the thief's crew would surely have been noticed.
3. How did the thief know the couple didn't have kids or somebody else inside?
4. The note, tickets, doorman, and neighbors, are evidence.
5. Who the heck would own a car in Manhattan?

after a Christmas Eve 1998 accident in which two guests and a park employee were injured when a rope tore away from the sailing ship *Columbia* and sent a metal cleat flying. The cleat struck the two guests, one of whom was declared brain-dead two days later. In 1999 a legislative movement was begun in California to regulate amusement parks. Disney has always been a leader in theme park safety; nevertheless, since 1955, there have been eight deaths at Disneyland, all but one (the cleat incident) being the result of guests actively ignoring safety instructions.

2. **There's Coca-Cola in the water fountains—false.** When Disneyland opened on July 17, 1955—but before enough tourists returned from the park to quash the rumors—the drinking fountains were reported to rain with Coca-Cola, ice cream was free, and Walt Disney personally greeted all the guests. This myth is patently false, as anyone knows who has ever attended any Disney theme park.

3. **Walt had a pied-à-terre in Disneyland—almost.** When New Orleans Square was dedicated in the summer of 1966, Walt and his brother, Roy, planned to build an apartment for themselves on the land above the Pirates of the Caribbean ride. After Walt's death in December, however, Roy decided not to proceed. The area became a VIP lounge called Club 33 and was the only place in the park where liquor could be served. The space is now the Disney Gallery and features exhibitions of concept sketches and limited edition art. The initials WD and RD can still be seen on the wrought-iron railing leading up to the second-floor gallery.

4. **Walt loved to ride "Pirates of the Caribbean" after hours—false.** Although Walt was fascinated by technology, and particularly liked the Audioanimatronic figures in his parks, he died on December 15, 1966, and "Pirates" did not open until March 18, 1967. He may have enjoyed some prototype trips, however.

5. **If you smoke pot in Disneyland or Disney World, they kick you out and ban you for life—unconfirmed.** Security, particularly undercover security, is tight in all Disney theme parks, and unruly "guests" (which is what patrons are called), for whatever reason, are shown the way out. In the 1960s, guests with long hair were barred because they didn't meet the park's (unwritten) dress code. There have also been charges that guests suspected of shoplifting are held in isolation until the matter is resolved. This tactic has garnered some very unfavorable publicity from irate guests who have told reporters afterward that they were forced to sign affidavits admitting guilt without benefit of counsel.

6. **There are hidden jokes in Disney cartoons—true.** Until *Variety* "outed" the practice in 1994, only a select few knew about the existence of "hidden jokes" (not messages) in Disney cartoons. As a consequence, all cartoons are examined frame-by-frame by the Disney video folks (get a life!), but a few that slipped past them (or never existed in the first place) are:

   - *Who Framed Roger Rabbit*: When Bob Hoskins and Jessica Rabbit are thrown from the Toon Town Taxi, Jessica's red dress goes flying and she isn't wearing underwear. Also, at the beginning of the film, Baby Herman gooses a woman as he leaves the soundstage.
   - When King Triton makes his big entrance at the beginning of *The Little Mermaid*, among the vassals he sweeps over in the crowd are Mickey and Goofy.
   - When Bianca and Bernard take flight with Orville the sea gull in *The Rescuers*, they fly past an apartment building in which a bare-breasted woman appears in two flash frames (so to speak).

7. **Walt's private screening—false.** This is a chilling rumor, despite there being no proof, because it meets all of the qualifications for a Disney legend: It's spooky,

✓ **REALITY CHECK**

Spanish Fly

There is no such thing as an aphrodisiac, but the legend persists that there is, and it is called Spanish fly. Medically, there is a substance called cantharidin, which is a product of the European blister beetle, sometimes called the Spanish beetle (get it?). It is a severe irritant if used externally (which may contribute to its aphrodisiacal reputation; i.e., the fantasy that its effects can be relieved by sexual friction), and it becomes a powerful laxative if taken internally. *None of this is recommended without medical supervision.*

✓ REALITY CHECK

Al Capp's Leg

Stories about missing prostheses make grizzly urban legends, but here's a funny one that's actually true.

As a boy, "Li'l Abner" comic artist and social critic Al Capp (1909–1979) lost a leg "as the result of an unfortunate encounter with a trolley car," as he openly and glibly recounted it. The garrulous Capp also told how he once returned to his suite in London's Savoy Hotel after a night of hitting the pubs and, as was his habit, unfastened his wooden leg and tucked it safely under the bed.

"In the morning I rang for room service," he recalled, "and the waiter came up to the room. After I had given him my breakfast order, he glanced down and asked me, with typical British aplomb, 'And what will the gentleman under the bed be having?'"

it's brilliant, and it matches Walt's personality. After Walt died in 1966, his chief executives were escorted to assigned seats in the company screening room. There they were shown a film that Walt had made before he died in which he spoke to each of them by name and told them all what he expected them to do for the next five years. Although Disney was no stranger to long-range planning, the Disney archives have been unable to locate either the film or any foundation for the legend.

8. **Walt could never draw Mickey Mouse—half-true.** Although Walt was a competent artist, it was his employee Ub Iwerks who refined the character the world came to know and love as Mickey. Walt could draw a passable Mickey, but that's about it. He also didn't sign his name the way it appears in the world-famous trademark, although he would agreeably fake it for autograph purposes. There are still people who believe that Walt drew every frame of his animated films.

9. **Walt was such a rabid anti-Communist that he refused to let Nikita Khrushchev visit Disneyland—false but true.** Yes, Walt was anti-Communist, but he did not ban Premier Nikita Khrushchev when the Soviet leader visited California in 1955. Security experts from both the United States and the Soviet Union agreed that the 30-mile drive from Los Angeles to Anaheim, plus the crowds at the park, would compromise the VIP's safety.

10. **Walt is frozen and awaiting a cure—false.** After Walt Disney died he was cremated and given a discreet, private funeral (so as not to disturb the value of the company's stock, it is said). Nevertheless, the rumor persists that Walt is cryogenically preserved until such time as medicine can cure the cancer that killed him. The myth might be explained because of his affinity for science and technology, but it is absolutely false. Walt

Disney's ashes reside in a crypt at the Freedom Mausoleum entrance of Forest Lawn Cemetery in Glendale, California.

The Fried Scuba-Scooper

One of the more persistent urban legends is the one about the scuba diver in the forest fire. This prank usually zips around the Internet under the heading, "So you think YOU'VE had a bad day":

> Fire authorities in California found a corpse in a burned-out section of forest while assessing the damage done by a forest fire. The deceased male was dressed in a full wetsuit, complete with a dive tank, flippers, and facemask. A post-mortem examination revealed that the person died not from burns but from massive internal injuries.
>
> Investigators then set about determining how a fully clad diver ended up in the middle of a forest fire. It was revealed that, on the day of the fire, the person went for a diving trip off the coast some 20 miles from the forest. The fire fighters, seeking to control the fire as quickly as possible, called in a fleet of helicopters with very large buckets. The buckets were dropped into the ocean for rapid filling, then flown to the forest fire and emptied.
>
> You guessed it. One minute our diver was making like Flipper in the Pacific, the next he was doing a breaststroke in a fire bucket 300 feet in the air.

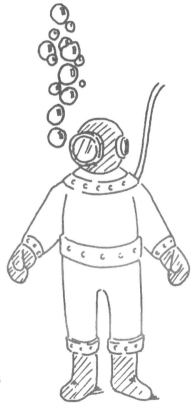

The image is incongruous at best and creepy at worst. One of its recent appearances was said to have been in the March 20, 1998, edition of the *California Examiner*, a newspaper serving the Philippine-American community, although it has been in circulation for at least five years. Its visualization in the 1999 movie *Magnolia* will probably embed it even deeper in the public consciousness.

Here's why it's fake. California and other fire-prone states do use "big scoopers" to transport large quantities of water from lakes

to raging fires. The craft are specially equipped airplanes, not helicopters, with a grid in the scoop that screens out anything larger than a Ping-Pong ball. The fact that a scuba diver was thus kidnapped, but not fish (which would be just as conspicuous in a forest), further disproves the story. The *California Examiner* would not respond to inquiries about how they feel having their name attached to an urban legend.

The Abducted Child

Myth: A disturbing story has been circulating for years about a parent and a child who visit a shopping mall. The child has to use the bathroom, and the parent waits outside. After some time has passed and the child still has not emerged, the concerned parent enters the bathroom and discovers, just in time, that the child is unconscious and being abducted by two adults. The parent thwarts the kidnapping and calls the police.

Truth: Before this story was told about shopping malls it was set in bus stations, city parks, airports, and any space big enough to have public bathrooms. Variations include:

- The child was a different gender than the parent, which explains why the parent didn't accompany the child into the bathroom at first.
- If the child was a girl, the felonious adults were intent on "slaving" her to a foreign country.
- If the child was a boy, the adults were predatory homosexuals who mutilated him in the course of the abduction.

Unlike racist and homophobic urban legends naming specific athletes or movie stars, this story feeds on people's xenophobia and intolerance as well as parents' natural concern for their children.

Tragically, an actual incident reminiscent of this urban legend took place in Primm, Nevada, on May 25, 1997. Jeremy Strohmeyer, a 20-year-old honor student from Long Beach, California, raped and

I'm Feeling Better!

His name is Craig Shergold, and you and 16 million other people sent him a get-well card in 1989 when he was 9 years old and had cancer. He's better now, but not the flow of cards that grew out of his legitimate desire (egged on by his mother and a family friend) to be included in the *Guinness Book of Records* and was allegedly supervised by a wish-granting charity. (The charity was not, repeat *not*, Make-A-Wish Foundation.)

Craig got his operation and his Guinness entry in 1991 and is now a healthy young man, but the wish people are still wasting resources dealing with the cards, letters, and calls that continue to arrive. According to correspondence with Guinness World Records, the Royal Mail still delivers 1,000 unwanted items of post each day. By their request, please *do not participate* in the Topsy-esque scheme. Check out *www.wish.org/craig.htm* or call 800-215-1333 for updates on this and similar chain letter hoaxes that exploit children and the organizations that really do help them. As for the Guinness people, they don't recognize records based on media appeals.

strangled seven-year-old Sherrice Iverson in the bathroom of the Primadonna Hotel-Casino. Claiming he had been in a "drunken and drugged haze," Strohmeyer pleaded guilty to the crime, adding that he strangled her after the rape to "stop her pain." He is now serving four life terms with no chance of parole.

Alligators and Marijuana

Myth: Alligators roam the sewer system of New York City. Easily the most popular and enduring urban legend, the venerable tale has not only spawned its share of jokes ("Flush twice, they're hungry down there"), and two horror movies (*Alligator*, 1980; *Alligator II: The Mutation*, 1991). The tale seems to have had its origins as far back as the 1920s when New Yorkers would visit Florida and return with live baby alligators as pets. Before long, any of the critters that hadn't died would outgrow their cardboard boxes (not to mention their cuteness). The New Yorkers, not wanting to feed them or leave their rent controlled apartments, would flush gators like dead goldfish. The survivors wound up in the sewers where they would thrive on the garbage. Anyone who ventured into Manhattan's sewer system did so at extreme risk.

Truth: Not a few people, having heard this tale, have undoubtedly sat on their toilets expecting to be bitten. Of course, it is completely false. Where to start? The traffic in baby alligators, if it ever existed, ceased long ago under the Endangered Species Act, not to mention basic awareness of cruelty to animals. The sewage system in New York is connected to waste treatment plants, not the municipal water system. Alligators breathe air; they would drown if they were flushed down the john. Finally, if they were there, Rudy Giuliani would have certainly had them all arrested by now and sent to New Jersey.

Corollary: There is a strain of albino marijuana growing in the sewers of New York. It is the result of hippies flushing their pot during the drug busts of the 1960s. It is albino because of the lack of sun, and it is incredibly potent because of all the chemicals in the silt on the sewer floor. Unfortunately, this valuable commodity can never be harvested because it's protected by all the alligators.

Little Mikey and Pop Rocks

Myth: "Little Mikey" died after swallowing several envelopes of Pop Rocks and washing them down with soda. His stomach exploded.

Truth: "Little Mikey" was a character played by child actor John Gilchrist who, in 1971 at the age of three, appeared in a television commercial for Quaker Life Cereal. In the commercial, which was repeated, mostly during children's programming, throughout the 1970s, Little Mikey was a "food tester" for his two older siblings who were skeptical about trying the product.

Pop Rocks were introduced to the market in 1974 and were an instant success for General Foods. A truly "fun" candy, they released trapped gas in the wet environment of the mouth, thereby creating a tingling sensation. They had the same effervescent quality as Fizzies or Alka-Seltzer except that they were made to be eaten as is, not diluted in water.

How Little Mikey, of all people, became connected with Pop Rocks, and why anybody would think they could be lethal, is one of the oldest mysteries in consumer public relations. It drove General Foods nuts when it struck. In 1979, the assailed manufacturer bought full-page ads in several newspapers in which the candy's inventor, William A. Mitchell, extolled its safety without once mentioning Little Mikey. The product was discontinued in 1983 but quietly reappeared in 1985 as Action Candy after Kraft Foods bought the manufacturer.

At last report, John Gilchrist was doing very well, thank you, as an advertising executive for CBS. So is Quaker Life, which in the late 1990s retooled their classic commercial to star, and to appeal to, 20-somethings.

Seagull Sense

Myth: Feeding Alka-Seltzer to sea gulls makes them explode.

Truth: Sea gulls may be scavengers, but they can certainly tell the difference between food and an over-the-counter remedy. This is a corollary to not throwing rice at weddings because the birds eat it, it expands in their stomachs, and they explode. People have also tried this on pigeons using Minute Rice, figuring it would cut the detonation time, but even pigeons are no fools. Somebody suggested throwing birdseed at weddings, but, hello, it's *seeds,* and who wants salad niçoise sprouting on the lawn?

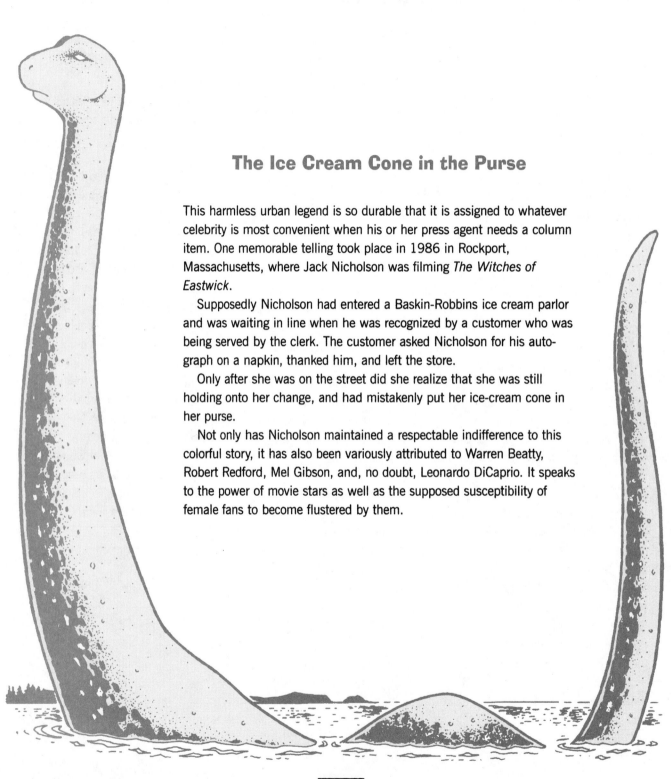

The Ice Cream Cone in the Purse

This harmless urban legend is so durable that it is assigned to whatever celebrity is most convenient when his or her press agent needs a column item. One memorable telling took place in 1986 in Rockport, Massachusetts, where Jack Nicholson was filming *The Witches of Eastwick*.

Supposedly Nicholson had entered a Baskin-Robbins ice cream parlor and was waiting in line when he was recognized by a customer who was being served by the clerk. The customer asked Nicholson for his autograph on a napkin, thanked him, and left the store.

Only after she was on the street did she realize that she was still holding onto her change, and had mistakenly put her ice-cream cone in her purse.

Not only has Nicholson maintained a respectable indifference to this colorful story, it has also been variously attributed to Warren Beatty, Robert Redford, Mel Gibson, and, no doubt, Leonardo DiCaprio. It speaks to the power of movie stars as well as the supposed susceptibility of female fans to become flustered by them.

The Choking Doberman

As meticulously researched by folklorist-scholar-author Jan Harold Brunvand in his urban legend book, *The Choking Doberman* title story concerns a woman who returns to the house one day to find her Doberman unable to breathe. She rushes it to the veterinarian who advises her to go home and wait for him to call with his diagnosis. When she gets home, the phone is ringing off the hook. It's the vet saying, "Get out of the house immediately and call the police!" She does. It turns out that the vet had removed three freshly severed fingers from the dog's throat, and reasoned that the intruder was still in the house. Sure enough, when the police get there, the intruder has passed out in the closet from loss of blood—and he is missing three fingers!

Brunvand tracked the tale back as far as a 1981 Phoenix, Arizona, *New Times* story in which the reporter admitted that it could not be verified. Logic alone dictates why it could never have happened:

- A dog big enough to bite off three fingers would be big enough to gulp them down.
- No pet owner would leave a dog that sick with a vet and just go home.
- If the dog was disabled by choking, and then was taken to the vet, the intruder would have time to flee the house.
- If the intruder had passed out from loss of blood, what threat could he be to the woman?

But the story characterizes what must be present in the "best" urban legends. There must be:

1. A vulnerable person (the woman)
2. A situation that seems obvious but turns out to be otherwise
3. Sudden dramatic jeopardy
4. A miraculous escape (In this case, it's a phone call, but in other stories it's "the lovers drive away," "the elevator

closed before the killer could lunge," or "the maniac drove to the next house instead.")

Sometimes a tired legend can be revived by attaching a name to it. Say, Eddie from TV's *Frasier* bit off an intruder's fingers. Naw, not Eddie.

The Vanishing Hitchhiker

Every kid is warned never to hitchhike. Here is one reason never to pick up a hitchhiker.

A man (although gender isn't important) is driving along a deserted highway and stops to pick up a hitchhiker (again, gender is not important) who insists on taking the backseat. The driver asks, "Where you going?" and the hitchhiker gives an address in a nearby town. After a few miles, the driver looks in the rear-view mirror and realizes the hitchhiker is gone. Curious to panicked, the driver continues to the address the hitchhiker had given. A man and a woman answer the door and the driver explains to them what happened.

"We've had other people tell us the same thing," the couple say. "You picked up our daughter/son at the very spot where she/he was killed by a drunk driver ten years ago."

The narrative makes several leaps of logic, but it remains riveting. It also bespeaks a time long past when drivers still stopped to pick up hitchhikers and nobody worried about crime. Doubtless it persists because it is spooky, nonviolent, and has a twist at the end like the best Saki (H. H. Munro) or O. Henry short stories. The tale itself has been around for a considerable time, and may even have served as inspiration for a 1941 radio play by Lucille Fletcher, which Rod Serling adapted in 1960 into a classic *Twilight Zone* episode. In the episode "The Hitchhiker," a mysterious man (Leonard Strong) plagues driver Inger Stevens. It turns out that he is the Angel of Death come to fetch her to the next world.

The Vanishing Hitchhiker, in all its forms, also addresses our age-old questions about spirits, Fate, and the things that swirl around us when nobody else is there—or so we think.

Rising to the Occasion

Variety, the show business trade paper, supposedly reported this bizarre death sometime in the mid-1980s, but no search of their archives reveals its appearance. It took place in Las Vegas, a town whose showmanship is second to none, in a casino lounge that features a piano that rises out of the floor on an elevator platform.

According to the legend, a man and woman somehow got into the closed theater and began making out on top of the piano. One thing led to another, and one of them accidentally clicked the UP button on the end of the keyboard with a toe, activating the elevator. Since they were too distracted to notice, the piano kept rising to the ceiling, crushing the man on top of the woman on top of the piano. The man suffocated in that position, and the horrified woman was unable to escape from underneath him, where she lay naked, hysterical, and pinned in place until the cleaning crew discovered them in the morning. (Unconfirmed.)

The Involuntary Kidney Donor

Myth: One morning a man wakes up to find himself in a bathtub full of ice. He discovers a fresh scar and stitches on his body and immediately calls an ambulance. In the hospital, emergency room personnel determine that he was drugged. X-rays show that one of his kidneys has been removed.

Truth: None. Typically, this is told as a cautionary tale against attending a certain bar or club, or walking through a particular park (an episode of NBC's *Law & Order* even exploited this myth), or associating with certain people. It also takes a swing at the controversial organ transplant allocation system in America.

✓ **REALITY CHECK**

Schrod

The fish isn't an urban legend, but the joke is. A man gets into a Boston taxi and, eager to sample the local dish for which the Hub is famous, asks, "Where can I get schrod in this town?"

"I musta had that question asked of me a thousand times since I've been driving a cab," the driver exclaims, "but that's the first time I ever heard it in the pluperfect subjunctive."

For the curious etymologist, if not the ichthyologist, *scrod* and *schrod* are both mild-flavored whitefish. But, according to New England tradition, the former refers to cod while the latter is haddock. The presence of the letter *h* is the clue.

Tapeworm Diet Pills

Myth: A new diet pill was tested and proved extraordinarily effective, except for one tiny complication: It contained a baby tapeworm. The theory behind the diet pill (and the myth) is that the tapeworm gets fat instead of the person. Unfortunately, the manufacturer couldn't figure out how to get rid of the tapeworm without referring the customer for surgery, so they could never market it.

Truth: Tapeworms (*Cestoda*) are parasitic flatworms that enter the body by means of infested meat or fish. They attach themselves to the intestine and live on the food that is swallowed by the host organism. They can grow to a length of several feet. Tapeworms cannot live in a pill and would never pass muster with the Food and Drug Administration anyway. Besides, logic proves that even if the tapeworm eats the food instead of the person, the total weight would still be the same.

First, organs can't be taken out and mindlessly switched like floppy diskettes. They must be cross-matched, prepped, and rushed through surgery. Because of the immunosuppressant medication typically administered to minimize tissue rejection, a sterile environment for harvesting as well as inserting is essential. Finally, if someone is desperate enough to knock you out and swipe your kidney, why would he or she bother to sew you up afterward?

The Earwig Express

Myth: An insect called an earwig enters your head through your ear and lays eggs. The eggs hatch in your brain and kill you.

Truth: The "bodily invasion" motif occurs repeatedly in urban legends, from the cockroach infestation of a girl's matted hairdo to garden snakes that squirm their way into various bodily orifices at summer camp. One that has wormed its way, so to speak, into folklore is the earwig.

In this nightmare, a small insect crawls into the ear and, after much pain and fear, works its way through the minute passages of the brain until it crawls safely out the other ear. All seems right, until the sufferer brings the bug to an insect specialist for analysis. "This is a female earwig," the entomologist reports grimly. "And it laid eggs." The earwig rumor is a close relative of the hiker who swallows a snake egg (it hatches), the tapeworm in the diet pill, and the woman who goes swimming and ingests an octopus egg (it hatches inside her and the tentacles branch out and . . . well, you get the picture).

Earwigs (*Dermaptera*) are nocturnal insects that live in wood and decaying plants and feed on smaller insects. They are about ¾ inch in length, brown in color, and produce a foul odor when crushed. They have multiple legs, front antennae, and small, horny pincers at the rear.

Most important, earwigs do not enter the human body (Although that's what they did in *Star Trek II: The Wrath of Khan.* Creatures very close in appearance to earwigs, called Ceti eels, and found on Ceti Alpha 5, were used to torture captured Starfleet officers.) The worst place earwigs enter is the human house or apartment.

In point of fact, the only thing that seems to be able to go in one ear and out the other is parental advice to a teenager.

There is, however, at least one actual parasite that *does* invade humans. It is the *Onchocerca volvulus* worm, which causes a disease known as river blindness. This disease may afflict as many as 18 million persons, mostly in tropical areas, Africa, and Central America. The adult worm is carried by black flies to the human skin, where it lays its eggs (causing terrible itching). The larvae then migrate to the retinas where they cause blindness. Lee Dye, in an article on Charles Mackenzie of the Michigan State University Department of Pathology for ABCNEWS.com, reports that "victims may have 100 million tiny worms in their skin."

Jerry Mathers—Killed in Vietnam

Myth: Jerry Mathers, the young actor who played Theodore "The Beav" Cleaver in TV's enduring series *Leave It To Beaver* was killed in the Vietnam War.

Truth: Just when we were getting used to hearing that Ken Osmond, who played the brown-nosing Eddie Haskell, was the rock star Alice Cooper (he wasn't), along came this rumor about Mathers. Research conducted by Barbara and David P. Mikkelson for their Urban Legend Reference Pages shows that Mathers, who did join the Air National Guard, had been rejected by the Marines. They explained to him that they would post him stateside rather than suffer negative publicity if anything happened to him in Vietnam. The false rumor that he had been killed surfaced in either 1968 or 1969, but (per the Mikkelsons) no two sources, including Mathers's 1998 autobiography, are consistent.

In any event, golly, if Mathers had been killed in action, he could never have costarred in *The New Leave It To Beaver* (1985–1989), could he?

✓ REALITY CHECK

The Dropping Dog

Truman Capote invented this urban legend but didn't admit to it for years. In the story, a man is visiting a friend who lives in a penthouse. While the friend is getting ready, Capote plays toss with the friend's dog. On one throw, the ball goes over the balcony, and the excited dog dives after it, plummeting to its death on the street below. In one version of the story, the guest merely leaves without saying anything. In the better version (which sounds like pure Capote), the dog's owner enters the room and asks where the pooch is. Responds the guest, "I don't know how to tell you this, but your dog was looking terribly depressed . . ."

The Poodle in the Microwave

Myth: A woman gives her pet poodle a bath. It's cold outside and she wants to dry it in a hurry to keep it from catching a cold, so she puts it in the microwave to speed up the process.

Truth: Unverified, but filmmaker Joe Dante used a twist on it in *Gremlins 2: The New Batch* (1990). Along with The Dropping Dog, The Cat in the Dryer, The Parakeet in the Vacuum, The Frog in the Blender, Let's Feed the Goldfish Vodka, and other humans-hurting-animals story, this persistent urban legend plays into some people's dislike of particular species and the stereotypes that accompany them.

Bring Out Your Dead

Mark Twain was traveling in Europe when he received word that the American newspapers were printing stories that he had died. Twain sent back the telegram: "Reports of my death have been greatly exaggerated."

Despite improvements in communications, or maybe because of them, such things still happen. Near Christmas 1997, for example, a rumor spread through Hollywood that actor Scott Baio had died. It happened to be the same day (December 18) that actor Chris Farley died. For some reason, Baio's name also was spread around. Baio, who was out of town at the time, returned to Los Angeles to find his answering machine innundated with messages from mourners (but if he was dead, why would they think that . . . oh, never mind).

On January 24, 1999, NBC struck out Joe DiMaggio, who didn't actually die until March 8, 1999. And the usually authoritative Leslie Halliwell's *Filmgoers and Video Viewer's Companion* put a question mark after writer-director Barry Levinson's name in their ninth edition, indicating that they weren't sure whether he had died in 1987. (He hadn't, as his post-1987 films *Wag the Dog* and the Oscar-winning *Rain Man* attest.)

Okay, okay, these things happen. Celebrities "of a certain age" are frequently asked by newspapers (notably the *New York Times*) to peruse drafts of their obituaries to ensure accuracy. This seems to be what happened on June 5, 1998, when the Associated Press accidentally transmitted an undated draft of Bob Hope's death notice. The report was seen by Sen. Dick Armey, whose staff should have known better. He passed the information to Rep. Bob Stump, whose staff should also have known better, who publicly mourned for the patriotic performer. C-SPAN automatically televised it, and Bob Hope, who was alive at 95, was surprised to learn he was dead.

False reports of death can have international repercussions. There's a long-lived legend that Soviet leader Josef Stalin once faked his own death to see which of his underlings would rejoice most; then he could purge the merrymaker. Stalin's fraud could not have been far from the mind of other world leaders when, in the early 1950s, erroneous reports leaked out that then-premier Nikita Khrushchev had died. Hours later, an update "corrected" the report by insisting that Khrushchev was alive, but a *teletype machine* in the Kremlin had died.

Of course, there was the "Paul is dead" rumor that circulated in 1969, insisting that Paul McCartney had died in 1965 and that George, John, and Ringo had been including secret messages in Beatles records ever since.

What's it like to be dead? The utterly charming actor Patrick McNee, best known as John Steed on TV's *The Avengers*, reports:

> ✓ **REALITY CHECK**
>
> ## Polly Want a Hoover?
>
> There are several renderings of this story, none of which is verifiable. A woman is vacuuming her house and decides that the birdcage is dusty. She sticks the nozzle inside and accidentally sucks her parakeet into the hose. In one version, she manages to reverse the machine to "blow," sailing the budgie across the room where it lands dazed and ruffled, but alive. In another version, she stops the machine and finds the bird safe in the receptacle bag. In a third version, she finds the bird in the receptacle bag, which, in this machine, is on the other end of the fan.

An actor called Patrick Magee died a few years back. I was in Australia at the time. They announced on U.S. TV that Patrick Magee, star of *The Avengers*, had died. So they rang up my daughter in Palm Springs: "Sorry to hear that your father's dead."

She said, "But I was talking to him 12 minutes ago in Australia."

They said, "No, he's dead, it's just the time difference."

Really and Truly Dead

Is it true what they say about the way Catherine the Great died? If you have to ask, you haven't heard her urban legend. Hers is one of many demises that have been exaggerated, clouded, or otherwise misrepresented over the years. Here's how Catherine and five other "greats" became "lates":

1. **Cleopatra (69–30 B.C.).** After betraying her husband, Marc Antony, by siding with Octavian Caesar in order to keep her throne, Cleopatra was held prisoner by Octavian's troops. When word reached her that Antony had taken his life, Cleopatra vowed to do the same. Her exact cause of death was never determined, although a statue of her, in which she wore an asp-shaped bracelet, seems to have started the rumor that she allowed herself to be bitten by a snake.

2. **Catherine the Great (1729–1796).** The Russian empress died of a stroke, not from falling off a horse (or vice-versa).

3. **"Diamond" Jim Brady (1856–1917).** Although it would have been poetic, Diamond Jim Brady (so-named because of the gem collection he acquired selling equipment to the railroads) did not die of "a busted bell." The morbidly obese *bon vivant* (400+ pounds), who suffered from diabetes and digestive problems, ignored doctors' advice to cut back on his epicurean habits. Forsaking New York, he took a $1,009-a-week apartment in Atlantic City. His last meal was a glass of water, which he asked his servant to fetch him at 4:30 A.M. on April 13, 1917. An hour later he was dead of a heart attack—plus ulcers, and kidney and liver failure.

4. **W. C. Fields (1880–1946).** The comedian (whose epitaph, incidentally, is *not* "On the whole, I'd rather be living in Philadelphia") died in a Pasadena, California, hospital of a stomach hemorrhage. Doctors had warned him off liquor, but friends had continued to sneak it in. He died on Christmas Day, which must have really angered the celebrated Grinch.

5. **Lenny Bruce (1925–1966).** The brilliant social critic had been forced into penury by a succession of courtroom defeats, and he descended into a world of drugs. On August 3, 1966, he was discovered on the floor of the bathroom in his Los Angeles home, a needle in his arm. The authorities declared it a morphine overdose, but rumors have circulated ever since that those same authorities purposely sold Lenny abnormally strong drugs as a way to silence and discredit him at the same time.

6. **Nelson Rockefeller (1908–1979).** The question about the former New York governor and statesman is not how he died, but where and with whom. First reports were that "Rocky" died of a heart attack alone at his office desk in Rockefeller Plaza. Subsequent reports revealed that he died in the living room of his town house on West 54th Street. And the 70-year-old Rockefeller wasn't alone, he was with a 31-year-old secretary; and there was no paperwork in the apartment, only dinner. The circumstances have never been clarified.

Harmful Urban Legends

Not all urban legends are harmless cautionary tales; sometimes they are designed to promote hate. In a society that no longer sanctions racism, sexism, and homophobia out of an awareness of political correctness, certain urban legends fly underneath the radar by using real names. For example, no evolved person would sanction anti-black jokes, yet there is a persistent urban legend that has a famous African-American (Reggie Jackson, Michael

✓ **REALITY CHECK**

Johnny Carson

As much as everybody swears he did it, Johnny Carson never made vulgar conversation with Zsa Zsa Gabor about her cat, or with Mrs. Arnold Palmer about what she did to give her husband luck before a golf tournament.

According to Helen Sanders at Carson Productions, he *did* accidentally trigger a national crisis . . . of sorts. A joke in his December 19, 1973, *Tonight Show* monologue mentioned a toilet paper shortage. The next day millions of Americans raced to their supermarkets in a frenzy of bathroom tissue buying, creating an actual shortage where the only thing that really existed was a punch line. Hi-Yo!

Jordan, Charles Barkley, Eddie Murphy) standing in the back of a hotel elevator with two large pet dogs. The door opens, a white woman enters and faces front. When the elevator reaches her floor, she starts to get out, but so does one of the athlete's dogs. Speaking to the animal by its name, Jackson/Jordan/Barclay/Murphy orders, "Get down, Lady." Immediately the white woman passenger kneels in fear.

The "Get down, Lady" story could work with a person of any color, but it is always told about a specific man who is African-American. In this way, racist jokes enter the mainstream disguised as a news item.

The other significant urban legend names a well known movie star (who is litigious, so he won't be named here) who supposedly turned up in a hospital emergency room one night as the result of an arcane sexual act involving a gerbil. The supposed practice, which is as rare as "crush" videos and has never been authenticated, involves somehow forcing a live rodent into one's anal orifice. As the animal suffocates, its movement produces a sexual thrill. Although anyone of any sexual orientation might indulge in anal stimulation, this practice is most often identified with the gay community. But you can't tell anti-gay jokes without being homophobic, so the name of this specific movie star is attached, and, suddenly, these jokes become acceptable.

Needless to say, both stories are false.

Death by Tanning

Myth: A man baked to death in a tanning machine.

Truth: When tanning machines were introduced in the late 1970s, they fell heir to the same urban legend that had cursed hot tubs, namely, the "technology turning on humans" myth. According to the tanning booth story, a customer falls asleep inside a tanning booth. The attendant forgets to turn it off and awaken him at the agreed-on time. The attendant, of course, remembers his obligation

in horror and rushes to extricate the man who has, by then, slowly baked to death. Given that the temperature in the booths never reaches cooking temperature, scientific (if not the culinary) veracity of this legend immediately quashes it. There would be a risk of dehydration and a hospital-worthy sunburn, however, just as you can get on the beach.

The hot tub story has survived the tanning machine fad because it contains a wisp of medical truth. In the myth, a partying couple enjoy too much champagne while bathing in their hot tub. They become drowsy and fall asleep. Instead of drowning, as might be expected, they are gently simmered to death like two immense knackwurst, which is pretty much what they look like when neighbors/children/the milkman/police discover them the next day.

As doctors and hot tub instructions caution users, prolonged immersion in water above 105°F. can profoundly affect the cardiac system. Combined with the effects of drugs or alcohol, drowsiness or sleep (at best) and pulmonary collapse (at worst) might result. Nevertheless, the water temperature would never get hot enough to boil anything (which would hardly matter at that point, anyway).

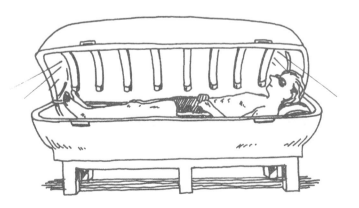

"Puff (But Don't Inhale) the Magic Dragon"

There's a maxim that nothing is as filthy as the mind of a censor, because a censor always finds the worst in everything. Certainly that explains why Rev. Donald Wildmon once accused Mighty Mouse of advocating cocaine use after seeing the cartoon rodent sniff a flower and smile, or why a publication published by Rev. Jerry Falwell insisted that Tele-tubby "Tinky Winky" is gay because he (she? it? them?) is purple, carries a purse, and wears a triangle.

But for longevity, nothing matches the rumor that the 1962 Peter, Paul & Mary children's song "Puff the Magic Dragon" is about marijuana. "Puff" was written in 1959 by Leonard Lipton, a 19-year-old Cornell University student.

"Puff" is not what you do with pot; "Jackie Paper" was not an addict or the name of rolling papers; and "painted wings and giant things make way for other toys" does not mean that Jackie "moved up" to heroin.*

All parties proclaim that it has nothing to do with drugs. Furthermore, Peter (Yarrow) even countered the rumor by describing how "The Star Spangled Banner" could be considered a drug song. By the Puff measure, "the dawn's early light" is when addicts shoot up, and "the rockets' red glare" alludes to the condition of red-eye that pot smokers evince.

As Freud supposedly said, sometimes a cigar is just a cigar.

Too Hot to Microwave

Myth: A microwaved cup of water exploded in a boy's face.

Truth: Water can, indeed, be superheated in a microwave oven to the point where it may "explode,"—or, more accurately, roil. This can happen in glass or china, but a particular culprit is the Styrofoam cup.

---

*See the Urban Reference Pages: *www.snopes.com/music/songs/puff.htm.*

Here's why: In a pot on the stove the water is allowed to form convection currents so the hotter water at the bottom flows to the surface. In a microwave oven, however, the "heat" (actually molecular vibration) may form pockets rather than convection currents, and water can be heated above its normal 212°F. boiling point. The insulating qualities of the Styrofoam cup may, in this case, worsen these "pockets," and a sudden disturbance can make them "pop." It happens in a subtler way when you dip a tea bag into microwaved water and it "fizzes."

The originators of these stories may genuinely be trying to help people. They just believe that the most effective way to do so is to personalize the case, albeit by using someone else as goat.

As to the boy who, for some inexplicable reason, stuck his face close to a cup of boiling water, he's like the lady who rested a cup of boiling coffee in her crotch, or the guy who tried to French-kiss a rattlesnake. *What were they thinking?*

Headlight Flashers

Myth: Never warn an oncoming driver that his headlights are off by flashing your headlights at him! It's a trick by street gangs who shoot flashers as an initiation rite.

Truth: Police gang units in major cities have denied this story ever since they first started hearing it in the mid-1990s. It feeds the lore that urban gang-bangers gain membership by killing someone they don't know as a demonstration of their mettle, and who would make a more senseless victim than a Good Samaritan?

Chapter 8

Damage Control

<u>Nibbled</u> <u>to</u> <u>Death</u> <u>by</u> <u>Ducks</u>
—book title, Robert Campbell

In their 1953 play, *The Solid Gold Cadillac*, Howard Teichmann and George S. Kaufman constructed a satire in which a little old lady brings General Motors to its knees with a series of niggling requests. Little did the playwrights realize that they were creating not only a classic comedy but also the strategy that cyber-hackers would use half a century later.

Since then, of course, the very nature of big business has changed. Once giant companies had manufactured the goods that kept Americans working, but the computer age changed the country into a service economy. No one fought this transformation with more vigor, or with less success, than organized labor. After trade agreements such as the North American Free Trade Agreement (NAFTA) sent factories into other countries, American workers changed from being craftsmen into being servants.

Reactionaries and revolutionaries alike railed against this shift, albeit for different reasons. The 1992 presidential candidacy of billionaire businessman Ross Perot, for example, was supported by a coalition of traditionalists who valued his anti-NAFTA stance as well as by remnants of the Woodstock generation who didn't like the growing influence of multinational corporations. Both sides shared the view that, as intransigent as the U.S. government might be, at least it followed the Constitution. Corporations, they noted, owe allegiance only to their stockholders.

Yet, in the 1990s, as the stock market soared beyond all imagination and more people got richer than ever before, it was hard to argue that anything was going wrong. It didn't matter that, at the start of the year 2000, 1 percent of the people held 90 percent of the money, and fully 25 percent of American children went to bed hungry. Like all revolutions, discontent bubbled up from the bottom. This time, though, it was not workers marching in the street or antiwar protesters demonstrating at the Pentagon, it was a cyber-community of lone hackers who were the grains of sand slowing the machinery of commerce.

It's hard to ascribe radical motives to hackers and hoaxers. Of the corporations that really are building bombs, polluting the environment, and toppling nations, why do the cyber-saboteurs always target the sites that auction lawn furniture? Even the hackers who broke into the FBI's Web site did little more than throw a virtual moon. It doesn't excuse them, but, unlike the social movements of the '60s and '70s whose goals were to stop war and eliminate racism, today's hackers and hoaxers have no game plan.

But it's a deadly serious one. When someone starts a hoax about a corporation, management doesn't lose jobs, workers do. When a product division folds, a fast-food franchise closes, or a Web site is attacked, it affects the company from the bottom up, not the top down.

How a company reacts when it is assailed is a study in crisis management. Those who face a hoax head-on (such as the people of Coca-Cola, Diet Pepsi, Tylenol, Kentucky Fried Chicken, and Procter & Gamble) find that the problem either goes away or retreats to its rightful place among nutcases. Those who stonewall a problem, however, do so at their own risk; invariably they are the companies and products about whom one consistently hears urban legends. Hoaxers count on an uptight company shriveling like a spider on a hot skillet when it's so much easier to protect itself with simple truth.

Cyber-vandals are like a three-year-old who wants to see if he can reach the cookie jar on top of the refrigerator. So what if the fridge falls over and smashes, the cookie jar breaks, and others cut their feet on the pieces of pottery? Little Johnny got his treat. Ironically, two phrases come to mind in this contest: the first is from Thomas Jefferson, whose Declaration of Independence cites "life, liberty and the pursuit of happiness" as an inalienable right. The second is from Spider-Man (Stan Lee) who realized what today's hoaxers apparently do not: "With great power comes great responsibility." Since hoaxers probably know more about the latter than the former, what follows may shed some light on both.

(*Note:* Remember that all product myths are false unless specifically proven true.)

✓ **REALITY CHECK**

You Can Get Your Car Back

When asked whether it would be feasible to commit the crime of car theft, a federal judge once confided, "Of all the car thefts that are committed, perhaps one in ten is solved. Of that one in ten, perhaps another one in ten actually goes to trial instead of being plea-bargained. And if it goes to trial, the chances are only one in ten that there will be a conviction. And even if there is a conviction, there is usually probation, so the chances of going to jail are maybe one in ten. So if you're asking me whether you should steal a car, I'd say hell, yes."

Then he added, "If you want a lighter sentence, always commit a crime that the judge or jury can relate to."

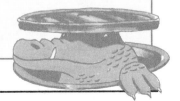

✍️ INTERVIEW

Crisis Management

Even though the law treats corporations as individuals, that doesn't necessarily make them human. So when a corporation finds itself under attack by boycott, urban legend, or product mishap, the staff can be just as clumsy as the average person in dealing with it. Robin Cohn is a crisis management consultant who is frequently summoned to advise corporate clients on how to deal with such problems. She came to national attention by her handling of the January 13, 1982, Air Florida #90 crash in Washington, D.C., and has since (discreetly) helped other clients weather similar storms. Her book, *The PR Crisis Bible*, is published by St. Martin's Press.

Segaloff: What's the first thing a company should do when they hear of an urban legend or rumor?

Cohn: Find out where it's coming from. Is it coming from a chat room, is it coming from a competitor? From the questions that people ask when they call you, you can pretty much tell. For example, I had one company that started getting phone calls from customers saying that their product had a flaw in it and why didn't they tell them, and so on. They were able, through the customers, to track down that it was in a chat room, and from that they were able to track it down to a guy they happened to know because he bugged them all the time. Nowadays people are using monitoring services and [Internet detectives].

Segaloff: Why is it that corporations can spend millions of dollars for advertising, yet it doesn't have the power of one person mentioning something in a chat room?

Cohn: First of all, something that is written has more validity. Second, everybody knows that an advertisement is paid for by the company. So, in terms of real credibility, the public is sophisticated enough to know that an ad is just that.

Something in a chat room sounds legitimate. There's a saying that if you want everybody to pay attention, whisper. There's also such a prejudice toward big business these days [that] if the rumor has any validity, people expect it to be correct.

Segaloff: When you're called in for crisis management to a company that's under siege, how do you coach them, and whom do you coach?

Cohn: It starts at the top. If we're talking about a serious crisis, the initial response has to come from the CEO or the president or someone of a high-ranking level. If it's something that's going to affect the health and well-being of its customers, or the public in general, or its employees, or even something environmental, then these top people have to address it. In the case of a CEO who is not very good on camera—if it's as serious as Bhopal, for example—he can still come out, read the statement, and then turn it over to the other high-ranking individual who will serve as spokesperson. But if the top person isn't out there, it looks like he's hiding.

Fast-Food Chicken

Myth: Kentucky Fried Chicken has been selling genetically engineered chickens and/or rats and/or ersatz chicken.

Truth: False, false, and false. There have been jokes for years that Colonel Sanders was trying to breed chickens with six drumsticks, but nothing like the rumors that:

1. "Kentucky Fried Chicken stopped using chicken in favor of a genetically engineered meat that's cheaper, and that's why they changed their name to KFC." Hello! Isn't KFC's slogan still "We do chicken right"? One KFC hoax specifies "a study at the University of New Hampshire" to authenticate itself; no such study exists. The reason the company changed its name was to de-emphasize the word *fried* in their expanding menu, as well as to position their product more effectively in a broader marketplace (in other words, to shed the urban and Southern stigma).
2. "They use rats instead of chicken, which is why the pieces don't look like the chicken you fry at home." Rats are not and have never been used. America's fast-food franchises have strict hygiene standards. Interestingly, whenever there's been an outbreak of food poisoning, it's been in beef products. But you're right that the chicken you get in fast-food restaurants doesn't look the same as when you cut up a chicken at home. Blame it on the thick layers of crunchy crust that everybody loves.
3. "They use pressed chicken." Although some chicken items (such as breaded cutlets) in some restaurants (not KFC) may be processed and reshaped chicken, they are definitely chicken *meat*. The same holds for fish fillets, which are pressed and re-formed, unless you've hooked a loaf-shaped fish lately.

KFC is a subsidiary of Tricon Global Restaurants, Inc., the same people who own Taco Bell and Pizza Hut. Their Web site (*www.kfc.com*) provides additional information.

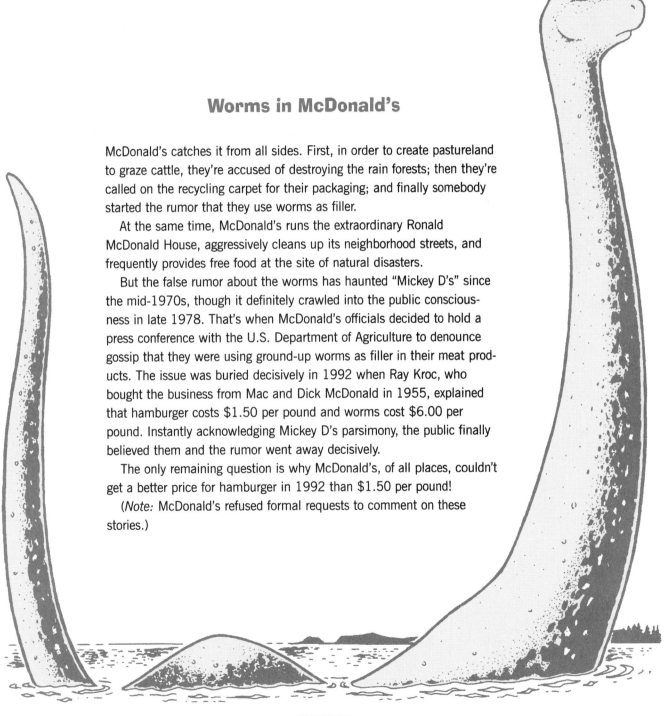

Worms in McDonald's

McDonald's catches it from all sides. First, in order to create pastureland to graze cattle, they're accused of destroying the rain forests; then they're called on the recycling carpet for their packaging; and finally somebody started the rumor that they use worms as filler.

At the same time, McDonald's runs the extraordinary Ronald McDonald House, aggressively cleans up its neighborhood streets, and frequently provides free food at the site of natural disasters.

But the false rumor about the worms has haunted "Mickey D's" since the mid-1970s, though it definitely crawled into the public consciousness in late 1978. That's when McDonald's officials decided to hold a press conference with the U.S. Department of Agriculture to denounce gossip that they were using ground-up worms as filler in their meat products. The issue was buried decisively in 1992 when Ray Kroc, who bought the business from Mac and Dick McDonald in 1955, explained that hamburger costs $1.50 per pound and worms cost $6.00 per pound. Instantly acknowledging Mickey D's parsimony, the public finally believed them and the rumor went away decisively.

The only remaining question is why McDonald's, of all places, couldn't get a better price for hamburger in 1992 than $1.50 per pound!

(*Note:* McDonald's refused formal requests to comment on these stories.)

The Roach Eggs in the Taco

Myth: A girl got roach eggs in her saliva glands from eating a taco at Taco Bell.

Truth: This racially tinged fabrication has been forwarded to a fare-the-well on the Internet, often with the heading, "I can't believe this!!! Disgusting!!! I got goose bumps!!" The rumor describes how "this girl" (never named) ate a chicken taco and, that night, her jaw became swollen. Eventually doctors found that her saliva glands had become infested with eggs from the female cockroach the girl ate in the taco. It ends, "If they hadn't figured out what was going on, the eggs would have hatched inside the lining of her mouth." The message refers disbelievers to the November 19, 1999, *New York Times*.

Following the modus operandi of Internet pranksters, this story ignores biology (roach eggs are in pods inside the female), anatomy (chewed-up anything couldn't "climb" into saliva glands), and chemistry (saliva and stomach acid kill bugs).

There is, indeed, a mention of Taco Bell in the November 19, 1999, *New York Times*. It is an item about a 270-pound football player who got stuck in a restaurant's drive-through window! Clearly, the perpetrator of this hoax cleverly chose a date that would respond to a Web search for "Taco Bell" and assumed that nobody would pay the *Times* $2.50 to retrieve it. It turns out that the incident, which involved University of Kansas defensive end Dion Rayford, had been characterized incorrectly by he Lawrence, Kansas police department. The (less interesting) truth is that on November 17, 1999, Rayford poked his head into the take-out window of Taco Bell and yelled at an employee who has misfilled his order.

Procter & Gamble's Corporate Logo

The most inexplicable rumor attacking a product or corporation has got to be the one suggesting that the Procter & Gamble

Company is somehow associated with the Church of Satan. The "proof" offered by those who invented and continue this myth (whoever they are) has to do with the "moon and stars" trademark supposedly being satanic, and alleged appearances by P&G executives on TV talk shows where they admit to their demonic associations.

Not only are those allegations false, but P&G has gone to considerable effort (*www.pg.com*) to deny them and offer detailed rebuttal. The company's supporters in this effort include not only the talk shows (Jenny Jones, Phil Donahue, Sally Jessy Raphael) but an ecumenical list of bona fide religious groups.

According to P&G's research, the rumor began in the early 1980s. The company itself began in 1851 when Mr. Procter and Mr. Gamble manufactured Star Candles and used the moon and stars logo, as the company says, "to help identify the quality products made by P&G through a visual symbol, since many people in the 1800s could not read. The half moon was chosen because it was a popular symbol for those times and widely used. The 13 stars represented the 13 original colonies. The trademark was officially registered with the U.S. Patent Office in 1882."

However, trying to handle the problem by having Durk Jager (chairman, president, and CEO) appear on a talk show would merely confirm the rumor that "someone from P&G went on TV," as well as provide words that could be taken out of context. Clearly, truth has no meaning to the hoaxers.

Proving something false that is already false is like trying to prove it's night by turning on a light. Procter & Gamble's reaction is part of a growing specialization within the public relations profession that might best be called "corporate damage control." It also raises questions of why, of all targets, P&G was chosen. Some think it might have been a form of industrial sabotage by a competitor. Others see malice on the part of some radical Christian sect that wants to aggrandize itself by screaming "Satan" in a crowded supermarket.

Spider Eggs in Bubble Yum

Here is another impossible scheme that gripped America in the late 1970s. Maybe it was the uniqueness of the product: a pillow of chewing gum that gave way without a fight. Like any new kid who was different, Bubble Yum attracted rumors: It was made soft by spider eggs, and a girl got her head infested, sneezed, and her face got covered in a sticky web. Before you could say "arachnid," an urban legend was born.

LifeSavers, the company responsible for Bubble Yum, had already cut back on advertising so they could meet the unprecedented demand for the gum. But when rumors hurt sales, they were forced to take ads proclaiming "Somebody is telling very bad lies about a very good product." Obviously, the myth was false for any number of reasons, but it left a bookmark in the memory of anyone who ever heard it.

When Milkmen Attack

In the days when dairies still made home deliveries, the sight of the white-suited, milkman driving his delivery truck was as familiar in the American landscape as the iceman had been a generation earlier. Those were the days when milk still came in bottles, and when local dairies competed fiercely for the door-to-door trade.

Getting a customer to change from The Other Guy meant greater revenue on a milkman's route, and some MIW (Men In White) occasionally engaged in a homegrown form of industrial sabotage. They would fill a hypodermic syringe with lemon juice, go to a house that did business with a competing dairy, and inject the lemon juice through the cardboard lid of their competitor's milk bottle. By the time the customer woke up and carried the bottle inside, the milk would be curdled. After this had happened a few times, the housewife would switch dairies. Alas, milkmen are gone now that dairies are vast conglomerates. Such progress has meant not only the loss of personal service, but also a shortage of off-color jokes about milkmen.

Un-advertised Benefits

Sometimes, myths about consumer products are true, but the manufacturer can't say so. Alka-Seltzer is a respected remedy, but the company has never been able to come out and say that it works for hangovers. Preparation-H is a valued treatment for—well, you know what it's used for. But it also reduces swelling when applied as a balm beneath puffy eyes. Uncarbonated Coca-Cola syrup is a time-honored palliative for upset stomachs (in fact, in 1885, it was originally sold only in pharmacies). And Accent Meat Tenderizer (MSG) works wonders when applied externally to reduce swelling from bee stings and mosquito bites.

These are perfectly acceptable uses, yet they may be seen as too unsavory to brag about or to associate with a mass market product. Even though (wink wink), everybody "knows" about them.

Tie Me Hamburger Down, Sport

The persistent urban legend that kangaroo meat once turned up in a Jack-in-the-Box hamburger is an example of how a lie can spread when it is not addressed. Let it be said from the start that "Jack" has not, and never did, sell kangaroo meat.

Here's how it started, but not how it ended.

On August 14, 1981, the *Washington Post* reported that the U.S. Department of Agriculture was on the alert for shipments of horsemeat labeled as beef that had been discovered at fast-food distribution points in six western states. The horsemeat (not kangaroo meat) was first discovered at a beef processing plant in San Diego, California, owned by Foodmaker, a Ralston-Purina subsidiary that also owned the Jack-in-the-Box restaurant chain. The meat was not reported by a worker in the plant but by a USDA inspector who said that the 60-pound block "did not look right."

A follow-up *Post* article on August 26, 1981, said that the USDA was beginning "new testing procedures to keep horse and kangaroo meat out of beef imports in the wake of evidence that Australian horse meat was served as beef in some fast-food restaurants in the western United States." The restaurants were not named. By October 4, 1981, the scandal was being called "Slaughtergate" and the Australian government was looking into it, too. The consensus was that Australians (not Americans) were "eating a lot of 'roo meat and not knowing it."

Kangaroo meat, by the way, is perfectly edible and is a widely available comestible Down Under. It is also clearly identified as such. Unfortunately, the way kangaroo meat is harvested—the animals are shot, field-dressed, and thrown on trucks to be driven hundreds of miles for processing—means that they may arrive befouled. The technical term was "4D" (diseased, dying, dead, and decayed). None of this meat has been reported as being used by any U.S. fast-food chain.

What has made this particular urban legend so troublesome is that it exists beyond the ability to prove or disprove it. USDA records from 1981 have been destroyed, and Freedom of Information Act documents are incomplete. According to USDA insiders, however, the joke that went around the Meat Grading department at the time was that "kangaroo meat comes in three grades: Hop, Skip and Jump." There was even a recorded parody of the Australian folk song, "Tie Me Kangaroo Down, Sport" that went "Tie Me Hamburger Down, Sport."

(*Note:* Jack-in-the-Box, Inc. would not respond to five phone calls and a certified letter to their Corporate Communications representative.)

Intravenous Pepsi Case Study

The summer of 1993 was made more exciting by the alleged presence of hypodermic syringes in at least two cans of Diet Pepsi. The first was "discovered" on June 9 in Tacoma, Washington, and, after television reports were broadcast, another was "found" a few days later in Cleveland, Ohio. By midmonth there was a rash of claims on file from citizens who said they had likewise been surprised.

At the same time, PepsiCo, Inc. (the parent company based in Somers, New York) began aggressively denying that anything other than Diet Pepsi could be found in Diet Pepsi cans. Their reaction has become a case study in responsible and effective corporate crisis management. It involved four steps:

1. Put public safety first.
2. Find the problem and fix it.
3. Communicate to reporters on the reporters' schedule.
4. Be accountable for solving the crisis.

Immediately on learning of the incident, Pepsi North America President & CEO Craig Weatherup and FDA Commissioner David Kessler held a televised press conference, appeared on ABC-TV's

Tachistoscopes

In the 1950s it was rumored that movie theaters were using "subliminal suggestions" to send audiences to the concession stand. This feat was supposedly accomplished in 1957 with a tachistoscope, a device used by one James Vicary during a run of *Picnic* in Fort Lee, New Jersey. A kind of slide projector that could flash words on the screen at 1/3,000 of a second, too fast to actually read but slow enough for the mind to absorb, the tachistoscope was touted as making everybody suddenly get the urge for soft drinks.

Despite the legend, its effectiveness was never publicly confirmed. A 1976 book by Wilson Bryan Key (who also claims that the word *sex* can be seen on Ritz Crackers, which increases their sales appeal) reported that the tachistoscope was patented in 1962 and 1966 by Dr. Hal Becker of the Tulane Medical School.

The tachistoscope's frightening potential for influencing voting or social attitudes has never been explored, or, for that matter, proven to sell soda pop. In 1974 the FCC banned its use on TV, which runs at an unvarying 30 frames per second and can't possibly exhibit a 1/3,000 image anyway.

(*Note:* For those who want to see some examples in film, check out *The Graduate,* which features flash-frames of breasts and thighs during Mrs. Robinson's seduction of Benjamin; and *Fight Club*, in which Brad Pitt makes several one-frame appearances to Edward Norton before his character is actually introduced.)

 **INTERVIEW**

Things Go Better with Mickey

Remember when "they" told you on the playground that if you took a bunch of aspirin and chugged a bottle of Coke, you'd catch a buzz? Or that the soft drink has cocaine in it? Or somebody once found a dead rodent in a bottle of Coke? Well, the Atlanta-based Coca-Cola Company remembers it, too, and Robert E. Baskin, their director of Corporate Media Relations & Communications, took the time to set the record straight about this legendary soft drink.

Segaloff: Has anybody ever actually complained about finding a dead mouse or a mouse skeleton in a bottle or can of Coke?

Baskin: There has never been a case of a mouse or mouse skeleton actually found in a can or bottle of Coca-Cola. This being a sometimes difficult world, there have, regrettably, been instances in which criminals have tampered with finished packages after they have purchased them and attempted to defraud either a retailer or our Company by inserting a foreign substance. But even these instances are extraordinarily rare.

Segaloff: Did the advertising slogan "Coke adds life," when translated into Chinese (as the Internet rumor says), really come out "Coke brings your dead relatives back from the grave"?

Baskin: The slogan "Coke adds life" was correctly translated to say "Coke adds life." Frankly, we have never heard your version of the translation before.

Segaloff: Can you really get a buzz by chugging Coke and aspirin?

Baskin: You'll have to ask a physiologist or physician about this. If I drink Coke when I take an aspirin, I satisfy my thirst and relieve my headache!

Segaloff: Is there now, or was there ever, cocaine in Coca-Cola?

Baskin: While the formula for Coca-Cola remains a secret, it has been a constant. It has not changed in one hundred and fourteen years. And cocaine was never an ingredient.

Segaloff: Why does Coke seem to taste different in different parts of the country?

Baskin: Coca-Cola is identical across the country and around the world. Taste is subjective. The best Coke I've ever had was in Burkina Faso, a country in equatorial Africa. But that may have been because it reminded me of home.

Segaloff: Why does it taste better in the classic eight-ounce bottle?

Baskin: I, too, think it tastes better in the eight-ounce bottle, but our flavor chemists tell us that there is no difference. Obviously, taste is impacted by the mind.

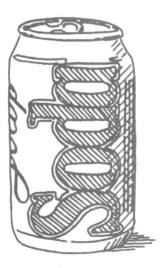

SLAPP Suits

What happens when the First Amendment right of free speech collides with a corporation that doesn't want its dirty laundry aired in public? Something called a SLAPP suit, that's what.

In the mid-1980s, corporations besieged by protesters, commentators, pamphleteers, and other organized opponents started filing Strategic Lawsuits Against Public Participation (SLAPP). The tactic was not so much to defend themselves as to silence anyone who spoke out against them. The expense alone, even when they were vindicated, would deprive an ordinary citizen of his or her right to voice an opinion. Courts have increasingly blocked SLAPP suits on the grounds that they are infringements on the U.S. Constitution. For their part, corporations can still sue for libelous content, so protesters need to make sure they can substantiate their claims. Generally speaking, though, the last thing a culpable corporation wants is to have its internal documents exposed during pre-trial depositions.

"Sex Sells Cars" Myth

Ever notice that there are two kinds of car commercials on television? First, there's the super-slick kind that shows the vehicle whooshing along the open road, slashing through jungles, climbing mountains, and curing rare diseases. Then there is the crude local kind where a man in loud clothing walks through a parking lot full of cars, screaming, "Hi! I'm Crazy Conroy! Come on down!"

Guess which sells more cars? That's right: Crazy Conroy. The slick "corporate" spots are designed to create a mystique for the car, and an image for the brand name, and to subtly target what people they want to buy each model of car (check out the gender, age, and race of the actors). The local dealership ads are designed to make the funny car salesperson into a celebrity so that they have an advantage closing the deal ("Wow! Crazy Conroy sold us our car!"). Interestingly, it's too early to know which of these ad types—if either—inspires the people who buy cars online.

Nightline, and blanketed the news media with press releases. They ran video of how Pepsi produced its beverage, irrefutably showing that it would be impossible to put anything in a can while it was speeding along the assembly machines under Pepsi's supervision. They also stressed the penalty for filing false product tampering claims (five years in prison and $250,000 in fines) and encouraged use of the words *hoax* and *copycat*, all the while putting a human face on the predicament. Rebecca Madeira, Pepsi Cola Company public affairs vice-president, working with company executives, got the press to temper its hysteria with logic and reportage. The company's 24-hour telephone hotline was kept updated. Everything was coordinated with the company's 400 bottlers to ensure that the information given out would be consistent.

As "syringings" continued across the country, it became clear that it was impossible for the fault to have been Pepsi's. So many cans from so many different bottlers were supposedly tainted that it had to be the work of independent people who thought they could shake down the company.

Finally, on June 16, Pepsi obtained a videotape of a Colorado woman caught on a convenience store's surveillance camera trying to slip something into a Diet Pepsi can. The FDA asked Pepsi not to release the tape until an arrest was made, but as soon as the tamperer was detained, the footage hit the airwaves. On June 21, 1993, Pepsi ran newspaper ads headlined, "Pepsi is pleased to announce . . . nothing." Because of the company's forthright response, the story disappeared, and Pepsi went back to fighting its traditional battle against Coca-Cola.

No criminal charges were brought against the Seattle man who made the original complaint. Apparently a mixup occurred involving a diabetic family member who used the can to dispose of her insulin syringe. As for the Colorado woman who was arrested for product tampering, Colorado's Attorney General's office explains that the state has no codified criminal records, so it impossible to report on her fate.

(*Note:* The Pepsi-Cola Company provided some of the information for this report.)

Andy's Last Hoax Backfires

Even the most polished public relations machine can backfire, especially when venturing into the uncharted waters of cult celebrity worship. Such was the fate of Universal Pictures' 1999 biographical film *Man on the Moon,* starring Jim Carrey as the late comedian Andy Kaufman.

Comedian hardly defines the challenging, maddening, existential talent of Kaufman, who died in 1984. At least that is what they say. The unconventional way he conducted his career raised doubts about his death even as he was being lowered into the ground. This is because Kaufman was a master of the put-on. On and off stage he would portray characters such as "Andy, the guy who works in the kitchen," the mittle-European "Taxi" driver Latka Gravas, Elvis Presley, and his masterpiece, the irritating lounge entertainer "Tony Clifton." When Kaufman was in a character, he refused to answer to his real name, a trait that those around him often found as annoying as it was impressive.

So were his conceptual antics. He seriously challenged women to wrestling matches. He meant it when he goaded a professional male wrestler into tossing him butt-over-brains on a TV show. He performed his spot-on Elvis impersonation on a *Saturday Night Live* sketch trashing the King, and then announced, on the air, that he did not approve of what he had just done. Then, in 1984, as if to top himself, he died of lung cancer. Since he was not a smoker, it just didn't follow, and his fans knew it.

So when Kaufman's obsessive life became the subject of *Man on the Moon*, starring Jim Carrey and directed by Milos Forman, Universal Pictures logically attempted to capitalize on what they perceived as the same cult-worship that had grown up around Elvis, Lenny Bruce, Sam Kinnison, James Dean, and other icons of the counterculture. They began an "Andy Lives" poster and Internet campaign. They had Kaufman's creative partner Bob Zmuda dress as Tony Clifton and get ejected from the Emmy Awards. They designed print and TV ads for the film that made it look as if the printer and TV station were running them wrong. And they staged

Restaurant Myths

"They" (and who, exactly, are "they"?) say that if you work in a restaurant you'll never eat there again; it has to do with knowing the intimate details of how they prepare the food. Other restaurant myths (some of which are true) include:

- Doctors are the worst tippers (11 percent); working people are the best (20 percent or more), especially other service workers.
- Waitpersons dislike serving two women sitting at a table because they take too much time to order, and then stay forever. The argot for this is *campers*.
- If you order meat well done, the chef knows you don't care how it tastes and you may get a lesser cut.
- A restaurant is only as good as the bread it serves.
- The third restaurant in a given location is the one that succeeds.
- Customers tend to order the same thing they had last time at the same restaurant.
- Never eat at a restaurant on Monday night; that's the head chef's night off.
- Never order the fish on Monday; it's probably been there since Friday.
- Never eat at a restaurant that has a "help wanted" sign in the window; they're short-handed and service will be bad.
- If you really want to do something nice for your waiter or waitress, leave a cash tip when you pay by credit card. The credit card company takes 3 to 6 percent service charge, and some restaurants deduct it from the tip.

an "incident" at a prerelease press conference at which Zmuda/Clifton hazed Carrey.

The film opened on Christmas Day, 1999, in 2,078 theaters across America. In general, the critics liked it; but the public stayed away, and the film was completely ignored at Oscar time. What went wrong?

Nothing.

The *Man on the Moon* promotional campaign did just what it was supposed to do: it accurately presented the film to the public. Unfortunately, the filmmakers and distributor ignored the fact that Andy Kaufman may have been a genius, but he rankled the public so much while he was alive that the film about him promised to do the same. In wielding the vast publicity machine on behalf of their product, the experts succeeded in helping millions of people make up their minds against them. It even worked against Jim Carrey, who gave one of the most brilliant and daring performances of his career.

Wherever he is, Andy must be smiling perversely and saying, "Dank you berry much."

Star Trek Sentencing

Myth: A man is convicted of a crime. At the penalty hearing, the judge asks him if he has anything to say before the sentence is handed down. The man taps a button on his shirt and says, "Beam me up, Scotty, there are hostile life forms down here."

Truth: There's no way to confirm this, but if the shirt was orange or he was an ensign, he probably got the death penalty.

Appendices

Appendix A

Bibliography

This book does not pretend to track down the origin of urban legends. Those who wish to explore the wandering lineage of these fables should consult the excellent series of books by folklorist Jan Harold Brunvand, author of *The Vanishing Hitchhiker: American Urban Legends and Their Meaning* and other titles, as well as the many Web sites, listed here, devoted to such cultural archaeology.

Anger, Kenneth, *Hollywood Babylon.* 1981 ed. New York: Bell Publishing Co., 1975.

Anouilh, Jean. *Becket or the Honor of God.* Translated by Lucienne Hill. New York: Coward-McCann, Inc., 1960.

Anti-Defamation League. *The Protocols of the Learned Elders of Zion: A Hoax of Hate,* Posted at *www.adl.org/special%5Freports/protocols/protocols_intro.html,* 1999.

Baden, Michael M., M.D., with Judith Adler Hennessee. *Unnatural Death: Confessions of a Medical Examiner.* New York: Ivy Books, 1989.

Balio, Tino, ed. *The American Film Industry.* Madison, Wisconsin: University of Wisconsin Press, 1985.

Barth, Jack. *American Quest.* New York: Simon & Schuster, 1990.

Bartlett, John. *Bartlett's Familiar Quotations.* 16th ed. Edited by Justin Kaplan. New York: Little, Brown, 1992.

Baskin, Robert E. Letter to Nat Segaloff, author.

Behlmer, Rudy, ed. *Memo from David O. Selznick.* New York: Viking Press, 1972.

Belkin, Gary, and Don Fauser. *V.D. Blues.* Presented by Educational Broadcasting Corp. New York: Avon Books, 1973.

Blatty, William Peter. *The Ninth Configuration.* Screenplay, 1980.

——*Twinkle Twinkle, Killer Kane,* New York: Doubleday, 1966.

Blum, Daniel H. *A Pictorial History of the Silent Screen.* New York: Grosset & Dunlop, 1953.

Boller Jr., Paul F., and Ronald L. Davis. *Hollywood Anecdotes*. New York: Ballantine Books, 1987.

Boller Jr., Paul F., and John George. *They Never Said It*. New York: Oxford University Press, 1989.

Botkin, B. A., ed. *A Treasury of American Folklore*. New York: Crown Publishers, 1944.

Brewer-Giorgio, Gail. *The Elvis Files*. New York: Shapolsky Publishers, Inc., 1990.

Brooks, Louise. *Lulu in Hollywood*. New York: Alfred A. Knopf, 1974, 1982.

Brooks, Tim, and Earle Marsh. *The Complete Directory to Prime Time Network and Cable TV Shows*. 6th ed. New York: Ballantine Books, 1995.

Brownlow, Kevin. *Hollywood: The Pioneers*. London: William Collins Sons & Co., Ltd., 1979.

Brunvand, Jan Harold. *The Choking Doberman*. New York: W. W. Norton & Co., 1984.

Burnam, Tom. *More Misinformation*. New York: Ballantine Books, 1980.

——*The Dictionary of Misinformation*. New York: Thomas Y. Crowell, 1975.

Capp, Al. Interview with Nat Segaloff, author.

Carey, Mary. *A Compendium of Bunk*. Springfield, Ill.: Charles C. Thomas Publishers, Ltd., 1976.

Carroll, Robert Todd. *The Skeptic's Dictionary*. Posted at *http://dcn.davis.ca.us/~btcarrol/skeptic/bigfoot.html*, 2000.

Clarke, Kenneth. "Diaries Trial Opens." *London Daily Telegraph*, August 21, 1984.

Cohen, Herb. *You Can Negotiate Anything*. Secaucus, N.J.: Lyle Stuart, Inc., 1980.

Cooper, Joe. "Cottingly: At Last the Truth." *The Unexplained*, no. 117, 1982. Posted by Donald Simenek at *www. lhup.edu/~dsimanek*.

Corman, Roger, with Will Jerome. *How I Made a Hundred Movies in Hollywood and Never Lost a Dime*. New York: Random House, 1990.

Corson, Ben, John Downey, Alice Tepper Marlin, Jonathan Schorsch, Emily Swaab, and Rosalyn Will. *Shopping for a Better World*. 3rd ed. New York: Council on Economic Priorities, 1990.

Crispen, Patrick Douglas. *MAP09: Spamming and Urban Legends*. Posted at *http://mobbiusweb.com/~mobius/Roadmap/map09.html*.

Culture Jammer's Encyclopedia. *www.syntac.net/hoax/ index.html*.

Darrow, Clarence. *The Story of My Life*. New York: Charles Scribner's Sons, 1932.

Della Femina, Jerry. *From Those Wonderful Folks Who Gave You Pearl Harbor*. Edited by Charles Sopkin. New York: Simon & Schuster, 1970.

Department of Mineral Services, National Museum of Natural History, Smithsonian Institution. "Hope Diamond." *Encyclopedia Smithsonian*. Posted at *www.si.edu/resource/faq/nmnh/hope.htm*.

Donaldson, Norman, and Betty Donaldson. *How Did They Die*. Vol.2. New York: St. Martin's Press, 1980.

Dummar, Melvin. Interview with Nat Segaloff, author.

Dye, Lee. "A Warrior Against Disease." ABCNEWS.com Science. Posted at *http://abcnews.go.com/sections/science/DyeHard/dye18.html*, 2000.

Ecole Chronology Project. "The Ecole Initiative." Posted at *http://cedar.evansville.edu*, 1995.

Emery, David. About.com Urban Legends Web Site. Posted at *http://urbanlegends.about.com*, 2000.

Fargis, Paul, and Sheree Bykofsky, eds. *The New York Public Library Desk Reference*. 2nd ed. New York: Prentice Hall, 1993.

Fletcher, Connie. *What Cops Know*. New York: Pocket Books, 1990.

Forbes, Malcolm, with Jeff Bloch. *They Went That-A-Way*. New York: Ballantine Books, 1988.

Foster, Freling. *Keep Up with the World*. New York: Grosset & Dunlop, 1949.

Franklin, Benjamin. *Poor Richard's Almanack, 1733*. Posted at *www.sln.fi.edu/qa98/musing9/almanack1733.html*.

Funk, Charles Earle. *A Hog On Ice & Other Curious Expression*. New York: Harper & Row, 1948.

Funk, Wilfred. *Word Origins*. New York: Wings Books, 1950.

Gabler, Neal. *An Empire of Their Own*. New York: Doubleday, 1988.

Givens, Bill. *Son of Film Flubs*. Secaucus, N.J.: Carol Publishing Group, 1991.

Goodman, Ezra. *The Fifty Year Decline and Fall of Hollywood*. New York: Simon & Schuster, 1961.

Goodman, Walter. *The Committee: The Extraordinary Career of the House Committee on Un-American Activities*. New York: Farrar, Straus and Giroux, 1968.

Green, Abel, and Joe Laurie Jr. *Show Biz from Vaude to Video*. New York: Henry Holt and Company, 1951.

Grossman, Gary H. *Saturday Morning Television*. New York: Dell Publishers, 1981.

——*Superman from Serial to Cereal*. New York: Popular Library, 1976. (Reissued: *www.supermanbook.com* and *www.georgereevesbook.com*)

Halliwell, Leslie. *Halliwell's Filmgoer's and Video Viewer's Companion*. 9th ed. New York: Harper & Row, 1988.

Harris, Robert. *Selling Hitler*. New York: Pantheon Books, 1986.

Hartner, Richard. *Piltdown Man.* Posted at *www.tiac.net/users/cri/piltdown.html*, 1998.

Haver, Ronald. *David O. Selznick's Hollywood.* New York: Alfred A. Knopf, 1980.

Hay, Peter. *Movie Anecdotes.* New York: Oxford University Press, 1990.

Hayduke, George. *Getting Even: The Complete Book of Dirty Tricks.* New York: Paladin Press, 1980. Republished, New York: Lyle Stuart/Carol Publishing, 1995.

Henreid, Paul, with Julius Fast. *Ladies' Man—An Autobiography.* New York: Coward-McCann, 1983.

Hirsch, E.D. Jr., Joseph F. Kett, and James Trefil. *The Dictionary of Cultural Literacy.* Boston: Houghton Mifflin Company, 1988.

Horan, James D. *The Wild Bunch.* New York: New American Library, 1958.

Hoxsey, Harry M. *You Don't Have to Die.* New York: Milestone Books, Inc., 1956.

Huntington, Tom. "The Man Who Believed in Fairies." *Smithsonian Magazine,* September 1997.

Johnson, Christopher Jay, Ph.D., and Marsha G. McGee, Ph.D., eds. *How Different Religions View Death and Afterlife.* Philadelphia, Penn: The Charles Press, 1991.

Juliano, Dave. *The Jersey Devil.* Posted at *www.serve.com/shadows/jd.htm*, 2000.

Katz, Ephriam. *The Film Encyclopedia.* 2nd ed. New York: HarperCollins, 1994.

Katzeff, Paul. *Full Moons.* Secaucus, N.J.: Citadel Press, 1981. Republished in 1988 as *Moon Madness.*

Kevan, S. M. "Perspectives on Seasons of Suicide." *Social Science and Medicine.* (14D: 369–78,1980.)

Kewzer, Gil. "King Tut's Curse Due to Fatal Spores?" *Canadian Medical Association Journal*, December 15, 1998.

Key, Wilson Bryan. *Media Sexploitation.* New York: New American Library, 1976.

Kirsch, J.P. "Donation of Constantine." *The Catholic Encyclopedia.* New York: Robert Appleton Company, 1909.

Knutson, Mark C. *The Remarkable Criminal Financial Career of Charles K. Ponzi.* Posted at *www.usinternet.com/ users/mcknutson/Pbankrup.htm*, 1997.

Kohn, Alfie. *You Know What They Say . . .* New York: HarperCollins, 1990.

Kovalik, Dr. Thomas. *Ned Buntline: King of the Dime Novels.* Posted at SamHar Press, *www.story-house.com*, 1996.

Krystek, Lee. *Unnatural Museum: Howard Carter and the Curse of the Mummy.* Posted at *www.unmuseum.mus.pa.us/ mummy.htm*, 1997, 1999.

——*Unnatural Museum: The Piltdown Man Hoax.* Posted at *http://unmuseum.mus.pa.us/piltdown.htm*, 1996.

Maltin, Leonard. *Movie & Video Guide.* 1999 ed. New York: Plume/Penguin Books, 1999.

Mankiewicz, Frank, and Joel Swerdlow. *Remote Control.* New York: Times Books, 1978.

Mankiewicz, Joseph L. *More about All about Eve, A Colloquy with Gary Carey.* New York: Random House, 1972.

Mann, Laurie D. T. *Dead People Server.* Posted at *http://dpsinfo.com*, 1997–2000.

Manners, Jane. "Can't Keep a Good Man Down." *Brill's Content*, pp. 82–85. April, 2000.

Marcus, Jon. "The G-Man: Melvin Purvis." *Boston Magazine*, pp. 42–45; 69–70. January, 1999.

Marinacci, Michael. *The Yellow Kid.* Posted at *http://pw2.netcom.com/~mikalm/weil.htm*, 1997.

Maurer, David W. *The American Confidence Man.* Springfield, Ill: Charles C. Thomas Publishers, Ltd., 1974.

Mayer, Arthur. *Merely Colossal.* New York: Simon & Schuster, 1953.

McNee, Patrick. Interview with Nat Sagaloff, author.

McWilliams, Peter. *Ain't Nobody's Business If You Do.* Los Angeles, Calif.: Prelude Press, 1996.

Meyers, Richard. *For One Week Only: The World of Exploitation Films.* Piscataway, N.J.: New Century Publishers, 1983.

Mikkelson, Barbara and David P. Mikkelson. Urban Legends Reference Page. Posted at *www.snopes.com*, 1995-2000.

National Geographic, "Wintering on the Roof of the World." October, 1962.

Nimoy, Leonard. Interview with Nat Segaloff, author.

O'Connell, Alan, and David Welch. Crop Circle Pages. Posted at *http://indigo.ie/~dcd/intro.htm*, 1997.

O'Connor, John. *Broadway Racketeers.* New York: Mayfair Publishing Co., undated (c. 1930).

O'Donnell, Pierce, and Dennis McDougall. *Fatal Subtraction.* New York: Dell Publishing, 1992.

Ogilvy, David. *Ogilvy on Advertising.* New York: Vintage Books, 1985.

Oxford University Libraries Automation Service. *Prophesies of Nostradamus.* Posted at *www.lib.ox.ac.uk/internet/news/faq/archive/nostradamus.html.*

Packard, Vance. *The Hidden Persuaders.* New York: Pocket Books, 1957.

Panati, Charles. *Panati's Parade of Fads, Follies, and Manias.* New York: HarperCollins, 1991.

——*Panati's Extraordinary Endings of Practically Everything and Everybody.* New York: Harper & Row, 1989.

BIBLIOGRAPHY

Perot, Ross. *United We Stand.* New York: Hyperion, 1992.

Phillips, D. P., and J. Liv, "The Frequency of Suicides Around Major Public Holidays. *Suicide and Life-Threatening Behavior.* (17:142, 1987.)

Polanski, Charles. *The Congressional Medal of Honor Society.* Posted at *www.cmohs.org.htm*, 2000.

Potter, Carole. *Knock on Wood & Other Superstitions.* New York: Bonanza Books, 1983.

Poundstone, William. *Big Secrets.* New York: Quill/William Morrow & Co., 1983.

Ramsaye, Terry. *A Million and One Nights.* New York: Simon & Schuster, 1926, 1954.

Rintels, David W. *Clarence Darrow for the Defense.* New York: Doubleday & Company, 1975.

Rohde, Stephen F. Interview with Nat Segaloff, author.

Rosten, Leo. *The Joys of Yiddish.* New York: Pocket Books, 1968.

Sagan, Carl. *The Demon-Haunted World.* New York: Random House, 1995.

Schickel, Richard. *The Stars.* New York: Dial Press, 1962.

Schultheiss, John and Mark Schaubert, eds. *You Are There Teleplays, The Critical Edition, by Abraham Polonsky.* Northridge, Calif.: The Center for Telecommunication Studies, California State University, 1997.

Sehlinger, Robert W. *The Unofficial Guide to Disneyland.* New York: Prentice Hall, 1990.

Shipman, David. *Movie Talk: Who Said What about Whom in the Movies.* New York: St. Martin's Press, 1988.

Sifakis, Carl. *The Encyclopedia of American Crime.* New York: Facts on File, 1982.

Smith, Dave. *Disney A to Z.* New York: Hyperion Books, 1996.

Smith, Russell. *Incredible History of the Fabled Hope Diamond.* Posted at *http://camalott.com/~rssmith/hope.htm.*

Sowards, Jack B. (screenplay). Story by Harve Bennett and Jack B. Sowards. *Star Trek II: The Wrath of Khan,* Calif.: Paramount Pictures Corporation, 1982. Screenplay published by Pocket Books, NY.

Spain, Patricia Ward. *History of Hoxsey Treatment.* Posted at *www.healthy.net/library/books/options/Hoxsey.htm,* 1999.

Spignesi, Stephen J. *The Odd Index.* New York: Plume, 1994.

Stambler, Irwin. *The Encyclopedia of Pop Rock and Soul.* Rev. ed. New York: St. Martin's Press, 1989.

Teichmann, Howard. *George S. Kaufman, an Intimate Portrait.* New York: Atheneum, 1972.

Trager, James. *The People's Chronology.* New York: Holt, Reinhart & Winston, 1979.

TV Guide. "TV's Most Notorious Legends," *TV Guide,* July 25, 1998.

Varasdi, J. Allen. *Myth Information*. New York: Ballantine Books, 1989.

Walker, Samuel. *In Defense of American Liberties*. New York: Oxford University Press, 1990.

Walters, Richard. *Hoxsey Therapy*. Health World Net, 1993.

Washburn, Charles. *The Cardiff Giant: A Narrative and Chronicle of the Hoax*. Posted at *www.cardiffgiant.com/hello/html*, 1995.

Waters, John. *Crackpot: The Obsessions of John Waters*. New York: MacMillan, 1983.

Weems, Mason Locke. *The Life and Memorable Actions of George Washington*. 5th ed. (1800). Posted at *www.genealogy.org/~weems (Mason Weems)*, 1996.

Weil, Joseph R., as told to W. T. Brannon. *"Yellow Kid" Weil*. 2nd ed. Chicago: Ziff-Dam's Publishers, 1948.

Weissling, Thomas. *Predator Focus: Earwigs*. University of Florida. Posted at *www.ftld.ufl.edi/predator1.htm*, 2000.

Wilk, Max. *The Wit and Wisdom of Hollywood*. New York: Athaneum, 1971.

Winslow, John Hathaway, and Alfred Meyer. "The Perpetrator at Piltdown," *Science*, September, 1983. J. H. A. Winslow, 1983, 1998. Posted at *www.tiac.net/users/cri/winslow.html*

Wright, John W., ed., with editors and reporters of the *Times, The New York Times 1998 Almanac*. New York: Penguin Group, 1997.

Zicree, Marc Scott. *The Twilight Zone Companion*. New York: Bantam Books, 1982.

Zukor, Adolph, with Dale Kramer. *The Public Is Never Wrong*. New York: G. P. Putnam's Sons, 1953.

Appendix B

Further Readings

100 Folk Heroes Who Shaped World History, by Sarah Krall, Chrisanne Beckner (Bluewood Books)

Above Top Secret: The Worldwide U.F.O. Cover-Up, by Timothy Good (Acacia Press, Inc.)

Alligators in the Sewer: And 222 Other Urban Legends, by Thomas J. Craughwell (Black Dog & Leventhal Publishers)

Baby on the Car Roof and 222 Other Urban Legends: Absolutely True Stories That Happened to a Friend of a Friend of a Friend, by Thomas J. Craughwell (Black Dog & Leventhal Publishers)

Big Book of Hoaxes, by B. Taggart (Editor), Carl Sifakis (DC Comics)

Big Footnotes: A Comprehensive Bibliography Concerning Bigfoot, the Abominable Snowman and Related Beings, by Daniel Perez (Danny Perez Publishing)

Bigfoot Sasquatch: Evidence, by Grover S. Krantz (Hancock House Pub Ltd)

Bigfoot: And Other Legendary Creatures, by Paul Robert Walker, William Noonan (Illustrator), Walker Walker (Harcourt Brace)

Careless Love: The Unmaking of Elvis Presley, by Peter Guralnick (Little Brown & Co.)

Chupacabras: And Other Mysteries, by Scott Corrales, Marc Davenport (Introduction) (Greenleaf Publications)

Come Sail Away: UFO Phenomenon & The Bible, by Guy Malone (Seekyel Publishing)

Con Games 101, by Cecilia Patch, Brendan Moynihan (Infrared Press)

Confusion Incorporated: A Collection of Lies, Hoaxes & Hidden Truths, by Stewart Home (Codex Books)

The Cost of Deception: The Seduction of Modern Myths and Urban Legends, by John A. Williams (Broadman & Holman Publishers)

The Creature: Personal Experiences With Bigfoot, by Jan Klement (Allegheny Press)

Cryptozoology A to Z: The Encyclopedia of Loch Monsters, Sasquatch, Chupacabras, and Other Authentic Mysteries of Nature, by Loren Coleman, Jerome Clark (Fireside)

Cursum Perficio: Marilyn Monroe Brentwood Hacienda: The Story of Her Final Months, by Gary Vitacco-Robles (Writers Club Ltd.)

The Deepening Complexity of Crop Circles: Scientific Research and Urban Legends, by Eltjo H. Haselhoff (North Atlantic Books)

Elvis: Unknown Stories Behind the Legend, by Jim Curtin, Renata Ginter (Contributor) (Associated Publishers Group)

An Encyclopedia of Claims, Frauds, and Hoaxes of the Occult and Supernatural: James Randi's Decidedly Skeptical Definitions of Alternate Realities, by James Randi, Arthur Charles Clarke (Introduction) (St. Martin's Press)

Encyclopedia of Hoaxes, by Gordon Stein (Gale Group)

The Enigma of Loch Ness: Making Sense of a Mystery, by Henry H. Bauer (University of Illinois Press)

Evil Agenda Of The Secret Government, by Tim Swartz (Global Communications Inner Light Publications)

Fakes, Frauds, and Flimflammery: Even More of the World's Most Outrageous Scams, by Andreas Schroeder (McClelland & Stewart)

The Field Guide to Bigfoot, Yeti and Other Mystery Primates Worldwide, by Loren Coleman, Patrick Huyghe, Harry Trumbore (Illustrator) (Avon Books)

Folk Heroes and Other Strange Happenings, by A.D. Winans (Benway Institute Studios)

Ghosts and Other Mysteries, by Dorothy Burtz Fiedel (D.B. Fiedel)

The Great American Liar, by James E., Sr. Myers (Lincoln Herndon Press)

Great Exploration Hoaxes, by David Roberts, Jan Morris (Introduction) (Modern Library)

Great Hoaxes of the World: And the Hoaxers Behind Them, by Nick Yapp (Pubs Overstock)

The Great New England Sea Serpent: An Account of Unknown Creatures Sighted by Many Respectable Persons Between 1638 and the Present Day, by J. P. O'Neill (Down East Books)

Haunted Lakes : Great Lakes Ghost Stories, Superstitions and Sea Serpents, by Frederick Stonehouse (Lake Superior Port City)

Hollywood Urban Legends: The Truth Behind the Most Delightfully Persistent Myths of Films, Tv, and Music, by Richard Roeper (New Page Books)

*Honey, Mud, Maggots, and Other Medical Marvels: The Science Behind Folk Remedies and Old Wives' Tales,*by Robert Root-Bernstein, et al (Houghton Mifflin Co.)

How Con Games Work, by M. Allen Henderson (Lyle Stuart)

Hustlers and Con Men: An Anecdotal History of the Confidence Man and His Games, by Jay Robert Nash (M. Evans & Co.)

Incredible Technologies Of The New World Order; UFOs - Tesla - Area 51, by Commander X (Global Communications Inner Light Publications)

John Chapman: The Legendary Johnny Appleseed, by Karen Clemens Warrick (Enslow Publishers, Inc.)

Johnny Appleseed: A Voice in the Wilderness: The Story of the Pioneer John Chapman : A Tribute, by William Ellery Jones (Editor) (Chrysalis Books)

Last Train to Memphis: The Rise of Elvis Presley, by Peter Guralnick (Little Brown & Co.)

Legend: The Life and Death of Marilyn Monroe, by Fred Lawrence Guiles (Scarborough House)

License to Steal: Traveling Con Artists: Their Games, Their Rules, Your Money, by Dennis Marlock, John Dowling (Contributor) (Paladin Press)

The Life of P. T. Barnum: Written by Himself, by Phineas T. Barnum, Terence Whalen (University of Illinois Press)

The Loch Ness Monster: The Evidence, by Steuart Campbell (Prometheus Books)

Making Millions on Legal Con Games and Pyramid Schemes, by William W. Walter (Walston Publishing)

Monsters of the Sea: The Truth About the Loch Ness Monster, the Giant Squid, Sea Serpents, Mermaids, and Other Fantastic Creatures of the Deep, by Richard Ellis (The Lyons Press)

Mysterious America: The Revised Edition, by Loren Coleman (Paraview Press)

The Mystery of the Loch Ness Monster, by Holly Wallace, Chris Oxlade (Heineman Library)

Old Wives Tales: The Truth Behind Common Notions, by Sue Castle (Citadel Press)

Paul Bunyan, by Steven Kellogg (William Morrow & Company Library)

Pelicans and Chihuahus and Other Urban Legends: Talking About Folklore, by William Neville Scott, Bill Scott (University of Queensland Press)

Pentagon Aliens, by William Lyne (Creatopia Productions)

Phantom of the Pines: More Tales of the Jersey Devil, by James F. McCloy, Ray Miller (Middle Atlantic Press)

Philadelphia Experiment and Other Ufo Conspiracies by Brad Steiger (Inner Light Publications)

Scams from the Great Beyond: How to Make Easy Money Off of Esp, Astrology, Ufos, Crop Circles, Cattle Mutilations, Alien Abductions, Atlantis, chan, by Peter Huston (Paladin Press)

Scams, Scandals, and Skulduggery: A Selection of the World's Most Outrageous Frauds, by Andreas Schroeder (McClelland & Stewart)

Spiders in the Hairdo, Modern Urban Legends, by David Holt, Bill Mooney, William Mooney (Illustrator), Kevin Pope (August House Publishers)

Tall Tale America: A Legendary History of Our Humorous Heroes, by Walter Blair, John Sanford (Illustrator) (University of Chicago Press)

There's a Customer Born Every Minute: P.T. Barnum's Secrets to Business Success, by Joseph G. Vitale, Joe Vitale (AMACOM)

Too Good to Be True: The Colossal Book of Urban Legends, by Jan Harold Brunvand (W.W. Norton & Company)

UFO Diary of a CIA Operative, by Commander Alvin E. Moore (Inner Light Publications)

Urban Legends: The As-Complete-As-One-Could-Be Guide to Modern Myths, by Ngaire E. Genge (Three Rivers Press)

Urban Legends: The Truth Behind All Those Deliciously Entertaining Myths That Are Absolutely, Positively, 100% Not True, by Richard Roeper (Career Press)

Appendix C

Movies to Watch

The Abyss, 1914, 1989
Alien Terminator, 1995
Alien, 1979
Alien: Resurrection, 1997
Alien³, 1992
Aliens, 1986
Andy Warhol's Dracula, 1974
Attack of the 50 Foot Woman, 1958
Attack of the Giant Crab Monsters, 1957
Attack of the Giant Leeches, 1959
Attack of the Killer Tomatoes, 1978
The Baby, 1973
Bad Moon, 1996
The Beach Girls and the Monster, 1965
Beast from 20,000 Fathoms, 1953
Beast from Haunted Cave, 1959
The Beast of Yucca Flats, 1961
The Beast Within, 1982
The Birds, 1963
Black Sunday, 1960
Blackout, 1985
The Blair Witch Project, 1999
Blood Cult, 1985
The Boogens, 1981
The Boogey Man, 1990
Book of Shadows: Blair Witch 2, 2000
Breeders, 1996
Bride of the Monster, 1956

The Bride of Frankenstein, 1935
Cameron's Closet, 1987
Candyman, 1995
The Capture of Bigfoot, 1979
Castle of Evil, 1966
Children of the Corn, 1984
Chillers, 1988
Close Encounters of the Third Kind,
    1977
Conspiracy Theory, 1997
Contact, 1997
The Crawling Eye, 1958
Creature from the Black Lagoon, 1954
The Creature Walks Among Us, 1956
Crystal Force, 1992
Curse of the Black Widow, 1976
The Curse of Frankenstein, 1957
Curucu, Beast of the Amazon, 1956
Dead Alive, 1993
Deep Rising, 1997
Doomwatch, 1972
Dracula Vs. Frankenstein, 1971
Dracula, 1931
The Dunwich Horror, 1970
Earth Girls are Easy, 1989
Edward Scissorhands, 1990
The Electronic Monster, 1957
E.T. the Extra-Terrestrial, 1982

Frankenstein 1959, 1970
Frankenstein Meets the Wolf Man, 1943
Frankenstein, 1973, 1993
Frankenstein's Daughter, 1958
Gappa the Triphibian Monsters, 1967
Ghost Brigade, 1995
The Ghost of Frankenstein, 1942
Ghost Stories, 1986
The Giant from the Unknown, 1958
The Giant Gila Monster, 1959
Godzilla, 1998
Godzilla, King of the Monsters! 1956
Gorgo Versus Godzilla, 1969
Graveyard Shift, 1990
Gremlins, 1984
The Hands of Orlac, 1960
Harry and the Hendersons, 1987
House of Dracula, 1945
Independence Day, 1996
Invasion of the Body Snatchers, 1956
Invisible Ghost, 1941
JFK, 1991
King Kong, 1933, 1976
Legend of the Chupacabra, 1998
Leprechaun, 1992
The Little Shop of Horrors, 1960, 1986
Man Beast, 1955
Man Made Monster, 1941
Mary Shelley's Frankenstein, 1994
Men in Black, 1997
Mighty Joe Young, 1949

Mission to Mars, 2000
The Monster and the Girl, 1941
The Monster of Piedras Blancas, 1958
The Monster That Challenged the World, 1957
The Monster Walks, 1932
Nosferatu: The Vampyre, 1922, 1979
The Old Dark House, 1932
The Omen, 1976
Photographing Fairies, 1998
Plan 9 from Outer Space, 1956
Pterodactyl Woman from Beverly Hills, 1994
Q: The Winged Serpent, 1983
The Relic, 1997
The Return of Swamp Thing, 1989
Revenge of the Creature, 1955
The Shadow of Chinatown, 1936
The Slime People, 1962
Something Wicked This Way Comes, 1983
Starship Troopers, 1997
Swamp Thing, 1981
Tremors, 1989
Trog, 1970
The Usual Suspects, 1995
The Valley of Gwangi, 1969
War of the Worlds, 1953
Wolfman, 1979
The X-Files, 1998

Appendix D

Web Sites of Interest

52 Signs of Abduction by Aliens: *members.tripod.com/~Magic32/52questions.htm*

The AFU and Urban Legends Archive: *www.urbanlegends.com*

THE AREA 51 RESEARCH CENTER: *www.area51researchcenter.com*

Big Hoax: *www.bighoax.com*

Bigfoot Database: *www.moneymaker.org/BFRR/GDB*

Bigfoot Encounters: *www.n2.net/prey/bigfoot*

The Cardiff Giant: *www.beaujest.com/cardiff.html*

Cliff Pickover's Internet Encyclopedia of Hoaxes: *www.pickover.com/hoax.html*

Coast to Coast A.M. with Mike Siegel: *www.artbell.com*

Con Artists: *goddess.hispeed.com/conartists*

Culture Jammer's Encyclopedia: *www.syntac.net/hoax/index.php*

Doctor Mac's Virus Hoax Hotlist: *www.doctormac.net/Virushoaxes.html*

Don't Spread That Hoax: *www.nonprofit.net/hoax/hoax.html*

Elvis Presley Guide: *www.lycos.com/entertainment/celebrities/celebs/Presley.html*

The [encounters:] Forum: *ourworld.compuserve.com/homepages/erikf*

Evolution: *www.bloomington.in.us/~lgthscac/evolution.htm*

Hitler's Secret Diaries: *www.docsnavyseals.com/hitler's%20secret%20diaries.html*

HOAXBUSTERS Home Page: *ciac.llnl.gov/ciac/CIACHoaxes.html*

The Hoaxkill service: *www.hoaxkill.com*

Internet Hoaxes Email Rumors and Urban Legends: *urbanlegends.miningco.com/library/blhoax.htm*

Makeup Man and the Monster: *www.strangemag.com/chambers17.html*

Marilyn Monroe Official Site: *www.marilynmonroe.com*

McAfee.com - Virus Hoaxes: *vil.mcafee.com/hoax.asp*

Military Involvement in UFO Abductions: *www.cco.net/~trufax/trans/lammer.html*

The Museum of Hoaxes: *www.museumofhoaxes.com*

NASA's Moon Hoax: *www.redzero.demon.co.uk/moonhoax*

Nostradaums: Prophecies of Our Century: *http://web1.tusco.net/ourlady/index.htm*

Nostradamus Repository: *http://www.nostradamus-repository.org*

Old Wive's Tales and Other Horticultural Misinformation:
  stanly.ces.state.nc.us/articles/jim/wives.html

Old Wive's Tales: *www.uconect.net/~bstemple/oldwives.htm*

ParaScope: *www.parascope.com*

Piltdown Man: *www.tiac.net/users/cri/piltdown.html*

Piltdown Plot – The Map: *140.232.1.5/~piltdown/pp_map.html*

Popular Con Games and How To Recognize Them: *www.reports-unlimited.com/
  congame.htm*

A Review of Old Wive's Tales: *www.uconect.net/~bstemple/oldwives.htm*

Scams 101: *www.friendsinbusiness.com/scams*

Secrets Con Artists Don't Want You to Know: *www.fightback2000.homepage.com*

The SETI League: *www.setileague.org*

The Skeptic's Dictionary: *skepdic.com/tifraud.html*

Stiller Research Virus Alphabetical Hoax List: *www.stiller.com/hoaxa.htm*

Superstitions and Old Wive's Tales: *www.cameodesigns.com/superstitions3.html*

Swiss Historian Exposes Anti-Hitler Rauschning Memoir as Fraudulent:
  ihr.org/jhr/v04/v04p378_Weber.html

Symantec Security Updates: *www.symantec.com/avcenter/hoax.html*

The Truth About Computer E-Mail Viruses: *www.gerlitz.com/virushoax*

Truth About Computer Virus Myths & Hoaxes: *www.kumite.com/myths*

UFO Folklore: *www.qtm.net/~geibdan/framemst.html*

UFOs/Aliens: *ufos.about.com/science/ufos*

UFOs: Just the Facts CD-ROM: *www.ufofacts.com*

Urban Legends and Folklore: *urbanlegends.about.com/science/urbanlegends*

Urban Legends Reference Pages: *www.snopes2.com/info/search/search.htm*

Urban Legends: *www.Urban-Legends.ukf.net*

Urban Legends: *www.tikipub.com/urban-legends.html*

Virus Scares and Hoaxes: *www.tcsn.net/ddavis/virus_hoax.html*

Ye Olde Wive's Tales: *www.ida.net/users/dhanco/tales.htm*

Appendix E

Organizations and Museums

American Film Institute
2021 North Western Avenue
Los Angeles, CA 90027
Phone: (323) 856-7600
Fax: (323) 467-4578
or
The John F. Kennedy Center for the Performing Arts
Washington, D.C. 20566
Phone: (202) 833-AFIT
Fax: (202) 659-1970
www.afionline.org

American Folklife Center
Room LJ G-49, Thomas Jefferson Building
First Street and Independence Avenue, SE
Washington, D.C. 20540-4610
Phone: (202) 707-5510
Fax: (202) 707-2076
E-mail: folklife@loc.gov
http://lcweb.loc.gov/folklife

Better Business Bureau
4200 Wilson Boulevard, Suite 800
Arlington, Virginia 22203-1838
Phone: (703) 276.0100
Fax: (703) 525.8277
www.bbb.org

Center for Folklife and Cultural Heritage
750 9th Street, Northwest, Suite 4100
Smithsonian Institution
Washington, D.C. 20560-0953
Phone: (202) 275-1150.
Fax: (202) 275-1119
E-mail: info@folklife.si.edu
www.folklife.si.edu

Consumers Union
101 Truman Avenue
Yonkers, New York 10703-1057
Phone: (914) 378-2000
www.consumersunion.org

Dryden Flight Research Center
Mail Code T
P.O. Box 273
Edwards, CA 93523-0273
Phone: (661) 276-3446 or (661) 276-3460
www.dfrc.nasa.gov

Elvis Presley Enterprises, Inc.
P.O. Box 16508
3734 Elvis Presley Boulevard
Memphis, Tennessee 38186-0508
Phone: (800) 238-2000
www.elvis.com

Federal Trade Commission
Consumer Response Center
600 Pennsylvania Ave NW
Washington, D.C. 20580
Phone: 877-FTC-HELP
www.ftc.gov

International UFO Museum & Research Center
114 North Main Street
P.O. Box 2221
Roswell, New Mexico 88202-2221
Phone: (505) 625-9495
Fax: (505) 625-1907
E-mail: IUFOMRC@IUFOMRC.org
www.iufomrc.com

Jet Propulsion Laboratory
Public Services Office
Mail Stop 186-113
4800 Oak Grove Drive
Pasadena, CA 91109
Phone: (818) 354-9314
Fax: (818) 393-4641
www.jpl.nasa.gov

Kennedy Space Center
State Road 405
Kennedy Space Center, Florida 32899
Phone: (321) 452-2121
Fax: (321) 452-3043
www.kennedyspacecenter.com

NASA Headquarters
300 East Street SW
Washington, D.C.
www.nasa.gov

National Air and Space Museum
7th and Independence Ave, SW
Washington, DC 20560
Phone: (202) 357-2700
www.nasm.edu

National Archives and Records Administration
700 Pennsylvania Avenue, NW
Washington, D.C. 20408
Phone: (800) 234-8861
www.nara.gov

National Fraud Information Center
Phone: (800) 876-7060
www.fraud.org

National Institute for Consumer Education
G12, Boone Hall
Eastern Michigan University
Ypsilanti, Michigan 48197
Phone: (734) 487-2292
Fax: (734) 487-7153
Email: NICE@online.emich.edu
www.emich.edu/public/coe/nice/nice.html

National Museum of Natural History
10th Street and Constitution Avenue, NW
Washington, D.C. 20560
Phone: (202) 357-2700
www.mnh.si.edu

Smithsonian Astrophysical Observatory
60 Garden Street
Cambridge, Massachusetts 02138
Phone: (617)495-7461
http://sao-www.harvard.edu/sao-home.html

Index

Index

We Have
EVERYTHING!

Everything® **After College Book**
$12.95, 1-55850-847-3

Everything® **Angels Book**
$12.95, 1-58062-398-0

Everything® **Astrology Book**
$12.95, 1-58062-062-0

Everything® **Baby Names Book**
$12.95, 1-55850-655-1

Everything® **Baby Shower Book**
$12.95, 1-58062-305-0

Everything® **Baby's First Food Book**
$12.95, 1-58062-512-6

Everything® **Barbeque Cookbook**
$12.95, 1-58062-316-6

Everything® **Bartender's Book**
$9.95, 1-55850-536-9

Everything® **Bedtime Story Book**
$12.95, 1-58062-147-3

Everything® **Bicycle Book**
$12.00, 1-55850-706-X

Everything® **Build Your Own Home Page**
$12.95, 1-58062-339-5

Everything® **Business Planning Book**
$12.95, 1-58062-491-X

Everything® **Casino Gambling Book**
$12.95, 1-55850-762-0

Everything® **Cat Book**
$12.95, 1-55850-710-8

Everything® **Chocolate Cookbook**
$12.95, 1-58062-405-7

Everything® **Christmas Book**
$15.00, 1-55850-697-7

Everything® **Civil War Book**
$12.95, 1-58062-366-2

Everything® **College Survival Book**
$12.95, 1-55850-720-5

Everything® **Computer Book**
$12.95, 1-58062-401-4

Everything® **Cookbook**
$14.95, 1-58062-400-6

Everything® **Cover Letter Book**
$12.95, 1-58062-312-3

Everything® **Crossword and Puzzle Book**
$12.95, 1-55850-764-7

Everything® **Dating Book**
$12.95, 1-58062-185-6

Everything® **Dessert Book**
$12.95, 1-55850-717-5

Everything® **Dog Book**
$12.95, 1-58062-144-9

Everything® **Dreams Book**
$12.95, 1-55850-806-6

Everything® **Etiquette Book**
$12.95, 1-55850-807-4

Everything® **Family Tree Book**
$12.95, 1-55850-763-9

Everything® **Fly-Fishing Book**
$12.95, 1-58062-148-1

Everything® **Games Book**
$12.95, 1-55850-643-8

Everything® **Get-A-Job Book**
$12.95, 1-58062-223-2

Everything® **Get Published Book**
$12.95, 1-58062-315-8

Everything® **Get Ready for Baby Book**
$12.95, 1-55850-844-9

Everything® **Golf Book**
$12.95, 1-55850-814-7

Everything® **Guide to Las Vegas**
$12.95, 1-58062-438-3

Everything® **Guide to New York City**
$12.95, 1-58062-314-X

Everything® **Guide to Walt Disney World®, Universal Studios®, and Greater Orlando, 2nd Edition**
$12.95, 1-58062-404-9

Everything® **Guide to Washington D.C.**
$12.95, 1-58062-313-1

Everything® **Herbal Remedies Book**
$12.95, 1-58062-331-X

Everything® **Home-Based Business Book**
$12.95, 1-58062-364-6

Everything® **Homebuying Book**
$12.95, 1-58062-074-4

Everything® **Homeselling Book**
$12.95, 1-58062-304-2

Everything® **Home Improvement Book**
$12.95, 1-55850-718-3

Everything® **Hot Careers Book**
$12.95, 1-58062-486-3

Everything® **Internet Book**
$12.95, 1-58062-073-6

Everything® **Investing Book**
$12.95, 1-58062-149-X

Everything® **Jewish Wedding Book**
$12.95, 1-55850-801-5

Everything® **Job Interviews Book**
$12.95, 1-58062-493-6

Everything® **Lawn Care Book**
$12.95, 1-58062-487-1

Everything® **Leadership Book**
$12.95, 1-58062-513-4

Everything® **Low-Fat High-Flavor Cookbook**
$12.95, 1-55850-802-3

Everything® **Magic Book**
$12.95, 1-58062-418-9

Everything® **Microsoft® Word 2000 Book**
$12.95, 1-58062-306-9

For more information, or to order, call 800-872-5627
or visit everything.com
Adams Media Corporation, 260 Center Street, Holbrook, MA 02343

Available wherever books are sold!

Everything® **Money Book**
$12.95, 1-58062-145-7

Everything® **Mother Goose Book**
$12.95, 1-58062-490-1

Everything® **Mutual Funds Book**
$12.95, 1-58062-419-7

Everything® **One-Pot Cookbook**
$12.95, 1-58062-186-4

Everything® **Online Business Book**
$12.95, 1-58062-320-4

Everything® **Online Genealogy Book**
$12.95, 1-58062-402-2

Everything® **Online Investing Book**
$12.95, 1-58062-338-7

Everything® **Online Job Search Book**
$12.95, 1-58062-365-4

Everything® **Pasta Book**
$12.95, 1-55850-719-1

Everything® **Pregnancy Book**
$12.95, 1-58062-146-5

Everything® **Pregnancy Organizer**
$15.00, 1-58062-336-0

Everything® **Quick Meals Cookbook**
$12.95, 1-58062-488-X

Everything® **Resume Book**
$12.95, 1-58062-311-5

Everything® **Sailing Book**
$12.95, 1-58062-187-2

Everything® **Selling Book**
$12.95, 1-58062-319-0

Everything® **Study Book**
$12.95, 1-55850-615-2

Everything® **Tall Tales, Legends, and Outrageous Lies Book**
$12.95, 1-58062-514-2

Everything® **Tarot Book**
$12.95, 1-58062-191-0

Everything® **Time Management Book**
$12.95, 1-58062-492-8

Everything® **Toasts Book**
$12.95, 1-58062-189-9

Everything® **Total Fitness Book**
$12.95, 1-58062-318-2

Everything® **Trivia Book**
$12.95, 1-58062-143-0

Everything® **Tropical Fish Book**
$12.95, 1-58062-343-3

Everything® **Vitamins, Minerals, and Nutritional Supplements Book**
$12.95, 1-58062-496-0

Everything® **Wedding Book, 2nd Edition**
$12.95, 1-58062-190-2

Everything® **Wedding Checklist**
$7.95, 1-58062-456-1

Everything® **Wedding Etiquette Book**
$7.95, 1-58062-454-5

Everything® **Wedding Organizer**
$15.00, 1-55850-828-7

Everything® **Wedding Shower Book**
$7.95, 1-58062-188-0

Everything® **Wedding Vows Book**
$7.95, 1-58062-455-3

Everything® **Wine Book**
$12.95, 1-55850-808-2

Everything® **Angels Mini Book**
$4.95, 1-58062-387-5

Everything® **Astrology Mini Book**
$4.95, 1-58062-385-9

Everything® **Baby Names Mini Book**
$4.95, 1-58062-391-3

Everything® **Bedtime Story Mini Book**
$4.95, 1-58062-390-5

Everything® **Dreams Mini Book**
$4.95, 1-58062-386-7

Everything® **Etiquette Mini Book**
$4.95, 1-58062-499-5

Everything® **Get Ready for Baby Mini Book**
$4.95, 1-58062-389-1

Everything® **Golf Mini Book**
$4.95, 1-58062-500-2

Everything® **Love Spells Mini Book**
$4.95, 1-58062-388-3

Everything® **Pregnancy Mini Book**
$4.95, 1-58062-392-1

Everything® **TV & Movie Trivia Mini Book**
$4.95, 1-58062-497-9

Everything® **Wine Mini Book**
$4.95, 1-58062-498-7

Everything® **Kids' Baseball Book**
$9.95, 1-58062-489-8

Everything® **Kids' Joke Book**
$9.95, 1-58062-495-2

Everything® **Kids' Money Book**
$9.95, 1-58062-322-0

Everything® **Kids' Nature Book**
$9.95, 1-58062-321-2

Everything® **Kids' Online Book**
$9.95, 1-58062-394-8

Everything® **Kids' Puzzle Book**
$9.95, 1-58062-323-9

Everything® **Kids' Space Book**
$9.95, 1-58062-395-6

Everything® **Kids' Witches and Wizards Book**
$9.95, 1-58062-396-4

Everything® is a registered trademark of Adams Media Corporation.

**For more information, or to order, call 800-872-5627
or visit everything.com**
Adams Media Corporation, 260 Center Street, Holbrook, MA 02343

We Have
EVERYTHING KIDS'®!

Everything® Kids' Baseball Book
$9.95, 1-58062-489-8

Everything® Kids' Joke Book
$9.95, 1-58062-495-2

Everything® Kids' Money Book
$9.95, 1-58062-322-0

Everything® Kids' Nature Book
$9.95, 1-58062-321-2

Everything® Kids' Online Book
$9.95, 1-58062-394-8

Everything® Kids' Puzzle Book
$9.95, 1-58062-323-9

Everything® Kids' Space Book
$9.95, 1-58062-395-6

Everything® Kids' Witches and Wizards Book
$9.95, 1-58062-396-4

Available wherever books are sold!

For more information, or to order,
call 800-872-5627 or visit everything.com

Adams Media Corporation, 260 Center Street, Holbrook, MA 02343

Everything® is a registered trademark of Adams Media Corporation.

About the Author

Nat Segaloff is a writer and producer with a background in newspapers, teaching, broadcasting, and film marketing. He has written, produced and/or directed for USA Networks, Turner Classic Movies, Disney, and The Learning Channel, and has written eight books, including the best selling *The Everything Etiquette® Book* and *The Everything® Trivia Book*. Previously a film critic/reporter for *The Boston Herald* and CBS Radio, he is the author of *Hurricane Billy: The Stormy Life and Films of William Friedkin* and has contributed monographs on screenwriters Stirling Silliphant and Walon Green to *Backstory III*. Among his documentaries for the popular "Biography" series on the Arts & Entertainment Network are episodes on comedian John Belushi, Shari Lewis & Lamb Chop, talkmaster Larry King, movie mogul Darryl F. Zanuck, and Marvel Comics icon Stan Lee.

He is former co-founder, with John de Lancie and Leonard Nimoy, of the science-fiction production company Alien Voices. He lives in Los Angeles and really tries to return phone calls.